CONVERGENCE
OF CATASTROPHES

GUILLAUME FAYE

CONVERGENCE

OF

CATASTROPHES

TWILIGHT OF
THE MODERN WORLD

ARKTOS
LONDON 2025

ARKTOS
Arktos.com fb.com/Arktos arktosmedia arktosjournal

Original title: *La Convergence des catastrophes*
(Diffusion International Edition, Paris, 2004).

First English edition published in 2012 by Arktos Media Ltd.

ISBN
978-1-917646-72-7 (Paperback)
978-1-917646-73-4 (Hardback)
978-1-917646-74-1 (Ebook)

Translation
E. Christian Kopff

Editing
John Morgan and Constantin von Hoffmeister

Cover & Layout
Tor Westman

CONTENTS

A NOTE FROM THE EDITOR

There were no footnotes to the original French edition of this book. Therefore, all footnotes to Faye's text are my own. Wherever possible, references have been given to the English translations of texts; if a reference is to a work in another language, I was unable to locate an English version of it. All references to Web sites in the footnotes were verified as accurate and available during May 2012.

This translation was made directly from the original French edition published in 2004 by Diffusion International Edition. This edition was printed under the name Guillaume Corvus at the request of the publisher.

I would like to thank Professor E. Christian Kopff for the translation, as well as Jared Taylor for providing an excellent Foreword at short notice, and to Sergio Knipe, who translated the back cover text from the French edition. I also wish to express my gratitude to Matthew Peters, who did the bulk of the editing and proofreading for this volume, including painstakingly comparing the translation against the original French.

JOHN B. MORGAN IV
Bangalore, India, May 2012

FOREWORD

BY JARED TAYLOR

first met Guillaume Faye in Paris in 2003. On previous visits, I had met a few figures from the French Right, such as Alain de Benoist, Charles Champetier, Bruno Mégret, Bruno Gollnisch. Pierre Vial, and Jean-Yves Le Gallou. All were brilliant and charming men, fully engaged in the struggle to defend their nation and its culture.

But of all these remarkable Frenchmen, it was Guillaume Faye with whom I fell into the quickest intimacy. The two of us — a French dissident and an American dissident — discovered that we had been driven out of respectable discourse for the same reasons and by the same forces. I hasten to point out that Mr. Faye is a dissident of a much broader sweep than I. As readers of this book will find, nothing is safe from Guillaume Faye: politics, culture, sex, foreign policy, economics, or religion. But when it came to an understanding of race, of the biological foundations of European civilization, we were immediately old comrades.

Since that time, we have met on both sides of the Atlantic, and Mr. Faye has been a speaker at two conferences I have organized. In 2006, he spoke on 'The Threat to the West', and in 2012 his subject was 'America and Europe, Brothers-in-Arms: A French Point of View'.

I like to think that those trips have given Mr. Faye a more comprehensive view of the United States. As one of the founders of the French New Right, he shared that group's deep suspicion of Americans, and in his 2001 book *Why We Fight* he wrote at considerable length about 'the American adversary'.

I certainly do not support most of what the United States government does, but I believe Mr. Faye was mistaken when he wrote, for example, that Americans have tried to form alliances with Islam deliberately to weaken Europe. The multiculturalism and mass immigration that the United States promotes for all White countries certainly weakens them, but the American governments do not push these things only on others. They practice them relentlessly on their own people. The United States therefore does not weaken Europe deliberately. It weakens it, as it weakens itself, perversely and tragically.

Anyone with a vision of the West must look beyond governments to the people they misgovern, and what Mr. Faye and I discovered at that meeting in 2003 was, indeed, what became the theme of his 2012 talk: that the people of America and Europe *are* brothers-in-arms. I am not certain he knew it when he wrote *Why We Fight,* but Mr. Faye certainly knows it now: the struggle to save Europe is the struggle to save America. It is the struggle to save all the children of Europe, whether they live in Canada, Australia, South Africa, or anywhere else. When Mr. Faye warns of catastrophe for Europe and writes of his hopes for redemption, he warns and hopes for all of us.

For virtually any other member of the French New Right, it would be heresy to talk of Americans and Europeans as brothers-in-arms. Such language came naturally for Mr. Faye in his recent talk, because he spoke of the American and European peoples rather than their rulers. As he pointed out, the people are the roots from which culture, civilization, and everything else grows, and if the European peoples — wherever they live — are replaced by others, all is lost.

Of course, in this book Mr. Faye warns that catastrophe looms no matter what we do: 'It is impossible to stop the headlong race of contemporary planetary civilisation to the abyss, because there exists no power with the decisive will to do so. How to change the direction of six billion people?'

And he warns that it is the people of the West who are the worst prepared: '[W]e have never been less prepared: invaded, devirilised, physically and morally disarmed, the prey of a culture of meaningless-ness and masochistic culpability. Europeans have never in their history been as weak as at this very moment when the Great Threat appears on the horizon.'

The goal of this book is not so much to avert catastrophe, much as I might hope it could, as to prepare for the new age that will dawn after the catastrophe.

For some, Mr. Faye is nothing more than a prophet of doom, but in my view, for at least the last ten years, he has been Europe's foremost spokesman for our people. Thanks to the translations by Arktos, his books are now available to the English-speaking world.

I particularly welcome this translation by E. Christian Kopff, whom I have known for nearly twenty years, and for whom I have the highest admiration. He has fully captured the slashing, uncompromising style that makes Mr. Faye so provocative and so memorable. I cannot think of a better match of author, publisher, and translator to bring these important ideas to new readers, and I envy them the pleasure of their first encounters with the work of Guillaume Faye.

JARED TAYLOR

Oakton, Virginia, 3 May 2012

Jared Taylor has been the editor of the journal *American Renaissance* since 1990, and founded the New Century Foundation in 1994, both of which have been among the most prominent institutions to analyse the problems being faced by those of European descent worldwide. He is also the author of *Paved with Good Intentions: The Failure of Race Relations in Contemporary America* (New York: Carroll & Graf, 1992); *The Real American Dilemma: Race, Immigration, and the Future of America* (Oakton, Virginia: New Century Foundation, 1998); and *White Identity: Racial Consciousness in the Twenty-First Century* (Oakton, Virginia: New Century Foundation, 2011).

AN EXPLOSIVE COCKTAIL

'The modern world is like a train full of
ammunition running in the fog on a moonless
night with its lights out.'

— ROBERT ARDREY[1]

For the first time in its history, humanity is threatened by a convergence of catastrophes.

A series of 'dramatic lines' are approaching one another and converging like a river's tributaries with perfect accord (between 2010 and

---

1   Robert Ardrey (1908–1980) was a widely read and discussed author during the 1960s, particularly his books *African Genesis* (1961) and *The Territorial Imperative* (1966). Ardrey's most controversial hypothesis, known as the 'killer ape theory', posits that what distinguished humans' evolutionary ancestors from other primates was their aggressiveness, which caused them to develop weapons to conquer their environment and also leading to changes in their brains which led to modern humans. In his view, aggressiveness was an inherent part of the human character rather than an aberration. Ardrey's ideas were highly influential at the time, most notably in the 'Dawn of Man' sequence of *2001: A Space Odyssey*, and also in the writings of GRECE, in which Ardrey was frequently cited.

2020) towards a breaking point and a descent into chaos. From this chaos — which will be extremely painful on the global scale — can emerge the new order of the post-catastrophe era and therefore a new civilisation born in pain.

Let us briefly summarise the nature of these lines of catastrophe.

The first is the cancerisation of the European social fabric. The colonisation of the Northern hemisphere for purposes of permanent settlement by the peoples of the global South, which is increasingly serious despite the reassuring affirmations of the media, is pregnant with explosive situations; the failure of the multiracial society, increasingly full of racism of all kinds with different communities becoming more and more tribal; the progressive ethnic and anthropological metamorphosis of Europe, a true historical cataclysm; the return of poverty to Western and Eastern Europe; the slow but steady growth of criminal activity and drug use; the continual disintegration of family structures; the decline of educational infrastructure and the quality of academic programs; the disruption of the transmission of cultural knowledge and social disciplines (barbarisation and loss of needed skills); the disappearance of popular culture and the increasing degrading of the masses by the culture of spectacles.[2] All this indicates to us that the European nations are moving toward a *New Middle Ages*.[3]

---

2   Presumably a reference to 'society of the spectacle', a term coined by Guy Debord (1931–1994), a French Marxist philosopher and the founder of the anarchist Situationist International. The spectacle, as described in his principal work, *The Society of the Spectacle*, is one of the means by which the capitalist establishment maintains its authority in the modern world — namely, by reducing all genuine human experiences to representational images in the mass media, thus allowing the powers-that-be to determine how individuals experience reality.

3   This is a concept developed by the French author Alain Minc, in which he predicts a coming time of chaos and hardship resembling the Middle Ages, which will end in the development of a much smaller, but more sustainable, global economy. He discusses this idea in *Le Nouveau Moyen-âge* (Paris: Gallimard, 1993).

But these factors of social breakdown in Europe will be aggravated by the economic and demographic crisis which will only get worse and end by producing mass poverty. By 2010 the number of active workers will not be large enough to finance the retirements of the 'grandpa boomers'. Europe will collapse under the weight of old people; then its ageing countries will see their economies slowed and handicapped by payments for healthcare and retirement benefits for unproductive citizens; in addition, the ageing of the population will dry up technical and economic dynamism. In addition to these problems, the economy will increasingly resemble the Third World because of the uncontrolled immigration of unskilled populations.

Modernity's third dramatic line of catastrophe will be the chaos of the global South. By displacing their traditional cultures with industrialisation, the nations of the South, in spite of a deceptive and fragile economic growth, have created social chaos that is only going to get worse.

The fourth line of catastrophe, which has recently been explained by Jacques Attali,[4] is the threat of a world financial crisis, which will be much more serious than the crisis of the 1930s and will bring about a general recession. The harbinger of the crisis will be the collapse of the stock markets and currencies of the Far East, like the recession that is striking this region.

The fifth line of catastrophe is the rise of fanatical religious cults, principally Islam. The rise of radical Islam is the backlash to the

---

4   Jacques Attali (b. 1943) is a French economist who was an advisor to Mitterrand during the first decade of his presidency. Many of his writings are available in translation. Faye may be referring to Attali's article 'The Crash of Western Civilisation: The Limits of the Market and Democracy', which appeared in the Summer 1997 issue of the American journal *Foreign Policy*. In it, Attali claimed that democracy and the free market are incompatible, writing: 'Unless the West, and particularly its self-appointed leader, the United States, begins to recognise the shortcomings of the market economy and democracy, Western civilisation will gradually disintegrate and eventually self-destruct.' In many ways his arguments resemble Faye's.

excesses of the cosmopolitanism of modernity that wanted to impose on the entire world the model of atheist individualism, the cult of material goods, the loss of spiritual values and the dictatorship of the spectacle. In reaction to this aggression, Islam has radicalised, just as it was already becoming once again a religion of domination and conquest, in conformity with its traditions.

The sixth line of catastrophe: a North-South confrontation, with theological and ethnic roots, will appear on the horizon. It is increasingly likely to replace the risk of an East-West conflict, which we have so far avoided. No one knows what form it will take, but it will be serious, because it will be based on collective challenges and sentiments much stronger than the old and artificial partisan polarity of the USA and USSR, capitalism and Communism.

The seventh line of catastrophe is the uncontrolled increase of pollution, which will not threaten the Earth (which still has four billion years to look forward to and can start evolution over again from zero), but the physical survival of humanity. This collapse of the environment is the fruit of the liberal and egalitarian myth (which was once also a Soviet myth) of universal industrial development and a dynamic economy for everyone.

We can add to all this the probable implosion of the contemporary European Union, which is increasingly ungovernable, the risks involved with nuclear proliferation in the Third World, and the probability of ethnic civil war in Europe.

The convergence of these factors in the heart of a globalised and very fragile civilisation allows us to predict that the Twenty-first century will not be the 'progressive' continuation of the contemporary world, but the rise of another world. We must prepare ourselves for this tragic possibility with lucidity.

Believing in Miracles

We are dealing with a general prejudice inherited from the egalitarian and humanitarian utopias, like the philosophy of Progress, according to which 'we can have everything at the same time' and that reality never has negative consequences.

People believe they can have their cake and eat it too. They imagine, according to the liberal faith, that an 'invisible hand' will spontaneously restore a harmonious equilibrium. I shall mention a few examples of believing in miracles:

- Imagining that the dogma of the unlimited economic development of every nation is possible without massive pollution and ecological catastrophes that will destroy this very development. This is the illusion of indefinite development.

- Believing that a permissive society will not produce a social jungle, and that you can obtain at the same time libertarian emancipation and self-disciplined harmony. We see this drama being acted out in the shipwreck of our schools, where violence, insecurity, ignorance, and illiteracy are arising out of the illusion of progressive education, an educational method which rejects any form of discipline for its students.

- Believing that it will be possible to preserve retirement systems and social and medical entitlements while remaining faithful, in a period of demographic decline, to the ideal of 'solidarity of distribution'. This is the illusion of the Communist conception of solidarity.

- Believing that large-scale alien immigration is compatible with the 'values of the French Republic' and the preservation of the civilisation of the nations and peoples of Europe; and that Islam can become secular and blend in with republican values. Believing also that we can renew the working population by importing immigrants, when these immigrants are unskilled welfare recipients and our responsibility. Imagining also that by regularising the status of masses of illegal immigrants, it will be possible to assimilate them and avoid the arrival of new masses, although we observe exactly the opposite. This is the illusion of the benefits of immigration.

- Extolling the assimilation and integration of aliens while wanting to preserve and maintain their special characteristics, their original cultures, their memories and native mores. This is the communitarian illusion, one of the most harmful of all, which is particularly cherished by 'ethno-pluralist' intellectuals.

- Imagining that by cancelling Third World debt we can encourage their economic growth and prevent new indebtedness in the future. This is the Third Worldist illusion.

- Demanding at one and the same time that we abandon nuclear energy programs and replace them with power plants using natural gas, coal and petroleum, while advocating the reduction of polluting gases. This is the ecologist's illusion.

- Thinking that a world economy founded on short term speculation based on computerised markets and replacing monetary policies with the caprice of financial markets will guarantee a lasting 'new growth'. This is the illusion of the new economy.

- Believing that democracy and 'republican values' will be reinforced by eliminating 'populism', that is, the direct expression of the will of the people.

I could make the list longer. In all these matters, believing in miracles can be explained by the incorrigible optimism of the secular religion of egalitarian progressivism, but also by the fact that, although it has reached an impasse, the dominant ideology does not dare deny its dogmas or make heartbreaking revisions, while clinging to the idea that 'the storm will never come'. The whole thing is explained by the sophisms of bogus experts, whose conclusions are always that everything is going well and getting better and that we have the situation under control. They are like a driver who speeds through a red light and justifies it by explaining that the faster he drives, the less time he spends in the intersection and therefore reduces the risk of a collision.

Man, a Sick Animal

Paul MacLean,[5] Konrad Lorenz,[6] Arthur Koestler,[7] and Jean Rostand[8] have sensed that man is a sick animal, endowed with a brain that is too large. Conscience is perhaps, on the evolutionary scale, an illness and intelligence a burden. Man has lost touch with his natural survival instincts. We have not been on the Earth for a long time and it may be

---

5　Paul D. MacLean (1913-2007) was an American neuroscientist who developed the triune theory of the human brain, postulating that, over the course of its evolution, the brain was actually made up of three distinct elements: the reptilian complex, the limbic system, and the neocortex. As a result, human behavior is the product of all three tendencies.

6　Konrad Lorenz (1903-1989) was an Austrian ethologist who won the Nobel Prize in 1973. He was a member of the National Socialist Party during the Third Reich. He speculated that the supposed advances of modern life were actually harmful to humanity, since they had removed humans from the biological effects of natural competition and replaced it with the far more brutal competition inherent in relations between individuals in modern societies. After the war, his books on popular scientific and philosophical topics earned him international fame.

7　Arthur Koestler (1905-1983) was a Hungarian writer who, in his 1967 book *The Ghost in the Machine*, speculated that the triune model of the brain as described by Paul MacLean was responsible for a failure of the various parts to fully interconnect with each other, resulting in a conflict of desires within each individual leading to self-destructive tendencies.

8　Jean Rostand (1894-1977) was a French biologist who was a proponent of eugenics as a means for humanity to take responsibility for its own destiny. He was also a pioneer in the field of cryonics.

that, from life's point of view, or Gaia's,[9] we are a failed species, an abortive experiment; and that, especially by destroying the ecosystem that supports it, the *suicidal* human race is hastening its own disappearance.

Our neocortex, which some biologists compare to a tumour, does not function sufficiently in symbiosis with our reptilian brain. This is 'cerebral schizo-physiology', the source of a chaotic and self-destructive culture: wars, religious fanaticisms, frenzied exploitation of nature, aberrant demographic proliferation or, on the other hand, catastrophically low birth levels, frustrating natural selection, etc.: *Homo sapiens sapiens* does not deserve the name he has given himself. He is not 'wise', only intelligent. But he will perhaps perish from this excessive intelligence, which is pushing him to excess, *hybris*[10], and is making him lose every instinct of collective survival and all capacity to 'feel' the dangers that are piling up.

The Golem Parable, or the Machine That Went Mad

Humanity has lost control of the forward rush of the technological and globalised civilisation born in the Nineteenth century. We should remember the parable of the Golem, the Jewish allegory from Prague, in which a mud figure brought to life by magic escapes its maker, becomes an autonomous and out of control entity, and then starts spreading terror.

Today's little Jules Vernes[11] are mistaken. Optimistic and short-sighted mechanics, they are only making the situation worse. More

---

9   Gaia is the Ancient Greek name for the goddess of the Earth. In recent decades, the name has been adopted by ecologists, who use it to depict the combined components of the Earth as a living organism with its different parts acting in symbiosis with one another, rather than as a resource merely intended to be exploited by humans.

10   Latin: 'pride'.

11   Jules Verne (1828–1905) was a French novelist who is regarded as the inventor of the science fiction genre. Several of his books are notable for their predictions of future technological developments.

than that, they are not in control of the machine and have no idea where it is heading. There really is a pilot in the airplane, but he is convinced that he is driving a locomotive.

Among the inescapable trends at work today, there are other risks that are unforeseeable today but which will make things worse (or perhaps better, but this is less likely), or else create new tendencies or new earth-shattering phenomena. At any rate, it is hard to see any positive signs. All the indictors are flashing red.

In futurology, there are only two types of extrapolation from current trends that one can make with a high degree of probability: the weak and the strong. Today predictions are typically based on *weak extrapolations*. These latter are, for example, the pursuit of economic growth, linear and continuous technological progress, scientific civilisation, the affirmation of democracy everywhere in the world (who is telling us that Europe will be 'democratic' in 2030?); the lasting character of the United Nations; the effectiveness of antibiotics in the next century, and so on.

We are less concerned with *strong extrapolations*, which have a good chance of being realised in the next twenty years: the demographic disequilibrium of North and South that will grow massively; the unavoidable ageing of the indigenous European population; the growth of mass immigration into rich countries; the worsening of pollution, atmospheric warming and the exhaustion of resources, which is growing worse regardless of what measures may be taken today on a global level (and they are not being taken); the rising power of Islam; the worsening of social disintegration in Europe along ethnic lines, etc. All these strong extrapolations are headed in the direction of the system's breakdown, and are what we might call 'pessimistic'.

The 'Billiard Ball' Theory

The current implicit ideology that dominates the world, especially in the West, still continues to profess, officially, the *utopia* inherited from the egalitarian philosophy of the Enlightenment (Eighteenth century), positivism[12] and scientism (Nineteenth century): to create a situation where, in a few decades from now, some eight billion people will live on the planet with a good standard of living and democracy for all. All this resembles the billiard player who imagines that after four or five rebounds his ball will automatically fall into the hole. These professors of ballistics are playing golf, but they do not know it.

It is a quasi-certainty that this persistent belief in *progress* and *modernity*, concepts which the political classes of the West are always jabbering about and which are totally obsolete, will never see its objectives occur. The dream will shatter into pieces. *Constraining forces*, a *physical* wall, makes this ideology resemble a mass of intellectual stupefaction and *belief in miracles.*

The demanding parameters, mentioned above, based upon the assumption that current realities will persist and that current projections for the future will be realised, are not taken into account. No one is looking at the dashboard or the fuel gauge. Only the short-term counts, but for how much more time? The majority of the elites do not concern themselves with the long term, or even the middle term, in this civilisation of the here and now. The fate of future generations does not interest the decision-makers at all. They care only about their own careers.

***

They are helped by the *experts* in every field, who practice constant disinformation and *censorship of pessimism*, taking advantage of the

---

12 Positivism holds that the only knowledge which can be considered reliable is that which is obtained directly through the senses and via the (supposedly) objective techniques of the scientific method.

good old Coué method of optimistic autosuggestion:[13] 'Everything is going badly, so, to reassure myself, I say that everything is going well.' Actually pessimism would be more convincing, since it incites people to improve matters and to try to cure the disease. Alas, I think that is already too late. *We have passed the point of no return.*

The majority of intellectuals, media people, politicians and businessmen maintain a language of *utopian optimism*, clinging to their dogmas and making a gross travesty of reality: 'republican assimilation is making progress and will continue to make progress in France'; 'we are on the path to control massive illegal immigration'; 'Islamism is in decline'; 'we are on track to win the war on terror'; 'economic growth will resume next year and, because of the economic recovery, unemployment will go down' (when tomorrow comes, erasing it will cost nothing); 'we are going to establish democracy in the Near East'; 'we can stop using nuclear power and reduce pollution by making more efficient use of other resources, even if we go back to power plants that use petroleum, natural gas and coal'; 'we are going to find the money to pay for the costs of healthcare insurance without increasing public borrowing'; and so on.

We go forward each time either by lying and misrepresenting the objective situation, or by deliberately ignoring the parameters and changes that are taking place.

If elites of all different kinds pretend to believe this nonsense, public opinion (once upon a time we used to say, 'the people') subscribes to it less and less. Pessimism is present everywhere, like a sort of presentiment of a coming apocalypse. Already in 1995, an IFOP[14]

---

13   Émile Coué (1857–1926) was a French psychologist whose method involved repeating 'Every day, in every way, I am getting better and better' at the beginning and end of each day in a ritualized fashion, believing that this would influence the unconscious mind in a manner that would allow the practitioner to be more inclined toward success.

14   The Institut français d'opinion publique, or French Institute of Public Opinion, is an international marketing firm.

poll published in the Leftist newspaper *Libération* revealed that to the question, 'In ten years will we live in a better world?' 64 % of those polled responded in the negative. They were not mistaken.

'Catastrophe Theory' and 'Discrete Structural Metamorphoses'

In his 'catastrophe theory' French mathematician René Thom[15] explained that a 'system' (whether physical-chemical, mechanical, climatic, organic, social, civilisational, etc.) is an *always fragile ensemble* that can *suddenly* lurch into chaos, without anyone anticipating it, as a result of an accumulation of factors. It is the famous 'drop of water that causes the cup to overflow'. Every system is *unstable* and every civilisation is mortal, like everything in the universe. But sometimes the collapse is violent and sudden. For a long time a system can be worn away from inside by an endemic crisis; it holds out for a long time and then, suddenly, everything tips over. We find here the law of viral and bacterial biology: incubation is slow, but the final attack is as fast as lightning. A tree, apparently in good health, falls down during the first storm, although no one suspected that its insides were eaten away.

History offers us examples of sudden and unforeseen collapses: the Amerindian civilisation after the Spanish invasion, or else the Egyptian empire facing the assault of the Romans. I am defending the thesis that this is what awaits today's global civilisation in the next twenty years. We are going to hit a very sudden *breaking point* arising from the simultaneous convergences of great crises. It is easy to envisage spectacular and rapid historical reversals.

---

15 René Thom (1923–2002) was a French mathematician who made many achievements during his career, but is best remembered for his development of catastrophe theory. The theory is complex, but in essence it states that small alterations in the parameters of any system can cause large-scale and sudden changes to the system as a whole.

***

It is always necessary to beware of *surprises*, these unforeseen and sometimes discrete transformations, which turn everything upside down. They radically modify a system's structure, without making a loud noise and suddenly, their consequences explode and change everything. That is what is heading for us today. They are 'discrete structural metamorphoses'.

We believe that we are still living in world X, when we are already in world Y, and the house of cards of the old world collapses without warning. These metamorphoses do not always make the front pages of newspapers; they take place without making a fuss. They constitute history's infrastructure, not its ephemeral surface.

The founding of the Fifth Republic,[16] the fall of Communism, the results of American elections, etc., are *events* that depend on the superstructure. On the other hand, what we have called the 'discrete structural metamorphoses' will have incalculable consequences. For a generation they have been increasingly frequent and rapid. They are transforming the face of our civilisation.

Let us mention some cases. In France and Belgium, and soon in other countries, the number of active practitioners of Islam is soon going to surpass that of the Christian churches; the depopulation of Europe has begun as the radical ethnic modification of its population; the Spanish language has already equalled and even surpassed English in the American Southwest; some twenty nations possess the technology for making nuclear weapons; in a number of Western countries the traditional family is collapsing and a demographic coma is in place; the 'casino economy', purely speculative and unregulated, stretches over the entire world, especially in China, which still calls

---

16 The Fifth Republic began after the collapse of the Fourth Republic in 1958 as a result of the crisis in Algeria, bringing Charles de Gaulle to power and resulting in the drafting of a new constitution. It has remained in effect up to the present day.

itself 'Communist'; antibiotics are less and less effective against bacterial epidemics, and so on.

We are in control of none of these structural metamorphoses. And very few people are aware of the power of their interaction.

We Must Stop Believing in Sorcerers: Techno-Science Gone Mad

The elites who direct the Western world, the over-credentialed 'experts', are pulling the wool over our eyes. They possess neither strategy nor mastery of analysis and are satisfied with *tactics*. The real problems are never investigated. The solutions are rhetorical or electoral. The good apostles, bureaucrats with MBAs from prestigious schools, are only masters of words. No improvement is in sight. The Golem's inexorable march continues.

The burden of 'doing nothing' is the heaviest. But the experts and specialists (once called 'savants') are consoling us. They play the role sorcerers played in ancient societies.

***

No one is directing science and technology any longer and, far from improving the human condition as they used to, they are making it worse, notably by exhausting resources and destroying the environment. The modern myth of 'development', which is venerated more than ever all over the world, leads to its opposite, a gigantic regression, a race to the bottom. No authority, no international planning has emerged. Globalisation is anarchy. The backdrop of this fatal movement is generalised individual consumerism, the search for the highest possible standard of living, unbridled enthusiasm for the free market, the speculative economy and the cult of 'taking each day as it comes'.

Similarly, *democracy* has to be seen as an aggravating factor, for this type of regime removes any central authority that can, when it sees the storm appearing, react in an emergency. Liberal democracy

favours improvidence, the law of the market, and short-term calculation by individuals or corporations. If once upon a time this type of
regime was efficient, today it seems incompetent, as it shows every day,
to stem the rise of dangers.

International conferences on the environment are a futile waste of
time. Just as there is no control over mass immigration, so the destruction of fish reserves and our forest heritage, the increased emission
of greenhouse gases, the demographic gap between North and South,
etc., are out of control. Even the authorities who arise to reverse the
catastrophic course of events, whether they represent countries or the
United Nations, do not succeed in correcting the direction of the cargo
ship that is going full sail, faster and faster, towards the reefs.

***

But we are reassured by the 'experts' and are still fascinated by techno-
science, believing that it will solve all our problems using some new
form of magic. Computers, the electric or low-polluting engines, organic agriculture, and pharmaceutical research will not prevent the return of famines and epidemics or the exponential growth of pollution.
It is too late. The machine is racing. Intellectuals and 'philosophers'
have been telling us over and over again for decades that 'the myth
of Progress' is dead. On the contrary, it has never been in such good
shape, especially in the developing countries of the South. We are victims of the psychological condition of *derealisation*, a loss of the sense
of reality of what is happening. Our contemporaries have persuaded
themselves that 'catastrophe cannot happen' and that this civilisation is
at the same time *eternal* and continually getting better and better, that
it will never experience a reversal, and *a fortiori*[17] not a collapse. Not
only is this a possibility, but it will happen, and very soon.

What comforts us in this gloomy illusion is our techno-scientific
environment, which we consider to be *indestructible*, when on the
contrary this global civilisation is a colossus with feet of clay. The

_____

17   Latin: 'an argument with a stronger foundation'.

politicians and the experts, who possess neither audacity nor imagination, reject every *radical solution*. They always prefer little solutions, tactical or rigged, compromises that please an electorate with cold feet, always respecting the status quo. They believe, like King Arthur, that 'the fortress is impregnable' when no one is guarding the walls.[18]

The groundswell — or rather the different groundswells arriving at the same time, demographic, strategic, sociological, economic, environmental — is arrogantly ignored. In France we even use the surreal expression 'sustainable development'! The dominant ideology, which calls itself rationalist, is really magical. In every area it plays the role of an 'ideology of sleep'.

***

We must not forget — and it is one of the central theses of this work — that *mini-catastrophes reinforce one another*, multiplying their effects among one another to produce a global mega-catastrophe. An accident (of an airplane, for instance) is the result of a series of causes and never just one: for example, the conjunction of a technical problem in the controls, bad weather and pilot error.

It is the same with the situation we are living through, or rather that we are soon going to be living through. For example, the natural calamities produced by global warming aggravate the famines caused by other economic and demographic causes and thus make the economic situation even worse and push the populations of the South to emigrate to the North, thus destabilising the West still more. Growing poverty in certain countries feeds religious fanaticism that, in turn, complicates political instability. And so on.

The system is holistic and interactive, which explains the acceleration of the arrival of the breaking point, since a multitude of crises converge at the same moment, without anyone being able to treat them separately.

---

18 King Arthur's Camelot was frequently left unguarded while his knights were engaged in lengthy quests.

1

TOWARD THE COLLAPSE OF THE TERRESTRIAL ECOSYSTEM

It is Already Too Late

The planet Earth is not in danger. She has millions of years of revolving to recover. It is the human species that, by degrading the ecosystem, is putting itself at risk. Nothing will be done to stem present developments, and it is already too late. The prognosis is negative.

While the human population keeps growing at a pace commensurate with the greed of 'development', ecological resources and capacities continue to crumble. Let us briefly summarise the breaking points.

1) Emissions of greenhouse gases are going to provoke uncontrollable climate disruptions. Their rapidity will surpass our capacity to adapt to them. Global warming, rising ocean levels, the multiplication of cataclysms (floods, droughts, localised deep cold spells, etc.) are going to be added to all the other factors of destabilisation discussed elsewhere.

2) The exhaustion of natural resources. Reserves of petroleum, natural gas and coal will not last long in the face of ever-growing needs and costs. 'Renewable energies' cannot make up the difference. Humanity lives today as though it were the beneficiary of the resources of *four planets*. Add to this generalised deforestation, desertification of entire areas and the accelerated shrinking of fishing and agricultural reserves. These last problems are provoked by uncontrolled pollution and the intensive exploitation of soil and marine reserves. Let us not forget the stagnation or degradation of drinking water, by the triple effect of exponential increase in water usage, the pollution of water tables and growing drought zones. The bill must be paid very soon.

Extensive famines are likely to result from these phenomena. These disasters will be added to other lines of catastrophe and will make them worse.

3) Pandemics. AIDS will probably turn out to be only a first warning. It has not been controlled and continues to progress at a steady pace. It is possible that it will explode suddenly, especially if a giant crises occurs before preventive measures can take effect. We are beginning to see the emergence of many new contagious diseases, both viral and bacterial, whose strains mutate easily and which are resistant to all known antibiotics (the result of their overuse): powerful new forms of plague, cholera, tuberculosis, and previously unknown pathologies as well.

The demographic explosion of the human species over the past century is due to the reduction in mortality — especially infant mortality — caused by the progress of medicine and hygiene. But this tendency is in the process of reversing itself. 'Science', which is believed to be omnipotent, will be dialectically bypassed and negated by the consequences of its own powers. A demographic implosion in the course of the Twenty-first century is certain.

***

A global civilisation that destroys its planetary capital has no chance of surviving. Oddly, the Earth's population, on the whole, has followed the Western logic of pursuing the indefinite maximisation of wealth, which is, however, contrary to the ancestral wisdom of India or China, which is based on a cyclical view of history.

The planet Earth is simply not capable of answering the needs of an excessively large humanity that always wants more. Notions of 'justice' and 'injustice' are no longer relevant. Morality is disappearing in the face of physical obstructions, while ideologies are stuttering in the void. One can always say that the peoples of the global South have a 'right' to the same liberties as those of the North and that it is unjust that they cannot take advantage of them. But this purely moral discourse will change nothing in the Earth's capacities. Since the beginning of the Industrial Revolution (about 1850) the Earth's resources have been exploited by humanity at a pace that is much too fast. The breakdown will take place, by successive shocks, beginning in 2010–2015.

How Times Have Changed!

The World Meteorological Organization (WMO) issued a warning on 2 July 2003: 'The Earth's climate is breaking down'. The tone is alarmist and novel for an organisation characterised by extreme prudence and scholarly reserve. Extracts from its latest report: 'Recent scientific evaluations indicate that, since mean temperatures continue to increase from climate change, the number and intensity of extreme events ought to increase.' The year 2003 and the decade 1993–2003 have turned out to be the warmest in Europe since the existence of meteorological records 200 years ago. In the United States, in May 2003, a record number of tornadoes (562) caused 41 deaths. In Asia, monsoons, cyclones and floods are putting their fragile economies in danger. The report also says, 'New analyses of short-term climate developments indicate that for the northern hemisphere the rise of temperatures in the Twentieth century has been the highest of every century in a thousand years.' Not only are temperatures rising, but the rate of increase is speeding up. In the past 143 years the warmest have been 1998, 2001, 2003, and each year beats the record of the preceding one.

The WMO predicts, in no particular order, the end of winter sports in Europe (with massive loss of snow) about 2015, sub-Saharan climate in Spain beginning with 2020 with the possibility of Mediterranean climate in Sweden, the drying-up of the Loire valley, lack of drinking water, and so on.

***

Two studies, published by American and Australian researchers in March 2004, tell of an alarming increase in the worldwide emission of greenhouse gases, due in large part to the burning of fossil fuels. One more warning bell rings amidst the general indifference.

The Australian researchers of the CSIRO (Commonwealth Scientific and Industrial Research Organisation) have verified a disturbing increase of CO_2 (carbon dioxide) emissions, which are held responsible for global warming, during 2002 and 2003. 18.4 billion tons were released into the atmosphere in 2002 and 17.1 billion in 2003, a 40 % increase over the 13.3 billion tons released on average annually in the course of the last ten years. These results have been confirmed by the American NOAA (National Oceanic and Atmospheric Administration), which has noted a sudden increase in the concentration of CO_2 in recent years. Marc Gillet, Director of the Observatoire National sur les Effets du Réchauffement Climatique (ONERC), estimates that 'it would be very troubling if similar rates of increase were verified over a longer period.'

Let us recall that since 1800 the concentration of carbon dioxide has increased by 36 %, which has probably never been seen before in the history of terrestrial ecology. Three-quarters of CO_2 emissions are generated by fossil fuels (natural gas, petroleum, coal) and the rest are the consequences of deforestation and the multiplication of giant forest fires, such as those that have recently taken place in the United States, Indonesia and Australia. So, because of the uncontrolled economic growth of Asia, especially China, whose coal reserves are considerable, we can expect a significant increase in CO_2 emissions, from increased burning of petroleum and coal. Asian countries are not bound by the Kyoto Protocol[1] to any commitment to reduce their CO_2 emissions.

Do not worry, however. This insane race of economic growth will end suddenly in the course of the Twenty-first century because of the climatic cataclysms they are going to provoke, but also perhaps by the exhaustion of petroleum resources that is appearing on the horizon.

Countdown to the Climate Bomb

The Earth is threatened not only by localized, short-term climactic events (heat waves, droughts, floods, cyclones, etc.), but by epochal climate change more violent than any other in the past. The evidence is piling up: glaciers in meltdown everywhere in the world, droughts in Africa, tropical heat waves in Europe, the construction of man-made islands in the Maldives to counter the rising ocean, the break-up in the Arctic of the largest glacier platform, which is 3,000 years old, and so on. All this is small potatoes compared with the near future, especially the depletion of the ozone layer, which inhibits plant growth and can accelerate deforestation and falling yields from farming.

---

1   The Kyoto Protocol is an effort by the United Nations to reduce greenhouse gas emissions worldwide, its first phase being the period between 2008 and 2012. It was signed on 11 December 1997 and went into effect in February 2005. Non-developed nations were not required to reduce their emissions, however, and this includes India and China, the world's two largest population centres and both are among the largest emitters. Other Asian countries, including Indonesia and Thailand, are also among the top emitters, yet are not bound by the treaty. The United States signed, but refused to ratify the treaty on these grounds, and Canada withdrew in 2011. The Kyoto Protocol ultimately laid the groundwork for future climate agreements, including the Paris Agreement of 2015, which broadened participation and shifted toward nationally determined contributions.

It is too late to react, since the lifespan of greenhouse gases in the atmosphere is measured in centuries. Even if we were to stop today or were to drastically reduce all greenhouse gas emissions, we would not escape an accelerated global warming due to the gas emitted in the Twentieth century. At any rate, nothing is being done to stop the process and emissions continue to increase at an exponential rate from the failure of the Kyoto Protocol, the American refusal to reduce industrial pollution and the impressive growth of Asian economies.

Granted this, it is very probable according to our general catastrophe scenario that the emission of pollutants is going to stop suddenly in the neighbourhood of 2020, but not voluntarily! It will be the direct consequence of the giant economic crisis and the collapse of the industrial societies. All the same, even after the global catastrophe, which will see a gigantic technological (and demographic) regression of the entire human species, humans will have to confront frightful climate conditions, the legacy of millions of tons of pollutants emitted over two hundred years.

***

The IPCC (Intergovernmental Panel on Climate Change), an international scientific organisation formed in 1988, which relies on the scientific expertise of the entire world, has published three reports since 1990, each more troubling than the previous one. The IPCC estimates that the Earth's temperature could increase by 1.4°C to 5.8°C by the end of the Twenty-first century. Jean-Marc Jancovici is a graduate of the École Polytechnique, the leading French expert on climate change, and the author of *L'effet de serre*[2] and *L'Avenir climatique*.[3] He estimates that temperatures may rise even higher and may increase by 10 degrees in two centuries!

---

2   Hervé Le Treut and Jean-Marc Jancovici, *L'effet de serre: allons-nous changer le climat?* (The Greenhouse Effect: Will We Change the Climate?) (Paris: Flammarion, 2004).

3   *L'avenir climatique: quel temps ferons-nous?* (The Climate of the Future: How Much Time Do We Have?) (Paris: Éditions du Seuil, 2002).

He wrote in the journal *Terre Sauvage* in February 2004: 'Twenty thousand years ago, in the last ice age, the median temperature of the Earth was about 10°C, while today we have reached 15°C. And yet we had ice three kilometres thick over Scandinavia, an ocean lower by 120 metres and an arctic steppe in France. Five degrees more means quite simply an epochal climate change that would bring temperatures unknown since man's appearance on Earth. With ten degrees more, it is even possible that we would reach temperatures unknown since life existed on Earth!'

In addition, this change would occur at a fantastic speed, which would prevent any adaptation. Jancovici estimates that this climatic cataclysm will compromise the survival of part of the human species and will probably entail the emergence of totalitarian regimes. In fact, confronted with dramatic change of this nature, democratic regimes are impotent: 'Tocqueville[4] already explained, more than 150 years ago, that democracies are short-sighted and are not systems well adapted to long-term challenges. ... He explained perfectly how democracies bring individualism and mass consumption. Democracies can respond to immediate threats, like war. But do democracies exist that are capable of dealing with an insidious but irreversible danger? This is an open question.'

***

Jancovici, who is an engineer, thinks, with a certain forced optimism, that an emergency solution would include a drastic reduction in our

---

4   Alexis De Tocqueville (1805–1859) was a French political thinker best known for his work, *Democracy in America,* which was based on his experiences while travelling in the United States. Although Tocqueville was a democrat who opposed the monarchy of his day, he also opposed the socialist radicals. In his study of the U.S., he praised America's democratic system, but disliked Americans' obsession with money and their contempt for elites, since even though the latter is what enabled them to do away with the old colonial aristocracy, it also caused them to disregard the most intelligent members of their society, coining the term 'tyranny of the majority' to describe it.

levels of consumption, as well as strongly increased use of nuclear energy (a source that does not emit pollutants), as well as underground carbon gas storage systems. He has no faith in wind power, which is specious, not only because of its exorbitant cost, but also because of the very low output of the new windmills when compared to the needs for electric power. He explains, 'Our social project ought to include an explicit will to seize the problem head-on and adapt everything (transportation, housing, industrial activity, budgets, use of free time, individual acts, etc.) accordingly, which is far from being the case today. This would require political courage, but also great efforts by consumers and we all are consumers. … The bad news is that there is no panacea that we can simply apply to correct the problem, while continuing to consume as we do today. To speak frankly, the tragedy is that even the lifestyle of a supermarket cashier or a factory worker is not sustainable today.'

Even if such a scenario of voluntary saving and responsibility takes place, it would not be enough to halt climate catastrophe. But it will not take place. Nobody is ready to lower or even moderate private levels of energy consumption, and especially not in the 'developing countries' of the Third World. Despite the rise of 'Green' parties — self-proclaimed ecologists, who seem to be neo-Trotskyites more than defenders of nature — the governments of the world care nothing for the questions we have just discussed, except for issuing declarations or organising 'seminars', or else elaborating timid treaties that are never ratified.

***

We are going to see the climate bomb explode. It will join the ranks of all the other problems and make them worse. A traditional society, based on rather simple technology, was resistant to climate risks, if only because of agricultural independence and cultural diversity. On the other hand, contemporary civilisation, which is highly specialised, hyper-technological, globalised, dependent on high speed transportation flow, psychologically ultra-sensitive to every disturbance, even small ones, is very *fragile* when faced with crises. The media only exaggerate the panic. The networks of production and transportation, on which we rely for all our supplies, are interdependent and so incapable of responding to a violent shock, especially a climatic one.

Let us recall, we have had warning signs: the two hurricanes of December 1999 that swept France, the repeated floods in the south of France, the unseasonable (although moderate) snowfalls that paralyse traffic, the heat wave of 2003 that upset the political order, and so on. But these pinpricks will open gaps in the social edifice and are insignificant compared to what probably awaits us.

How will our society react in perhaps less than twenty years, if Western Europe begins to experience winters like Siberia's (because of the melting of the Arctic ice cap that will entail the end of the warm Gulf Stream, followed in spring by torrential which will cause flooding, then in summer by drought and Sahara-like heat, without forgetting terrible autumn hurricanes? These will no longer be a question of 'accidents', but of a new status quo for the climate. It is likely that these phenomena will have grave repercussions on the economic, psychological and political equilibrium in a society as fragile and over-sensitive as ours.

It is impossible that the managers and political elites of today's Europe, who are marked by weakness in decision-making, an astonishing human mediocrity and a total lack of concern for the long-term, in short, by a lack of *character*, will understand or can handle such a situation.

***

Violent climate disasters are obviously going to increase all the other 'lines of catastrophe', especially in the countries of the global South, since they will pay the highest price. Certain areas could become almost uninhabitable when devastated by drought, heat, and rising ocean levels, which will only intensify mass immigration to the North, which will be increasingly mismanaged and contribute to major disruptions.

Confronted by Global Warming, the Utopias of the Ecologists

Because of greenhouse gas emissions, especially CO_2, the warming of the atmosphere is already beginning to cause significant climate disasters. According to Jean-Marc Jancovici, engineering advisor and President of X-Environnement, 'the consequences could be catastrophic and irreversible'. In fact, the difference in temperature between the glacial era and today was only 5 degrees. Back then the median temperature was only 10 degrees; now it has become 15 degrees in 10,000 years. If the greenhouse effect and global warming continue (and they will), the Earth's temperature will rise by 5 degrees in a century or even slightly less: what took 10,000 years to happen before will now happen in less than 100 years. The resulting shock and climactic cataclysms that follow will be of an unprecedented ferocity. We are seeing only the tip of the iceberg.

The failure of the 'Kyoto Protocol' that aimed at reducing the emission of pollutants, which was especially due to short-sighted American egoism, shows us that absolutely nothing will be done. Worse yet, even if by a miracle these emissions were stabilised or reduced, temperatures will continue to rise because of past pollution. So we know for a certainty that in the next twenty years these emissions will increase considerably, because of the unchecked industrialisation of the developing Asian countries, which care absolutely nothing about environmental matters.

European ecologists are proposing derisory measures — and will they follow their own suggestions? — for instance, reducing personal consumption, riding a bike instead of driving a car, taking the train instead of the airplane, eating natural tomatoes instead of greenhouse ones, reducing meat consumption, and so on. Even if these suggestions were voluntarily adopted by a large proportion of people in developed countries (which is unthinkable), these 'economies of energy' would change absolutely nothing in the state of the planet. Here again it is too late. In the Twenty-first century we are going to confront a climate shock worse than any mankind has ever experienced. And this 'line of catastrophe' will only be one among many others ...

***

Let me cite an example of the utopian character of the ecologists. Their excellent diagnosis is exceptionally clear, but they still believe that 'solutions' are possible: Serge Latouche, Professor at the University of Paris-Sud (Orsay), published a remarkable book in May 2003, *Justice sans limite*.[5] His diagnosis is that 'the Earth is at the end of its tether'. He views himself as a catastrophist (as do I), because he believes in the 'pedagogy of catastrophes'. For my part, I do not believe in it. Humans are incorrigible. For Latouche, 'the society of growth engenders catastrophes'. He says, 'Our mode of consumption, and by ours, I mean Europeans, would require two to three planets, if it were to continue in the same rhythm. The way Americans consume would require eight planets! And all this works only because the countries of the South are content with a tenth of the planet!'

Latouche looks upon 'growth' as a wicked witch. Growth is exhausting the environment, but without it the economy will collapse. So we are caught in the jaws of the trap: 'The least slow-down is a catastrophe: unemployment increases and there is no more money for culture or the environment.' The world is therefore condemned to a dramatic flight forward.

---

5   Serge Latouche, *Justice sans limites: Le défi de l'éthique dans un économie mondialisée* (Justice without Limits: The Challenge of Ethics in a Globalised Economy) (Paris: Fayard, 2003).

His solution is 'de-growth', that is, in fact, a reprise of the theme of 'zero growth' of the very prescient Club of Rome[6] in the 1970s. His basic idea was: 'We must live better with less. Growth involves enormous indirect costs, including increasing traffic, pollution, stress and so medical costs. So de-growth relies on questioning the set of beliefs on which the system rests: progress, science, the economy.' De-growth therefore extols a lifestyle that is rustic, neo-communitarian, based on localism (producing where one consumes) and drastic economies of energy. In short, it is a revolutionary model, breaking completely with what is practiced everywhere in the world.

***

This suggestion is really very old, since the American hippies had already formulated it in the 1960s. The problem is, whatever its theoretical relevance, such a suggestion has strictly no chance of being concretely followed or applied. Even poor countries aspire to only one thing: Western-style consumption and growth!

Professor Serge Latouche is aware of this fact, but he gets tangled up in contradictions when he responded in an interview in *Libération* (26 September 2003) according to the Third Worldist vulgate.

> Question: 'How do you apply the concept of "de-growth" in developing countries?'

> Answer (embarrassed): 'De-growth cannot obviously be applied in societies that do not know growth. We of the West know that, if the Chinese and the Indians follow our example and everyone buys a car, the planet will be a bloody mess. But what right do we have to forbid them access to the same things we enjoy? Let us offer another model for the rest of humanity and rediscover that happiness can be created by consuming infinitely less.'

---

6   The Club of Rome is a global think tank which was founded in 1968 to address the problems faced by humanity. In 1972 its members published a controversial book, *The Limits to Growth*, which held that the rapid increase in the global population combined with dwindling resources would lead to disaster if changes were not implemented.

We are flabbergasted by the utopian naïveté of this emeritus professor. So we are going to convince the Chinese and Indians to renounce mass consumption and adopt a 'green' lifestyle by setting a good example? Ridiculous! Here is the rationalist illusion of 'pedagogism', an illusion with deep roots in Leftist culture. This ecologist mentality is shared only by a fraction of the Western bourgeoisie who, moreover, do not even practice their own recommendations!

In all the countries of the South, the consumerist dream and desire for 'development' are very strong. Professor Latouche's model of 'degrowth' and all the analyses that lead to elaborating it certainly do not lack insight. But a society of this kind will not be imposed by human wisdom (which has never existed) nor by 'democracy' (which is always useless in emergencies), but by *constraint*, which will come from political tyranny or — the more likely case — from a *generalised catastrophe*. Professor Latouche predicts the latter case with impressive insight.

History teaches us that humans do not change their civilisation after deliberation, or by their own willpower, but in the wake of chaos that they themselves have provoked.

Violent Climate Change Is Going to Provoke Geopolitical Earthquakes

For an ever-growing number of scientists, climate change due to increased warming of the atmosphere (due to the emission of greenhouse gases) may well be much more radical and rapid than predicted. It will probably have major geopolitical consequences. The climatic upheavals that we are going to undergo will be much harsher than any we can imagine. The predictions are so precise and unsettling that Pentagon planners are worried and are including global atmospheric warming in their strategic calculations, according to an investigation by the American business magazine *Fortune*.[7] The author tells us, "The

---

7   David Stipp, 'Climate Collapse: The Pentagon's Weather Nightmare' in *Fortune* (26 January 2004).

threat that has riveted their attention is this: global warming, rather than causing gradual, centuries-spanning change, may be pushing the climate to a tipping point." The phenomenon has already started: 1997–2003 have been the warmest years on record. The oceanic-atmospheric system, on which the climate depends, could tip over into failure, like a ship rocked by the waves that capsizes without warning. If this scenario occurs — and the probability is becoming more and more likely — societies will not have time to adapt and the world's geopolitics will be turned upside down.

Core samples from the deep glaciers in the Arctic have shown that sudden catastrophic climate changes, occurring within a few years, have already occurred in the past.

***

Paradoxically, global warming may translate into Siberian winters in Europe and North America, because of the interruption of the warm current of the Gulf Stream caused by the meltdown of the ice packs, which will be followed by torrid summers. Right now we are experiencing increasingly mild winters, but this situation will not last. The northern hemisphere may also experience — in fact, it has already started — repeated hurricanes and giant forest fires as well as a series of floods and dramatic droughts. The 'temperate climate' of Western Europe may not last for long.

Satellite photos by NASA of the glacial cover at the North Pole show that between 1970 and 2003 there has been a reduction of 30 % in the ice pack. The same situation has been reported for the glaciers in high mountain ranges. David Stipp writes in *Fortune*, 'Over the past decade, data have accumulated suggesting that the plausibility of abrupt climate change is higher than most of the scientific community, and perhaps all of the political community, are prepared to accept.'[8]

---

8   David Stipp, 'Climate Collapse: The Pentagon's Weather Nightmare'.

The 2002 annual report of the American National Academy of Sciences confirms these sombre predictions. In the same year at the World Economic Forum at Davos, Robert Gagosian, Director of the Woods Hole Oceanographic Institution in Massachusetts, warned politicians from the whole world that it was necessary to take account of the major consequences of coming climate change. These 'politicians from the whole world' care only about votes ... The majority of scientists are no longer asking *if* climate catastrophe will take place during the Twenty-first century, but *when*.

***

One of the most respected Pentagon planners, Andrew Marshall, who has specialised since 1973 in 'threats to national security' and is a theoretician of anti-ballistic missile defence, and Peter Schwartz, a consultant for both Shell and the CIA, with help from climatologists, have published a highly alarmist report for the Pentagon.[9] The report concludes with speculation that something spectacular might occur around 2020. Let us summarise the principal warnings of this report that are relevant for a catastrophe scenario.

Median temperatures are going to fall *five* degrees in the northern hemisphere in America, Europe and Asia, but increase *six* degrees in southern Europe and the southern hemisphere, from 2010 to 2020. Agriculture all over the northern hemisphere will be handicapped by hurricanes and flooding rainstorms. Rising ocean levels due to the melting of the ice cap, combined with frequent storms, may make a number of cities and towns on the coast of northern Europe unliveable and lead to their evacuation, especially in Holland. Giant tornadoes and dust storms are going to become more frequent in the American South and Midwest.

---

9   Peter Schwartz and Doug Randall, 'An Abrupt Climate Change Scenario and Its Implications for United States National Security' (October 2003).

Climate upheavals will have the most serious consequences in Third World countries and the global South, which may increase the gap between rich and poor countries. Droughts, deforestation, the end of regular monsoon seasons and the flooding of coastal plains (phenomena that are already happening) will produce famines, scarcity of drinking water and massive displacement of populations. These in turn will lead to a general destabilisation, which will take the following forms, according to this report, which the Pentagon addressed to the White House:

1) Famines and uncontrollable epidemics may occur in all the countries of the global South, leading to the ruin of their agriculture, starting in 2010.

2) We can expect massive immigration larger than what we are experiencing today into the northern countries with unsustainable pressure from impoverished and starving masses.

3) China in particular will be affected by climate upheavals, especially by the risk of extreme flooding. The report predicts the destabilisation of the most heavily populated country in the world. There are similar risks for India, Pakistan, Indonesia and Bangladesh, which will become uninhabitable as a result of rising ocean levels.

4) Russia, which is in a demographic coma, but possesses significant natural resources, may experience relentless immigration pressure from all its southern neighbours. More generally the flow of refugees will increase tenfold everywhere on the planet, posing unsolvable problems and provoking civil wars.

5) All these phenomena will lead to nuclear conflicts in Asia, but also elsewhere, and 'nuclear arms proliferation is inevitable'.[10]

---

10   Peter Schwartz and Doug Randall, 'An Abrupt Climate Change Scenario and Its Implications for United States National Security', p. 19.

***

This report addressed to the Pentagon also predicts a certain number of disturbing scenarios, all based on peoples' vital need for access to resources that are increasingly scarce (food from farming or fishing, drinking water and fossil fuels).

1) North America (United States and Canada) is trying to create a bloc impermeable to massive immigration, following a fortress logic, while jealously preserving its water resources, of which it is depriving Mexico and Latin America, which are subject to drought.

2) The same fortress logic might animate all Europe and Russia to join together to dam up the explosive migratory floods of refugees from Africa and Asia. In both these cases the pressure of facts would sweep away the morality of human rights and re-establish the morality of 'every man for himself'.

3) The rapid climate catastrophe, plus the decline in petroleum reserves, will provoke 'aggressive wars [that] are likely to be fought over food, water, and energy'.[11] In the atmosphere of planet-wide generalised insecurity beginning from 2010, Korea (now reunified), Japan, Iran, and others, will possess nuclear weapons. Old ways of thinking will change as fast as the climate.

Neither the market nor technological progress will be able to handle this giant crisis, which will be fuelled even more by the rise in power of the Islamic countries. The archaeologist Steven A. LeBlanc, who teaches at Harvard and is cited in the report, noted that, in the past, wars for scarce resources were part of the human condition. In the near *future* we are going to return to this *archaic* situation, where armed conflicts caused the disappearance of 25 % of the population. His research shows that each time in human history when there was violent

---

11 Peter Schwartz and Doug Randall, 'An Abrupt Climate Change Scenario and Its Implications for United States National Security', p. 15.

climate change — especially after the last glaciation — war became the only solution to appropriate scarce resources.

***

The recommendations of the Pentagon report are astonishing. They first of all castigate the delaying of the political and scientific communities in admitting the emergency, as well as their disregard for the fact that it is human activity that is rapidly changing the Earth's climate.

It suggests, without putting too much faith in it (because it is already too late), taking every care to study and halt the phenomenon. It recommends survival measures that are to be adopted without second thoughts of the moral consequences ('no-regrets strategies'), even if they are violent, pragmatic and cynical, and even if they break with the ideology of human rights, in order to assure at all costs the security of North America, as well as its access to food, water, and energy, and its ability to defend itself against waves of immigrants fleeing climate catastrophe.

The Spectre of Shortages

In the journal *Ecologist*,[12] economist David Fleming predicts that 'to be sure, the planet's crude oil resources are going to last for a few more decades yet. However, the struggles over access and profits between countries and multinational corporations are already becoming fiercer.' On the basis of recent geological research he writes, 'Then, in the middle years of the decade 2010–2019, production by Middle East OPEC itself will start to fall, and decline will also set in for the combined total of both oil and gas. ... It can be expected to do so in, or shortly after, 2010. That will be the start of a sellers' market, putting the producers in control. The consequences will be devastating. ... Brief breakdowns in the supply of fuel can be survived; with sustained interruptions, however, the global market economy would cease to exist.'

---

12   David Fleming, 'The Wages of Denial', in *Ecologist* (1 April 2003).

In Fleming's opinion, this is the cause of American neo-militarism: 'America's determination to take military action to prevent the Middle East being closed-off as a reliable seller of oil can be thus be better understood as a case of self-defence.'

***

What should we think of 'renewable energies'? Opponents of nuclear energy regularly explain to us that, in order to avoid a situation where abandoning nuclear power leads to the construction of hyper-polluting fossil fuel-burning power plants (petroleum, coal and natural gas), we must turn to 'renewable energies', an expression repeated like a mantra. Unfortunately, the facts are stubborn. The largest wind power factory in the world, which is under construction in Tasmania and equipped with 79 giant windmills with three blades each, the Vestas V66 built in Denmark, will produce 130 megawatts (MW) of energy, or forty times less than a single French nuclear power plant with four reactors of the Cattenon or Nogent-sur-Seine type (5,200 MW). And these wind power farms, which occupy enormous areas of land, can be built only on a very small number of sites, which enjoy powerful and regular wind.

What about solar panels? To reach the electricity-producing power of a single average nuclear reactor (900 MW of the Cruas-Meysse brand) would require the land surface of an entire French province! What about the 'marine current turbines' built by the English? The ones planned for the Severn estuary near Bristol will produce ... a single megawatt and, at full power, 50 MW. In this case, too, the sites where they can be constructed in the world are few. The passive four helix pylons are buried in the estuaries of rivers, and tied to generators that are themselves connected to underwater electrophoretic cables. The ratio of energy produced to total cost is 60 % lower than with nuclear power. Therefore renewable energies can only provide backup energy.

***

A major problem for which it is hard to see a solution is the problem of 'blue gold', that is, drinking water, the shortages of which are beginning to be felt. In 2025 the Earth will contain 8.3 billion inhabitants (an increase of 45 % over today). There will not be enough drinking water for this population, because resources are disappearing, especially as a result of massive pollution but also from the growing droughts caused by climate change in the countries of the global South.

Conflicts and wars for the control of hydrologic and water-bearing basins can be predicted, as the WHO has done. Consider Lake Chad that has gone from 25,000 km2 to 2,500 km2 because of desertification. The privatisation of water and attempts to corner the market in water by business interests will only make matters worse.

Of the water on this planet, only 2.5 % is fresh water, but the majority of it is frozen or too deep. Only 0.007 % of the total is accessible to humans. Between 1900 and 2003, water consumption has multiplied seven times, or twice the rate of population growth, and 70 % of the water is used for farming irrigation. Currently a fifth of the world's population does not have access to water. This proportion can only increase.

***

The Earth is about to have a shortage of water. Already, in Italy, Greece and Spain there is a serious drought problem and a shortage of fresh water, especially for irrigation. The pollution of groundwater and rivers is compromising the food supply everywhere and is making the use of 'blue gold' more and more expensive. With worldwide demographic growth, the shortage of water is going to become a deadly weapon.

Today more than one and a half billion individuals live without access to clean water. In 2025 this number will be 3 billion, spread over 52 countries, not only in Africa and the Middle East, but also in Pakistan, China, India, and others. In order to feed their growing populations, governments are furiously developing agriculture (deforesting and polluting). This is making matters worse, since agricultural activity uses up aquatic resources.

The fourteen largest Indian rivers and 75 % of the Chinese river network are so seriously polluted that fish can no longer survive in them. 25 % of Bangladesh's inhabitants absorb arsenic every time they quench their thirst. Here is the frightening fact: today there is just as much water on the Earth as there was 2,000 years ago, but the human population is thirty times larger.

'Water wars' are inevitable. They are a significant factor in the potential wars between India and Pakistan or Israel and its neighbours. Water is one more factor destabilising the global system, that it will not be possible to contain.

Examples of Ecological Disasters

In 1995 a report of the highly official Security Council of the Russian Federation warned that the Russian population was menaced by an 'ecological disaster'. Poorly buried radioactive waste, polluted groundwater, decimated forests, and so on, can provoke 'degeneration of the population' in the Twenty-first century, if these threats are not halted. Nine years later there is no reason to think that they have been. The report noted, 'Russia is threatened by a very real ecological terrorism', which could well cause nothing less than 'the progressive extinction of the Russian population' in the course of the Twenty-first century. The report continues, 'Optimism for the future is sinking, disease is increasing and there are reports of a growing number of birth defects.' Add to this the demographic coma into which Russia is falling and which I shall discuss elsewhere.

***

The demographic explosion in Third World cities can no longer be controlled and constitutes a new line of catastrophe. The situation of

Manila, capital of the Philippines, is an emblematic case, which is also found in Mexico City, Lagos, Bombay, and others. In Manila, with 16 million inhabitants by 2010, as a result of the uncontrolled exodus from the countryside, ecological disaster is beginning to handicap the economy and threaten the health of its inhabitants.

The nine public drains, which are open to the sky, are overflowing. The 5,900 tons of garbage produced every day increases by 4.5 % a year. Wildcat drains pollute the water supply and poison the fish in Manila Bay, which is disappearing under the 800 tons of garbage that pour into it every day. Although legally prohibited, the incineration of wastes is growing and generates toxic emissions. The administration of water is catastrophic: 54 % of the water supply is unregulated. In the ever-growing shantytowns, when there are floods, which are more and more frequent, everything overflows and water that has been used mingles with garbage, contaminating drinking water and generating appalling sanitary conditions.

The Philippines' population growth is going to give an even more dramatic seriousness to these problems. In 2001, in the Tondo shantytown, a cholera epidemic was barely averted after killing nearly fifty inhabitants. Unhealthy conditions and poverty ceaselessly increase the gap between rich and poor and multiply the chances of social upheavals. The shantytowns, which are not connected to the water supply, are served by 'water carriers', who charge eight times the price paid by those who are connected to the water network. The groundwater is drying up or becoming polluted, making 'blue gold' increasingly rare and expensive.

The effect on neighbouring agriculture is that irrigation can no longer be practiced and rice has to be imported from Thailand. The Philippine government is totally powerless, overwhelmed by the scale of the problems.

All these facts are the same in a score of enormous cities that have grown too large in the countries of the South. They encourage all sorts of internal destabilisations, not to mention the temptations to emigrate *en masse* to the West.

And Let's Not Forget Epidemics

Where is AIDS in all of this? It is doing quite well, thank you. The pandemic is not slowing down, but speeding up. Here are the figures for 2001: 5 million new cases were reported, 66 % in Africa. 3 million infected are dead. There are 40 million HIV-positive cases reported worldwide and this number is likely lower than in reality. The number of HIV-positive cases and true AIDS cases should perhaps be doubled, since in the Third World it is often impossible to get an accurate count of AIDS victims. In Asia, the epidemic is rapidly increasing: 7.1 million are sick and more than a million are infected; in Western Europe, there are 560,000 sick and 30,000 recently infected; and in the United States, there are 940,000 sick and 30,000 infected, and AIDS is taking off again, since people are taking fewer precautions because of 'tritherapies', and because the use of intravenous drugs is on the increase. In Russia the epidemic is exploding: there are 800,000 infected and a rate of increase of 15 %.

In Paris the number of HIV-positive patients is beginning to increase, after falling for a number of years, increasing by 25 % for the last three years. 0.86 % of the population of Paris who were tested were found to be infected. This number is lower than the reality since subjects who are at risk get themselves tested more than others. The number of those who are infected without being aware of it and believe that they are protected from danger is probably high. The increase is greatest among women from 29 to 49 and men from 30 to 49. In the Île-de-France,[13] the 'rate of risk-taking' (sexual contacts that are unprotected or with multiple partners or intravenous drug use) has increased dramatically, especially among the young: 31 % among those younger than 25 years old! Almost one young person in three engages in unprotected sex ...

The annual report of the United Nations program UNAIDS says, 'AIDS stands a good chance of becoming unequivocally the most

---

13   The largest administrative region in France, containing Paris.

devastating disease that humanity has ever known.' Since 1982, the
AIDS epidemic has already killed 22 million people, but, according
to Dr. Peter Piot, Executive Director of UNAIDS, 'the worst is yet to
come.'

**

A new hyper-resistant form of the HIV virus has appeared. The HIV
retrovirus is much more likely to mutate than the virus we already
know. Medical treatments (the famous 'tritherapies') have allowed the
lives of those with AIDS to be prolonged to a very significant degree, as
well as to combat the three known forms of the retrovirus, HIV I, HIV
II and HIV III, and therefore, along with the regular use of condoms,
this has slowed the epidemic in the West. However, researchers at the
American National Institute of Health (NIH) and the University of
California have discovered in San Francisco, in early July 2003, the
appearance of a new form of HIV that is resistant to all treatments.

The explanation is that the enormous homosexual 'community'
in California is no longer taking precautions in the belief that AIDS
has been 'vanquished' by tritherapies. Those who are HIV-positive,
who no longer take care of themselves or use condoms, are 'over-
infecting' their partners, who are also HIV-positive. The HIV virus
then mutates, getting stronger and becoming invincible. This situation
is already affecting heterosexuals, who are developing the fatal illness
at an alarming rate, without any way to slow down the spreading contagion, as at the beginning of the 1980s. This news should be related
to the accelerating spread of AIDS in the entire world, of which we
have already spoken. The NIH report concludes, 'All this means that
America will probably never see the end of the virus by herself, unless
a breakthrough is made by the discovery of a vaccine or a definitive
treatment, two highly unlikely hypotheses. ... The conclusion of the
studies made in San Francisco is that the HIV infection has become
endemic in the United States.'

***

The International Conference on AIDS that took place in Barcelona at the beginning of July 2003 has shown that AIDS may well cause life expectancy in sub-Saharan Africa to sink to a level lower than in the Nineteenth century. In Botswana, 39 % of adults are HIV-positive and life expectancy is 26.7 years, as opposed to 75 years in the worst period of colonialism ... Several Africa countries are about to disappear from the map or return to the Stone Age. Of course, we Europeans should take the blame and hold ourselves 'responsible for this holocaust', in the words of the ethnomasochist[14] Simon Carr in *The Independent*. The problem is that the endangered populations all dream of fleeing to Europe. In France, for example, the principal carriers and spreaders of the virus are Africans: according to the Public Assistance of Paris, 79 % of those recently infected are of sub-Saharan origin.

***

The return of syphilis will not astonish anyone but the naïve. We used to believe that it had been definitely eradicated. It has come back, just like tuberculosis and mange and, perhaps very soon, cholera and the plague. The causes are always the same: a decrease in the use of pro-phylactics and anti-venereal precautions and the absence of medical check-ups of a very large foreign population, whose state of health and hygiene leave much to be desired. According to the Centre for 'Refugees' of Sangatte, in the Pas-de-Calais, several cases of mange (a contagious skin disease) have been observed in April 2002. Firemen who enter the Centre have to wear a TPUU.[15]

Here are the figures for France: 1990: 0 cases; 1999: 9 cases; 2000: 29 cases; 2001: 139 cases; since January 1, 2002: 240 cases, of which 199

---

14 Ethnomasochism, according to Faye in his book *Why We Fight: Manifesto for the European Resistance* (London: Arktos, 2011), is '[t]he masochistic tendency to blame and devalue one's ethnicity, one's own people'.

15 *Tenue de protection à usage unique*, or disposable biohazard suit.

are in Paris. 90 % of the infected are male homosexuals or bisexuals and 50 % are suffering from AIDS. Mange is a sexually transmitted disease caused by a type of bacteria called treponemes. It was a serious problem until the discovery of penicillin in 1945. But is there any way to guarantee that new, mutated forms of bacteria that will be resistant to antibiotics will not appear, as we have seen with other diseases?

***

And let us not forget that according to the Ministry of Health tuberculosis, which had once been eradicated thanks to antibiotics, is again spreading in France. The principal victims (and spreaders of the disease) are immigrants. 65 % of reported cases are of foreigners.

2

TOWARD THE CLASH
OF CIVILISATIONS

The Globalisation of War

A lready subject to a terrible degrading of the ecological state of its earthly environment, humanity from the beginning of the Twenty-first century is going to experience at the same time giant confrontations whose intensity will be much worse than the last two 'world wars'. At any rate, they were not 'world wars' in the strict sense, since they were fought over very limited areas of the face of the earth.

On the other hand, what we are going to experience will be a real 'worldwide' crisis and, in addition to classic wars, there will be civil wars and terrorism involving criminal organisations. Everything is beginning to be sketched out, but the logic of these conflicts has not yet reached a serious level. We have not seen anything yet. We are feeling the breath of the gentle, unhealthy breeze that precedes the devastating cyclone by a few hours.

The Cold War that opposed the West to the Communism led by the USSR was a sort of shadow boxing, a confrontation resting on artificial polarities, that is, ideologies. There was a game of creating fear and, obviously, nothing happened and Russian Communism sank (or imploded) without a sound. What is coming differs by nature. We are returning to the *archaic*, that is, the eternal condition of mankind, which the brief parenthesis of 'modernity' made us forget, in other words, the rivalry of peoples, of ethnic and cultural blocs and of civilisations.

***

In fact, despite or because of the techno-scientific homogenisation of the world, despite or because of the Western attempt to unify humanity culturally, local traditions and ethnic identities are becoming stronger in response. The speed of travel and communication, like the world's demographic density that makes the Earth seem like a crowded subway station, makes a potentially explosive situation out of the very ancient propensity to 'the clash of civilisations' — the title of Samuel P. Huntington's essay,[1] whose sound idea echoed around the world because it designates a real threat that all decision-makers perceive very clearly.

This 'clash of civilisations' will take different forms. It will bring together all the forms of war and conflict. Here are the principal fault lines:

1) A global confrontation with Islam.

    Whether we like it or not, Islam has entered its third phase of conquest, towards the 'Universal Caliphate'. The first two phases

---

1   Samuel Huntington (1927–2008) was an American political scientist who became infamous for serving as an advisor to authoritarian regimes, such as South Africa in the 1980s. He famously postulated that nations in the process of transitioning into modernity must be cautious about not introducing democracy too quickly into their societies, and that repressive measures can actually be necessary and beneficial in the short term. More recently, he became well-known for his 1993 essay 'The Clash of Civilizations' published in *Foreign Affairs*, which was later expanded into a book of the same name, in which he theorized that the changing world order following the collapse of Communism would be defined by conflicts between cultural blocs, such as the West and the Islamic world.

happened in the Seventh to the Eleventh centuries, as well as in the Sixteenth to the Eighteenth centuries. It is a question of a groundswell that the governments of Islamic countries, which are pro-Western out of temporary calculation, cannot disguise for long. Islam's principal weapon is its demographic vigour, in the face of Western countries that are experiencing depopulation. This confrontation will cover the planet and will usually take the form of civil war, with episodes of classic war.

2) The risk of a war between China and the USA.

The causes of such a war will be tied not only to the question of Taiwan, but also to rivalry over the status of superpower, especially economic superpower. China is a much more serious challenger for the USA than the defunct USSR.

3) The serious opposition between India and Pakistan.

Two nuclear powers opposed in every respect (from religion to harnessing water resources and territorial claims) are permanently on the threshold of open war. A lasting reconciliation is unimaginable. The contest will take place between Indian Hindus and Pakistani Muslims.

4) The conflagration in the Near East.

The infected wound in the world's heel is the Israeli-Palestinian question that is only going to get worse, since nothing can stop the protagonists of this inextricable situation, which opposes Judaism to Arab Islamism, from moving to extremes. By invading nearby Iraq, Washington and the 'neo-conservatives' followed an absurd perception of geopolitics and have only succeeded in making the infected wound a bit worse. Since the fall of the USSR, unilateral American imperialism has not stopped destabilising the world's equilibrium, especially in the Near East. This region will soon catch fire, with an intensity that we cannot yet imagine.

***

The world is threatened by the *conflagration of war*, at this paradoxical moment when there is endless talk of 'human rights' and 'peace'. The United Nations, a first draft of world government, has shown its impotence everywhere. From the Near East to the Balkans, including the suburbs of Europe and even Africa, we meet the logic of ethnic and nationalist confrontation, which belies the dominant ideology inspired by the pious hopes of Christian universalism.

Nothing will halt nuclear proliferation among states and terrorist groups. In all the countries of the Third World (the opposite of an emasculated Europe) ethnic and nationalist passions are strengthening the people. The *general atmosphere* of this humanity, this planet, this civilisation near its end is a generalised brawl. There is no way to prevent it, just as nothing will halt the conflict discussed above, because it is too late and we have reached the point of no return.

Toward the Most Bellicose Century in History

In the face of war, a certain number of contradictory paradoxes are revealed:

1) Pacifism, the universal lay religion of the Americano-centric West, along with the doctrine of tolerating zero casualties in war, is accompanied by an intensification of planetary violence, provoked, of course, by Islam, but also by America's 'collateral' strikes almost everywhere in the world since 1991 and by the murderous embargo against Iraq.

2) After the end of the Cold War, a belief was proclaimed in a 'New World Order', an 'end of history', world peace characterised by democracy and trade (*Pax Americana*). Now the Twenty-first century is preparing for us perhaps the most bellicose situation in the entire history of humanity. The enormous wars of the Twentieth

century will be smaller than those that we and our descendants are going to experience.

The factors are well known: the *de facto* conquest by massive Third World immigration into the North with the accompanying ethnic civil wars that immigration will provoke; the revival of Islamic *jihad* on a worldwide scale from Gibraltar to Indonesia, with a will ten times more bellicose, because it is *archaic*, than the will of the defunct USSR; the chance of a confrontation between China and the United States for control of the Pacific; but also, on a planet that has become crowded, and has seen the spread of nuclear weapons, multiplying conflicts of every sort between states; without forgetting that since 9/11 we are in the era of *macro-terrorism* and that we shall very probably see acts of nuclear terrorism, with devastating destabilising effects.

3) In spite of a publically proclaimed desire for world peace under its aegis (or that of NATO), the hypocritical United States has a vital economic need to develop its military-industrial complex and therefore to maintain fronts everywhere, like wounds that are always open.

4) In addition, two of the major figures at the beginning of this century, the United States and Islam, are two rival universalisms, two Manichean messianic cults, aggressive but related. Both function under a mode of religious fanaticism (the *Bible* and the *Qur'an*), both posit an absolute Good and Evil, a paradise and a hell, large or small Satans, and, in addition, function according to an imperialist logic that is direct and violent (not muffled like the former USSR). The 'warrior crusade for the Good and for expansion' appears in their two visions of the world.

***

Thus everything leads us to believe that, rather than a *peaceful globalisation* (the dream of the 'world state'), we are going to experience in the Twenty-first century a *bellicose globalisation*. Having passed through the era of continental wars that became world wars, and which returned from time to time, we are now going to see it followed by the era of a globalised war, endemic and protean in form, which will oppose states to other states, Islam to other civilisations — the Americano-centric West, and so on. War will assume the masks of classic wars, civil wars in the streets, terrorist wars, economic wars, and others.

We should have expected it. Human nature is martial and this trait cannot be eradicated, since it is innate. In the past when civilisations and peoples were relatively separated and intermingled only occasionally, conflicts were necessarily limited. In our day, in this first global century, when civilisations, ethnic identities and diverging interests have not disappeared by dissolving into a general melting pot, but, on the contrary, have been affirmed and exacerbated, and when technology gives a greater ability to wage combat, one can predict an all-out brawl in the heart of humanity. We are going to experience a permanent and multiform state of conflict, of which we see only the beginning, and which will automatically lead to the collapse, the breakdown of the current world order, as the result of serious perturbations linked one to the others — taking into account the extremely fragile character of the globalised economy.

Terror as Art of Living

In fact, in view of the attacks of September 11 on the United States — which marked the real beginning of the Twenty-first century — terrorism has changed its nature. This is *neo-terrorism*. The novelty is that it can now create *mass massacres* while before it used to be limited to less than 200 deaths per operation, when the most murderous was the possibility of detonating bombs aboard airplanes in flight. The use of sophisticated technologies has created this new situation. This allows us to revive Carl Schmitt's distinction between the conventional 'warrior' and the 'partisan' and to say that from now on the partisan will see his status and dangerousness equal, or rather surpass, that of the military apparatus of states.[2]

Let us not indulge in wishful thinking. We shall again see large-scale terrorist acts, perpetrated by Islamist fanatics (or others), this time using biological, chemical or nuclear weapons. This is the way terrorism makes its bloody entrance into history, no longer as a *minor threat*, but as a *major threat*, equal to and perhaps even worse than the threat of nuclear war between states.

What are the fearsome dangers that await us? They are seven in number:

1) More attacks by suicide bombers on airplanes, including small private planes and helicopters diverted from their route and loaded with explosives. In this regard precautionary measures against air piracy are of dubious effectiveness.

2) Attacks using airplanes or bombs on the ground against nuclear reactors.

3) Bioterrorism dispersing bacterial strains, not especially murderous in reality, but with a very significant psychological effect.

4) Dispersion in confined places (as in the Tokyo subway by the Aum Shinrikyo[3] sect) of poison gas or poisoning the channels of drinking water. The effect will be similar to number 3.

---

2   Carl Schmitt (1888–1985) was an important German jurist who wrote about political science, geopolitics and constitutional law. He was part of the Conservative Revolutionary movement of the Weimar era. He also briefly supported the National Socialists at the beginning of their regime, although they later turned against him. He remains highly influential in the fields of law and philosophy. He describes his ideas about the partisan in *Theory of the Partisan* (New York: Telos Press, 2007).

3   Aum Shinrikyo is a New Age cult based in Japan, the beliefs of which are derived from a variety of sources, including Buddhism. On 20 March 1995, some of its

5) Attacks by vehicles driven by suicide bombers containing more than one hundred kilos of explosives rolling through the heart of large cities. These will be as impossible to prevent as the attacks at Beirut against the French and American barracks.[4]

6) Exploding rudimentary or miniaturised atomic bombs in big cities or significant targets. This scenario was predicted in the 1980s by the political scientist Julien Freund.[5]

7) Exploding radiological 'dirty bombs' made from recycled plutonium in urban areas with devastating effects from the massive radiation.

We shall come back in the conclusion to all these forms of terrorism. In summary, we can now distinguish three types of terrorism: micro-terrorism (less than 200 deaths); macro-terrorism (thousands of deaths), which was inaugurated on September 11 in New York; and giga-terrorism (10,000 deaths and up), which we have not yet seen, but, you can be sure, *we are going to see.*

---

members released sarin gas into the Tokyo subway system, killing 30 people and injuring hundreds more. During the subsequent trial, the prosecution later claimed that the goal of the attack had been to bring about the downfall of the Japanese government. The group continues to exist under the name Aleph.

4   On 23 October 1983, two simultaneous suicide truck bombings hit the barracks of the United States Marines and of the French paratroopers in Beirut, who were part of the Multinational Force which was there to oversee the conflict between Israel and the Palestinians. Over 300 people, mostly American and French servicemen, were killed, and led to the withdrawal of the Multinational Force from Lebanon. The responsibility for the bombings has never been firmly established, although it is widely believed that the Lebanese Islamist group Hezbollah, acting on instructions from the Iranian government, carried out the attacks.

5   Julien Freund (1921–1993) was a student of Raymond Aron and Carl Schmitt. During the Second World War, he was a member of the French Resistance movement. After the war he became a professor of sociology at the University of Strasbourg. In 1980, in protest against the French educational system and its methods of teaching political science, he decided to retire. He was also a contributor to New Right publications in both Germany and France.

***

The greatest danger concerns giga-terrorism by nuclear attacks, next to which flying civilian airplanes against the Twin Towers of the World Trade Center may well turn out to be nothing more than a little bee sting, in comparison with the two forms of nuclear terrorism (atomic bombs and 'dirty bombs'). With all their misfortune, the Americans had one bit of crazy good luck: if the diverted Boeing, which crashed, they say, into one wing of the Pentagon, had instead struck the nuclear plant at Three Mile Island, which is located nearby, the radiation would have been enough to cause the evacuation of a large part of the East Coast of the United States — including New York and Washington — for fifty years!

In other words, nuclear terrorism could bring a superpower like the United States to its knees, with very small means in comparison with the enormous size of the military objective obtained. This is the radical novelty of neo-terrorism and its superiority to the safety precautions of normal states. While bombardment with laser-guided bombs or cruise missiles against military targets found in countries supposed to be 'helping the terrorists' costs a considerable amount and has meagre results, a 'trifling' operation with modest means (not even the cost of a single F-18 fighter-bomber) can have devastating results. This is the advantage of neo-terrorism: an enormous effectiveness in terms of costs and results.

Since the fall of the USSR, it is known that nuclear fuel is for sale virtually over the counter from the networks of the Russian mafia, and that scientists from the former Soviet Union are selling their services to anyone who can pay their price. In addition, there are the 'leaks' coming from Pakistan, which possesses nuclear weapons, the 'Islamic bomb' Bin Laden bragged about.

And then, by a sort of contagion, the attacks of September 11 and those that followed have certainly given ideas to groups of fanatics who are not especially Muslim or even 'political' in the classic sense:

networks of crackpots of all types, criminal groups or extremist movements of the extreme Left or extreme Right (like the Oklahoma City
bombing, perpetrated by American 'militias' of the extreme Right),
outlandish neo-Nazi or new Leftist revivals, and pseudo-religious
sects. Anything is possible. Giga-terrorism does not cost much and,
provided there is good organisation and good training, it has the technical means, beginning with hundreds of individuals, to destabilise a
planet of several billion people.

**

Neo-terrorism is like a virus confronting a lion. The mighty lion cannot detect the microscopic virus, but the virus can kill the lion and
not *vice versa*. Jean de La Fontaine[6] foresaw the situation in his fable
'The Lion and the Gnat'.[7] The weak challenges the strong or the mad
challenges the strong, as you please.

One of the characteristics of this mass neo-terrorism is that, unlike
classic terrorism, it can destabilise the West and the world economy,
which, since globalisation, has become disturbingly *fragile* and *vulnerable*. This is the domino effect. The most powerful terrorist actions
of the past did not succeed in affecting speculators or investors or
terrorising public opinion. It is extraordinary to learn that, after the attacks of September 11, a very large number of economic sectors entered
into crisis, from air travel to cinema, and even including tourism, and
all this from a simple psychological effect of panic multiplied by the
media. One estimate was that in Europe an entire growth point was
lost from the GDP. Unheard of!

---

6   Jean de La Fontaine (1621–1695) was a Seventeenth-century French poet.

7   In this fable, a gnat challenges a lion to a fight. The lion, enraged that he is
     being attacked by such a tiny creature, tries to kill the gnat as it attaches itself
     to various parts of his body, but the gnat is so small as to be able to evade the
     lion's strikes, and continues to annoy him. Exhausted, the lion finally gives up
     the fight.

There were two memorable images from that time. One was of President Bush just after the attacks, looking frightened in a command centre that was crowded with computers and television screens; the other — filmed on amateur video — was Bin Laden, surrounded by his lieutenants, standing like a new Muhammad, at the back of a cave, a Kalashnikov AKS-74U beside him, dressed in the traditional garb of an Eighth-century Bedouin, defying his enemy on all the world's televisions. It was the rise of the archaic *in the very heart of a sick modernity.*

***

I shall cite passages from an interview conducted by Luther Blisset with Paul Virilio,[8] a French philosopher, urbanist and specialist in 'speed', which was published by Sinergias Europeas, the Spanish bureau of Synergies européennes, on 6 October 2001. The journalist asks Virilio if, since September 11, we have not entered the Third World War. Listen to how Virilio responds: 'The Twentieth century started with the First World War in 1914. In 2001 we are witnessing the first war of globalisation. The difference between the two is one of extent. The First World War was limited essentially to Europe and we are now entering a globalised war. The attack on the World Trade Center in New York corresponds to the attack in Sarajevo in August 1914' (because the two events raised the curtain for a war). We are indeed entering the Third World War, but it will be a new type of war and a much more serious one. The philosopher Virilio explains that up to this point we have been dealing with *micro-terrorism*, which had no catastrophic impact. Now, however, we are dealing with 'large-scale global terrorism, of which the first symbolic sign was the fall of the Twin Towers of the World Trade Center. This large-scale terrorism will continue and become nuclear terrorism'. Virilio thinks that nuclear terrorism could take two forms, either 'anti-cities' (against civilian

---

8   Paul Virilio (1932–2018) was a French philosopher who wrote primarily about technology, as well as what the use of physical space tells us about the institutions that utilize it.

populations), or 'anti-forces' (against ports, factories, etc.). He believes that nuclear terrorism against civilian populations will become the dominant form. Then he makes the following acerbic remark: 'Bush, with his anti-missile system, is completely mistaken. He thought that the danger would come from intercontinental missiles, and in fact the attack came from three airplanes that belonged to American Airlines! I insist: we are dealing with a real war and not with "terrorism"'! Yes, to be sure, but in a war we need an enemy. This is a war against whom? Against Islam or against shadows? Virilio, as he usually does, offers a brilliant analysis, but it may be insufficient.

Let us first examine his analysis objectively. For Virilio, after the fall of the Berlin Wall, the Gulf War and Kosovo — which he calls conflicts of the 'post-Cold War' period — we are entering 'a new period of international war' that he analyses as follows: 'Formerly there existed an equilibrium of terror, which lasted up to the fall of the Soviet Union. With the fall of the towers of the World Trade Center we are entering the era of the disequilibrium of terror. Anything is possible, even the unimaginable!' In his opinion, 'the West is completely unprepared for this new form of war', and then adds, 'There are two forms of war: the classic and "substantial" conflict with armies and the "accidental" war with unpredictable modalities. In the Twentieth century, classic war could degenerate into a subversive war of partisans, guerillas, local terrorisms. But today, we are entering a form of war without openly declared enemies, without front lines, a furtive war.' In summary, no longer a 'world war', but a 'globalised' war, a blind war, without rules, without frontiers or sanctuaries, in which there are no low blows and even the most horrible ones are permitted, in a society 'delocalised' and animated by the 'speed of movement', where the invisible enemy strikes from within.

Virilio explains that Bush is confused because he 'cannot distinguish a clearly identified enemy'. In other words, Bush does not dare designate Islam, but instead the abstract enemy that is 'terrorism'.

Virilio explains that classic, territorial war, *à la* Clausewitz[9] (war between nations) is obsolete and the theory of anti-ballistic missile defence has been made ridiculous by September 11. The threat was not where everyone expected it.

Virilio gives a very impressive analysis, which must, however, be completed, for it seems insufficient. From our point of view his 'First War of Globalisation' opposes two different camps. Virilio forgets the historical dimension. He is too much of a sociologist. Islam has been trying to invade Europe for 1,300 years. On two previous occasions it failed, but it keeps returning obstinately to the assault and is never discouraged. This is the key element that Virilio neglects. War can change *forms* and does so eternally, but it always opposes two different camps: friend and foe, us and them. Between the two there is no mercy. Let us think about the expression, used in French and Spanish, '*nous autres*': the rest of us.

***

The struggle against terrorism that the United States and other Western countries say they are conducting is suffering from impotence since they do not dare to clearly name their enemies (radical Islam) and because, out of naïveté, they are allowing millions of foreign immigrants from the Third World and Islamic countries to set themselves up on their own soil, especially in Europe. The 52 million Muslims present in Europe, from Gibraltar to Russia, are breeding grounds for Islamist terrorists much more dangerous than the terrorist networks of the Near East! On the other hand, Europeans and Americans are completely blind to the coming of an ethnic civil war and a demographic submersion much more serious than 'terrorism'. It is not bombs and armed attacks, but rather ethnic submersion that destroys peoples. On the contrary, bombs and violence can wake them up. The principal

---

9   Carl von Clausewitz (1780–1831) was a Prussian officer and military strategist whose principal work, *On War*, continues to be regarded as one of the most important formulations of strategic theory.

weapon of war in every age has been the infiltration, naturalisation, and progressive seizure of power by foreigners. Battles and terrorist acts only accompany this basic movement, but are not its content.

In France, giga-terrorism may be accompanied by a repetitive micro-terrorism, as in Israel: a daily terrorist incident by a booby-trapped car or a kamikaze attack, with a 'strategy of tension'.[10] The real struggle against terrorism must succeed first in reducing and then eliminating the massive and organised presence of Islam in areas where it was not — or was no longer — present in the Twentieth century. This is the politics of containment, extolled during the Cold War by the Pentagon (McNamara)[11] against Communism, which was infinitely less dangerous than Islam. The strategy must be first to contain and then to repel Islam everywhere where it expands outside its historic territory.

**

Can Islamic terrorism strike the United States again? The experts of the American government are afraid that it will. Under the cover of anonymity (in a few cases they actually give their names), they confided in Lisa Myers of MSNBC News (16 September 2003). Here is a summary of the substance of their fears. First of all, as was perfectly predictable, the invasion of Iraq did not weaken the terrorist networks; in fact, it strengthened and spread them. George W. Bush's policies, which were supposed to reduce the risk of attacks against the

---

10 The term 'strategy of tension' was coined by Leftist groups in Italy in the 1970s, who claimed that the United States and domestic right-wing elements were responsible for terrorist attacks that were in turn blamed on left-wing groups, causing them to be discredited and for the population to call for stronger government powers to combat them.

11 Robert S. McNamara (1916–2009) was the United States Secretary of Defense from 1961 until 1968, including during the outbreak of the Vietnam War. While he did pursue the strategy of containment, the strategy itself was first developed by George F. Kennan (1904–2005) as an advisor to President Truman during the late 1940s, setting the tone for America's approach to the Soviet Union throughout the Cold War.

United States, only increased them. Finally, the new organisation that is suspected of having committed the attack against the headquarters of the United Nations in Baghdad, Ansar-al-Islam,[12] is supposed to have succeeded in infiltrating America, which, even more than before September 11, is the principle target of the *mujahideen*. Interestingly, this organisation is a mixture of radicalised Kurds and Islamist Arabs. 'There is no doubt that Ansar-al-Islam has succeeded in entering the United States. Our information is making us very nervous', explains FBI agent Patrick D'Amuro. The terrorists are supposed to have been involved in locating targets in six big cities, including New York, San Diego and Los Angeles. They may be preparing suicide attacks on a large-scale. Terrorism expert M. J. Gohel warns, 'They can be activated to perpetrate an atrocity in the United States, but also in Europe.'

***

Will there be a new September 11 tomorrow? It is necessary to expect giant Islamist attacks in the West, according to the warnings of the ambassador of Saudi Arabia to the United States, Prince Bandar ibn Sultan. The threat is precise. On 17 June 2003, the Director of MI5, the British domestic secret service, Eliza Manningham-Buller, announced in the course of a speech to the Royal United Services Institute, 'we are faced with the realistic possibility of some form of unconventional attack… Sadly, given the widespread proliferation of the technical knowledge to construct these weapons, it will only be a matter of time before a crude version of a chemical, biological, radiological or nuclear attack is launched at a major Western city and only a matter of time before that crude version becomes something more sophisticated.' She

---

12   The Canal Hotel, which was being used by the United Nations for its head-quarters in Iraq at the time, was bombed on 19 August 2003, killing 22 people, including the UN's Special Representative, Sérgio Vieira de Mello. At first, the group Ansar al-Islam was thought to be responsible, but subsequent investigation determined that Abu Musab al-Zarqawi's al-Tawhid wal-Jihad, later renamed Al Qaeda in Iraq, as the most likely culprit.

added that Al Qaeda remains capable of deadly terrorist attacks, and that the breeding grounds for recruiting potential terrorists is far from shrinking, a polite way of underlining the totally counterproductive nature of the 'Bush doctrine'. And then, in conclusion, she ventured this scathing quip: 'Breaking the link between terrorism and religious ideology is difficult.' So the head of MI5 accepts the thesis that Islamism necessarily produces terrorism.

***

What are the chances of large-scale Islamist attacks on the West? According to an investigation by Jeffrey Fleishman, reprinted in the London *Times* and the *Los Angeles Times*,[13] the Al Qaeda teams that perpetrated the anti-Western attack in Riyadh[14] have infiltrated Europe and the United States. Prince Bandar ibn Sultan, the ambassador of Saudi Arabia in Washington, announced, 'My gut feeling is that something enormous is going to happen in Saudi Arabia or in America.' He noted that intelligence services 'have detected a significant flood of chatter about terrorist activity, some regional but also international ones', while listening to relevant networks. The invasion of Iraq probably reactivated all these networks. The Prince numbered at 350 the active Saudi militant terrorists who are preparing for an action.

According to an article in *The Guardian*, 'Al Qaeda has returned and is stronger than ever.'[15] Jonathan Stevenson of the International Institute for Strategic Studies believes that the victories that Bush boasted of in dismantling terrorist networks have been nullified by significant new recruitment following the invasion of Iraq.

---

13 Jeffrey Fleishman, 'Some Plotters May Have Gone West' in the *Los Angeles Times* (20 May 2003).

14 On 12 May 2003, attacks were carried out on a compound in Riyadh which housed many foreigners, killing 35 and injuring more than 160, including many from the United States and Europe.

15 Richard Norton-Taylor, 'Al-Qaida is Back and Stronger Than Ever' in *The Guardian* (19 May 2003).

Is It a Question of War between Islam and the West?

The answer is very complicated. Officially, the Arabic and Islamic leaders declare, 'Of course not!' Bush and his allies as well as Putin echo them. The reality is much less clear.

Western, Arab and Pakistani leaders insist there is no question of the 'clash of civilisations' predicted by Samuel P. Huntington. Similarly, Bush and Blair swear they are not opposing Islam but 'terrorism'. This is a beautiful euphemism. In reality they are opposing 'Muslim terrorism', in a word, Islamism. Islamists believe the logic of terrorism is in theological agreement with the *Qur'an*. Is it an attempt to exorcise reality (to try to avoid new terrorist assaults) by calling the enemy by the abstract noun of 'terrorism'? An enemy, however, is never a concept, but *someone*. Carl Schmitt wrote, 'If you refuse to name your enemy, he will name you.' A very disturbing fact is clear: Muslims (Arab or Asian), both the masses and opinion shapers, all over the world, including Europe, applauded the September 11 attacks and those in spring 2002 in Russian Dagestan and Pakistan (aimed at Europeans), as well as Palestinian kamikaze attacks.

Let us not fool ourselves. Many Muslims, even secretly a good part of their elites, approve of terrorist activities. We are dealing with a kind of war that objectively and implicitly involves Islam, even if it does not involve all Muslims, but only the militant wing known as Islamist.

***

Let us not deceive ourselves. The United States, and probably Europe in the coming decade, are once again going to be the target of giga-terrorist operations. Here are the reasons: 1) The presence of millions of Muslims in Europe forms an extraordinary breeding ground for Islamists. We shall discuss this question later on. 2) The ineffectiveness of security measures like the Vigipirate system,[16] which are only for show and intended to reassure the population. 3) The material impossibility of observing everything, checking everything 24 hours out of 24. How is it possible to guard against kamikaze trucks that drive around the city, crammed with explosives? How to check day and night every kilometre of the TGV railroad network?[17] How is it possible to comb one by one through the suitcases loaded into airplanes' storage holds? 4) We should also remember the incredible porosity of the borders between the states of the European Union, as well as the moral objection to 'racial profiling'.

The only effective strategy against terrorism is *upstream prevention* to frustrate its assaults (as it was possible to foil the attacks planned against Strasbourg Cathedral and the American embassy in Paris). This will, however, prove more and more difficult because of two factors: 1) Muslim immigration, which allows some of them to mount their attacks protected from any European police investigation and to send commandos into Europe; 2) The extreme difficulty of infiltrating Islamist networks. The Israelis, although equipped with excellent intelligence services and agents who speak Arabic perfectly, have not succeeded in infiltrating effectively the Palestinian terrorist networks on their own soil ... Even when it does not reach the level of action, Islamist terrorism allows them to exercise an intolerable pressure on European countries through implicit blackmail. Out of fear of attacks, there is a discrete modification of foreign policy, and mosques and Qur'anic schools are supported — the politics of the ostrich and of 'moving back to be able to jump better'.

* * *

---

16   Vigipirate is France's national security alert system, created in 1978. Similar to the now-defunct Homeland Security Advisory System in the United States, it uses five colors (white, yellow, orange, red and scarlet) to represent varying levels of readiness in response to intelligence about terrorist threats.

17   TGV is France's national high-speed railway network.

Some imams admit that they want 'to conquer Rome and Europe'. Sheikh Yusuf al-Qaradhawi,[18] one of the Arab world's most influential Sunni religious leaders, in a sermon delivered Friday, 13 December 2003, which was retransmitted by the Qatar-based Al Jazeera channel, proclaimed, 'Islam will return to Europe as a victorious conqueror after having been expelled twice.' Then, on the Internet, he explained, 'The Prophet Muhammad predicted that Constantinople, the city of Hercules, would be conquered before Rome. Constantinople was conquered in 1453 by Muhammad bin Murad. We shall rebaptise Rome, the capital of Italy, Romiyya, for we hope and believe that we are going to conquer it in its turn.'[19] The Saudi imam Muhammad bin Abd al-Ramanal-'Arifi of the mosque of the King Fahd Defence Academy, announced, 'We will control the land of the Vatican; we will control Rome and introduce Islam in it.'

In a sermon delivered in November 2003 at the Al-Nour mosque in Khobar, Saudi Arabia, Sheikh Naser Mohammed Al-Naser, announced that after the conquest of Constantinople, today's Istanbul, would come the conquest of Rome. 'The "Second Conquest" [of Rome] will be carried out, Allah willing, and it is inevitable.'[20] He went on to assert that it will be necessary to conquer Constantinople a second time by re-Islamicising Turkey. Is this not what we see happening?

---

18   Sheikh Yusuf al-Qaradhawi (b. 1926) is an Egyptian theologian who has a regular programme on Al Jazeera, and is regarded as a Muslim public intellectual of global importance. He has worked with Egypt's Muslim Brotherhood, although has never held any official status. He opposed the September 11 attacks and supported the Arab Spring uprising in Egypt, and also issued a *fatwa* against Libya's Gaddafi in 2011. He has held a number of academic positions, including acting as a trustee for the Oxford Centre for Islamic Studies. Nevertheless, in response to some of his proclamations, including his support for attacks against Israel, he has been restricted from entering the United States since 1999, the United Kingdom since 2008, and France in 2012.

19   This *fatwa* was originally posted at *Islam Online* on 2 December 2002.

20   Reported by the Israel-based Middle East Media Research Institute (MEMRI) in 'Leading Sunni Sheikh Yousef Al-Qaradhawi and Other Sheikhs Herald the Coming Conquest of Rome' (6 December 2002).

Al-Naser thinks so: 'There are signs that it will again be conquered and will return to the hands of the Islamic state.'

In a sermon preached in the great Al-Aqsa mosque in Jerusalem, the Deputy Minister for Faith and Islamic Affairs of the Palestinian Authority, Yusuf Juma'a Salameh, said that those who believe that Islam's expansion stopped with the capture of Constantinople are mistaken. Affirming, in agreement with the *Qur'an*, that the expansion of Islam has no limits and that the next stage was the conquest of Europe, Salameh concluded, like a good orthodox Muslim, 'Islam had not reached its end in the world, because on the day it reaches its end, there will be no world: the sun will be extinguished, the stars will go out.'[21] Imam Mohammed Abd El-Karim also preached in April 2004 in the grand mosque of Khartoum in the Sudan that 'The Prophet told us of the conquest of Constantinople, the capital of the Byzantine state, and of the conquest of Rome, where the Vatican is situated... The Muslims attacked India and Allah conquered it for us, until they reached the borders of China. The Muslims conquered Constantinople, where Eastern Christianity is situated, and in the future, a mighty king will arise for the Muslims; through him, Islam will spread and Rome will be conquered...'[22]

These words do not come from marginal and extremist 'Islamists', but from respected international authorities in the Muslim world, often with reputations as 'moderates'. What do the friends of 'secular and tolerant Islam' and Catholic prelates, who are often accomplices of this development, think of them?

***

21   MEMRI, 'Leading Sunni Sheikh Yousef Al-Qaradhawi and Other Sheikhs Herald the Coming Conquest of Rome'.

22   MEMRI, 'Leading Sunni Sheikh Yousef Al-Qaradhawi and Other Sheikhs Herald the Coming Conquest of Rome'.

Commenting on the French translation of the book, *The Rage and the Pride*,[23] written by the celebrated left-wing Italian journalist, Oriana Fallaci,[24] Elizabeth Schemla, essayist and editor of the Web site Proche-Orient.info wrote in *Le Figaro* (8 and 9 June 2003): 'The profoundly disturbing element in her work is that she dares to be angry at Islam. This is the taboo subject *par excellence* in Europe, although no one knows why, unless it is the visceral fear inspired by a billion Muslims... Fallaci presents Islam as an untiring expansionist quest for sacred territory. Therefore, she refuses to differentiate between Muslim countries — of which she notes emphatically that not one is a democracy — and Muslims installed on European soil. This is very clear in reading her text. It does not matter whether they are Arabs, Africans, or Turks; Sunni, Shiite, secular, agnostics or atheists — whether they want to be or not, immigrants are the scouting parties of a military disposition that will be activated one day (i.e., a fifth column). For Fallaci, in these times of war declared all over the Earth by one part of the Muslim world, in order to convert all societies definitively to Islam, the distinction between moderates and extremists is already the sign of apostasy, a cop-out before the necessary confrontation ... People who oppose Fallaci lack the courage to open this important debate for the future of all Judaeo-Christian and Asian societies... Oriana Fallaci's scathing attack, far from being a symptom of any sort of populism, which it is helping us to understand, is rather an unbearable scream against the perversions of decadence.'

Ms. Fallaci's book does not distinguish between the violent Islamic combatant and the ordinary Muslim, and she is right to do so. On the

---

23   Oriana Fallaci, *The Rage and the Pride* (New York: Rizzoli, 2002).

24   Oriana Fallaci (1929–2006) was an Italian journalist who had fought as an anti-Fascist partisan in her youth. During her career, she was known for her coverage of wars and her often contentious interviews with world leaders, including Ayatollah Khomeini. After the September 11 attacks, she wrote three books that were extremely hostile to Muslims and Islam as a religion, sparking a great deal of international controversy.

other hand, her attacks on 'Arabs' are inappropriate. Ms. Fallaci defends an absolute philo-Americanism and the most extreme Zionist position with a militant extremism. If we must applaud the courage and lucidity of her denunciation of Islam as a serious threat, especially because of the reality of a colonising immigration into Europe, her presentation would have been more persuasive if she had avoided a passionate and vindictive tone, which always rouses suspicions of 'ressentiment'.[25]

***

Are there really plans to conquer and Islamicise Europe? Up until now, immigration for permanent settlement and the multiplication of Muslims seemed to be happening naturally. Only very lucid minds uncovered a concerted project for conquest. In a recently published book, *En el nombre de Alà*,[26] two Spanish authors, Enrique Montánchez and Pedro Canales (Montánchez is an investigative reporter for the journal *La Razòn*; Canales is a correspondent in the Maghreb for several Spanish magazines), claim there is a secret plan to re-Islamicise Europe, beginning with the reconquest of Andalusia by immigration, a plan directed by Morocco and Saudi Arabia. Saudi Arabia is supposed to have set up a massive system to finance mosques in Andalusia (from which the Muslims were driven in the Fifteenth century), while Morocco is to be in charge of furnishing the battalions of immigrants and sending them into, first, Ceuta and Melilla, Spain's 'Achilles' heels'.

Two other pieces of news: 30,000 Spaniards have already converted to Islam; and the terrorist networks — linked to Saudi Arabia — especially Al Qaeda, 'are using Spain as the logistical preparatory stage for

---

25 *Ressentiment*, literally 'resentment', has a much stronger meaning in French. It suggests the endless repetition of the disgust that one feels towards a person or thing, resulting in a deep-seated aversion that becomes part of a person's essential nature.

26 Enrique Montánchez and Pedro Canales, *En el nombre de Alá: la red secreta del terrorismo islámico en España* (Barcelona: Editorial Planeta, 2002).

launching attacks against targets in Europe'. Isabella the Catholic,[27] who liberated Spain from the Muslim yoke, must be turning in her grave ...

***

The response to all those who dream of a secular and moderate Islam, who believe that the fundamentalists are a minority and that Islam is not trying to conquer Europe is the confession of an eminent Muslim doctor, Muhammad Ibn-Guadi, an Islamic scholar at the University of Strasbourg, in a provocative article with the warning, 'Islam has always been political!' (*Le Figaro*, 17 June 2003). The general message of his article is that France has to convert to Islam, and that the ideal of republican secularism and assimilation are both impossible. 'Negotiating' with the real Islam is not a practical option.

He writes, 'There can be no "secular Muslims", there can be no reform in Islam simply because the advent of Islam is itself a reform... What those who desire dialogue between Muslims and Christians seem to forget is that Islam does indeed confirm earlier revelations, but that its objective is to correct those revelations... The notion found in Reformed Christianity of the separation of church and state is completely unknown to Islam. Religious institutions are not separate from civil institutions. The spiritual is inseparable from the temporal.' The Muslim professor explains correctly that Islam is first and foremost a political and social doctrine. 'Islam has always been political. The only form of political organisation known to Muslims is the Islamic state.' The author adds that Arab nationalism, an ephemeral form imported from the West, is dead.

Sarkozy should think seriously about these honest and lucid statements: 'Whether it shocks people or not, the fact that Muslims can declare that the *Qur'an* overrides the laws of the French Republic is

---

27 Isabela I of Castile (1451–1504), known as 'the Catholic', was Queen of Spain in 1492, when the 800-year Reconquista, which saw the expulsion or conversion to Catholicism of all Muslims and Jews in Spain, was successfully concluded.

perfectly correct in Islam. The efforts of Muslims who hope to rec-
oncile Islam and secularism are futile.' And now the confession of
the will to conquer Europe: 'Muslims cannot find themselves in non-
Muslim countries without apprehending it as a territory where Islamic
laws ought to prevail. There is France's problem in a nutshell.' Let us
mention also this extraordinary passage, where our learned professor
associates himself with Bin Laden and so wrings the neck of the absurd thesis of the 'two Islams', one moderate, the other fanatical: 'On 3
November 2001, Bin Laden declared to the Al Jazeera network, "Under
no circumstances should we forget this enmity between us and the
infidels. For, the enmity is based on creed." Unfortunately he was right.'

Ibn-Guadi is neither a terrorist nor an extremist, but a respected
professor with a salary from the French state. He is putting his cards
on the table. Let us thank him for admitting to us that that his 'faith'
has declared war on us.

∗∗∗

Our Islamophile intellectuals and politicians are going to be really
annoyed once more. The daily *Sydney Morning Herald*[28] got hold of
a secret 44-page manual published by Jemaah Islamiyah (a Southeast
Asian Islamist network based in Indonesia) entitled *General Guide to
the Struggle*. There we read: '[We have] love of *jihad* (holy war) in the
path of God and love of dying as a martyr... [Our enemies are] satanic
demons and satanic humans.' The objective is to carry Islam 'to the
four corners of the Earth'. There is no question here of 'defending' poor
Muslims 'under attack by the Judaeo-Crusaders'.

The manual describes a worldwide organisational chart of terrorist
combat structures, and explains how to plan attacks and communicate
secretly. It insists on the necessity of political and religious instruction
and military training of all the Muslim volunteers in the world. One

---

28   Wayne Miller, 'Secret Guide Details JI Plan for Conquest', in *Sydney Morning
     Herald* (1 September 2003).

member of Jemaah Islamiyah, a 'witness' of the bloody attack in Bali, assures us that 'this manual is the most important text after the *Qur'an'.* The terrorists in Bali followed the manual to the letter.[29]

***

Is 'secular Islam' making progress? Contrary to the dreams of the European political class who want to deal with a 'secular and moderate Islam', which has never existed except in their imagination, Islamist organisations are lifting their head in France and Belgium and now talk openly of applying *shariah* (Islamic law) in a Europe on the road to being conquered.

The fundamentalists of the Union of Islamic Organisations in France (UOIF), which has been gaining influence, declared in the course of their recent Muslim conference in Bourget that their members would never vote for candidates who would reject the application of Muslim law (mosques, Qur'anic schools, innumerable exemptions from the secularism of the French Republic) in areas with a large Muslim population.

This is the logic of Islam: to remove the mask of 'moderation' as soon as they feel they are sufficiently numerous.

In Belgium there is the same pressure from fundamentalists. The new President of the Belgian Muslim Executive (a converted Flemish university instructor, Omar Van den Broeck), in his book *L'islam occidentalement?* (Islam in the Western Way?), has expounded a fanatical vision of the conquest of Europe by Islam, one in perfect agreement with the *Qur'an.* He writes, 'The point of departure consists of the

---

29   On 12 October 2002, a popular nightclub on the Indonesian island of Bali was bombed, killing 202 people, including 88 Australians and other foreigners, and injuring hundreds more. Several members of Jemaah Islamiyah were said to be the perpetrators. A week later, Osama bin Laden released a statement claiming that the attack was in retaliation for Australia's support for the "war on terror" and other crimes against Muslims. One of the terrorists, Ali Ghufron, was said to be the author of the *General Guide to the Struggle.*

unconditional application of basic Islamic principles… This lived faith automatically implies individual obedience to divine law, to *shariah* and therefore to the *Qur'an*'s commands.' Then this Flemish convert, who is now the head of an influential Islamic organisation, praises the veil, criticises race mixing in the name of a (morbid) Muslim puritanism and explains that Islam 'cannot accept the division of the world into nations'. In other words, here is a frank profession of faith in the final objective of Islam, the Universal Caliphate, that is, the worldwide Islamic state. Arab Muslims have understood very well that there are no worse fanatics than European converts, who are animated by the 'zeal of the convert', collaborators, who are often recruited in extremist movements.

***

A report of Renseignements Généraux[30] of 5 August 2003 indicates that the department[31] of Essonne is a hotbed of fanatic Muslim pietism, the Tablighi Jamaat movement. This group is supposed to promote conversion, but also propagate Islamist vocations, i.e., terrorists, and is very well represented at the Fleury-Mérogis prison. Of the prison's 3,600 male prisoners, 1,000 are foreigners who have emigrated from Muslim countries and 80 are Islamists incarcerated for terrorism, who devote themselves to proselytising and recruiting. It is also reported that in this department (and therefore also elsewhere) 'converts represent a worrying phenomenon that is rapidly expanding' and are fertile ground for growing extremism. 'If one refers to the national studies estimating about 30,000 to 50,000 converts in the whole territory', there would be 2,000 in Essonne alone. The Islamic Centre of Évry-Courcouronnes 'claims two to three conversions a week'. The figures come to one a day for the province (20 times the number of

---

30   Central Directorate of General Intelligence was the intelligence arm of the French police. In 2008 it was merged into a new department.

31   In France, the various provinces are referred to as departments.

Muslim conversions to Christianity), and these converts for the most part 'have been immersed in Christian culture and education'. Are they dangerous? The answer is, 'converts, already thoroughly immersed in the Tablighi's religious fanaticism, constitute a breeding pond where Islamist jihadists come to fish ... conversion to Islam of fragile individuals undoubtedly involves a risk of terrorist drift'. Are they potential 'bagmen'?[32] 'Converts are all the more appreciated by radicals because their French nationality makes it easier for them to cross borders, to serve as puppets and to supply logistical support.' Converts were acting inside the Beghal terrorist network, which was fortunately dismantled just in time before it could commit a suicide attack against American interests in Paris.[33]

***

Many European mosques are really propaganda centres for civil war and holy war aimed at conquering Europe, as well as diffusing a constant defence of Islamic terrorism. And they are authorised, with the most complete blindness, by the European authorities.

---

32 In French, *porteurs de valise*, which was a term used to describe Frenchmen, usually Communists, who assisted the Algerian guerrillas in the 1954–62 Algerian War.

33 In July 2001, a French Algerian named Djamel Beghal was arrested at the airport in Dubai for falsifying his passport. It soon became apparent that he had been attempting to return to Europe after receiving training from Al Qaeda in Afghanistan. Under interrogation, Beghal confessed to attempting to relay instructions from Osama bin Laden to cell members in France, the Netherlands and Belgium to carry out simultaneous attacks on the U.S. embassy and the American cultural centre in Paris. The French authorities began their arm of the investigation on 10 September 2001. Many suspected terrorists were arrested in seven European countries and the United Arab Emirates as a result, many of whom were found to be in possession of large quantities of explosives and other tools related to the attack.

In Great Britain, the bastion of Islamism in Europe, a figure of 'British Islam', Abu Hamza al-Masri,[34] who, according to the Americans, is linked to terrorist networks, is the guru of the Grand Mosque (with a seating capacity of 1,500) in Finsbury Park in north-central London. He openly preaches *jihad,* and his Friday sermons are sold on cassettes and transmitted into every Muslim country through the Internet. Here are examples of some of his remarks: 'It is the duty of every Muslim to fight every law that is not inspired by God [therefore only *shariah* is valid, not European law]; we must fight every *kuffar* [non-Muslim], without distinction, and there will be a special reward and a privileged place in paradise for those who volunteer to fight, while Muslims who stay at home without fighting will have only a small place.' This information, which is in perfect agreement with the *Qur'an,* pulverises the belief in a difference between a 'peaceful' Islam and an 'aggressive Islamism'.

The following comes from other speeches by Abu Hamza: 'I do not preach Islam as the West would like it to be, but as God wants it to be. Some imams want to "moderate" Islam in order to please the West, but not me. I expound Islam as it is, that is, fighting against the West.

---

34   Abu Hamza al-Masri (b. 1958) is an Egyptian who fought alongside the Bosnian Muslims in the former Yugoslavia during the 1990s. He is missing his right hand and one eye, injuries which he claims to have received while fighting in Afghanistan (other accounts claim it was the result of an accident during explosives training). In addition to his duties as an imam, al-Masri also ran a group called 'Supporters of Shariah' in the United Kingdom, which advocated a radical Islamist agenda and voiced support for Osama bin Laden. In 2004 he was arrested under British hate speech laws. In 2004, the United States government also began extradition proceedings against al-Masri, accusing him of having aided in an attempt to establish an Al Qaeda-affiliated training camp in Oregon in 1999. He was also accused of recruiting for Al Qaeda through the Finsbury Park mosque. In April 2012, the European Court of Human Rights approved the extradition request. He was extradited to the United States later that year and, in 2015, was sentenced to life in prison without the possibility of parole for terrorism-related offenses. He is also the author of *Allah's Governance on Earth: Ruling Is Only for Allah* (BCM-Holographics, 2001).

... I do not belong to Bin Laden's networks, but I share some of their views. My sympathies and my prayers go to the Taliban and that is not a crime.'[35]

Some Muslim regimes (which are treated as impious tyrannies by Abu Hamza) have asked the British authorities to forbid Abu Hamza from preaching. Obviously in vain ... At the same time, the British simultaneously support Bush's crusade against the 'axis of evil' and authorise activities on their soil of the advance guard of the worldwide *jihad*. This is suicidal.

***

Samuel P. Huntington, a Professor at Harvard and former member of the White House's National Security Council, has predicted an ethno-political conflict of civilisations in the Twenty-first century in his book, *The Clash of Civilizations and the Remaking of World Order*.[36] His thesis is that ideological conflicts (like Communism against capitalism) are going to be replaced by ethno-cultural conflicts, the exact reverse of globalist theories of planetary unification. He declared in an interview: '[There is] a serious conflict between Muslim societies and non-Muslim societies. If one looks at the borders of a great block of Muslim countries stretching from Morocco to Indonesia, one sees along the borders of the Muslim world continuous fighting. is a continuous frontline. Bosnians versus Orthodox Serbs and Catholic Croats in the Balkans, Greeks versus Turks, Armenians versus Azerbaijanis, Russians versus Chechens, Russians versus Central Asian Muslims, India versus Pakistan. More generally, there are also conflicts between Muslims and Catholics in the Philippines and Indonesia, and between Jews and Arabs in the Middle East, and between Christians and Muslims

---

35 *The Times*, 6 May 2002.

36 Samuel P. Huntington, *The Clash of Civilizations and the Remaking of World Order* (New York: Simon & Schuster, 1996).

in Sudan.'[37] He could have added confrontations in Nigeria and the Ivory Coast and also ... Europe. At Roubaix, Marseilles, Birmingham, Brussels, and Frankfort, the 'frontline' has advanced deep into the heart of Europe.

***

Is there a chance of an Islamic Republic in France? The Kabyle[38] Rachid Kaci, founder of the Free Right (*la Droite libre*), writes in his essay, *La République des laches*:[39] 'The debate about the veil depends less on religion than on tactics, the goal of which remains above all political. It is a question of leading French society to be sufficiently immersed in Islam so that in the end this religion may be in a position to influence French law. The penetration of the veil into public schools is only a stage of this process. Once the principle is admitted, Islamists will raise their bids even higher. Have we not heard them demand, in the name of the equality of all religions before the law, that French schools and society devote the same attention to Muslim holidays as to Catholic holidays.'

Kaci does not discuss the problem of demography. What arguments will he use when Muslims will be in the majority, which is actually happening? Obviously he never calls for 'deportation', but he is lucid, when he criticises the lax politics of Sarkozy: 'These people have a political project, which is to create a Muslim community in France and manage it with a view to its final domination over the nation. This is their ambition. Do not doubt it for a minute.'

---

37 Hector Feliciano and Dijana Sulic, 'On Conflicts and Global Politics' in *New Straits Times* (17 March 1997).

38 The Kabyle people are the largest group of ethnic Berbers, and their home is in northern Algeria, although there are also large Kabyle populations in France and Canada.

39 *La République des laches: la faillite des politiques d'intégration* (The Republic of Cowards: The Failure of the Politics of Integration) (Paris: Syrtes, 2003).

China against the USA

China is preparing for war, but against whom? First the implacable facts: the People's Republic of China is increasing its military budget in the largest percentages of any nation on Earth. On 6 March 2001, Beijing announced an increase in military expenditure of 17.7 % in 2001, which will bring them to 141 billion yuan, or 19 billion euros or 120 billion francs. Western experts estimate that China's real military expenses are 'two to three times higher than the official figures' (*Le Monde*, 7 March 2001). This striking increase is the largest observed in twenty years and represents the thirteenth consecutive increase of more than 10 %.

Unlike Europe, which is disarming and reducing its military budgets, China is in the process of rearmament with a massive increase in its military power, higher than that of Germany between 1933 and 1940 and the increases in the United States after Pearl Harbor.

Why is China doing this? It has always been known that a country that is rearming is doing so for one of two reasons: either it feels threatened and wants to protect itself, or it wants to attack. Does China want to attack Taiwan, in order to conquer it again? No, because it does not need to rearm so heavily in order to retake Taiwan and it prefers a strategy of 'persuasion'. China wants to regain Taiwan peacefully, by threats rather than direct force. A war would ruin Taiwan's successful economy, which China needs. China envisages Taiwan as a future 'autonomous region', like Hong Kong.

A French correspondent, Régis de M., suggests, 'We need to compare the Chinese military budget and the depopulation of Russia.' So does China want to attack Russia? Clearly China could claim part of eastern Siberia, which Chinese immigrants are infiltrating. One remembers the Sino-Russian conflict over Amur in the 1960s.[40]

---

40 Sino-Soviet relations deteriorated seriously during the 1960s, culminating in a series of skirmishes on Damansky Island and in Xinjiang, bringing the two powers close to full-scale war.

This, however, is not China's geopolitical preoccupation. The Middle Kingdom feels no more threatened by Russia than by India (all the more so because the Russians still supply the Chinese with weapons, notably Sukhoi fighter-bombers). It is in China's interest to maintain good relations with these two continental powers. Then why is China rearming?

Because the Chinese sense the possibility of a major conflict in the Twenty-first century with the great thalassocratic superpower, the United States. China, a nation that (like France) is both maritime and continental, has understood that the Pacific — currently under American control — is going to become a locus of major friction. Let us not forget that the two military superpowers starting from 2015 will be China and the United States. So China foresees a situation similar to that of the 'Cold War' between the West and the USSR of the years 1947–1991. In the context of this rearmament, China is not increasing at all her territorial strength (which would be the case in the hypothesis of conflicts along her continental frontiers), but as though accidentally, 1) she is strengthening her naval and submarine fleets on the high seas — Beijing has plans to launch aircraft carriers — and her air force; 2) she is improving her rocket and nuclear capacities and preparing military spy satellites, 3) she is revaluing her currency to motivate her army. The Chinese are preparing for a 'post-modern' type of conflict, centred on electronic war, missiles, airplanes and submarines. This conflict would inevitably have a (partly) nuclear aspect. The Pentagon understands the situation perfectly. The recent crisis concerning the aerial 'accident' between a US Navy EP-3 spy plane, which was forced to land at Hainan, and a J-8 fighter of the Chinese People's Liberation Army[41] confirms the start of serious disputes between the two principal

---

41   This incident occurred on 1 April 2001 near the Chinese island of Hainan. The pilot of the Chinese plane was killed, and tensions between the two countries soared. An ambiguously-worded apology from the United States succeeded in defusing the incident, however.

waterfronts of the Pacific that will relegate the Jewish-Arab conflicts of the Near East to the status of regional quarrels.

***

What are the real reasons for the American anti-ballistic missile shield? In contempt for the SALT nuclear disarmament accords[42]—and in formal disagreement with China, Russia and France—Bush wants to endow his country with a shield of anti-ballistic missile interceptors capable of shooting down nuclear warheads launched against American territory while still in flight. In so doing, he is breaking the 'equilibrium of terror' that has avoided all nuclear warfare thanks to 'mutually assured destruction' (MAD), which rests on an implicit pact between the nuclear powers, according to which the aggressor, who is certain of being destroyed in retaliation, is dissuaded from launching its own nuclear weapons. If, however, a country—in this case the United States—possesses an anti-missile shield, it could permit itself any type of war against a nuclear power without fearing effective retaliation.

They tell us—and all the commentators pretend to believe it—that the Americans want to protect themselves from possible future missile attacks from 'rogue states': North Korea, Libya, Iran, Iraq, etc. This motive is a possibility, but secondary. In reality, there is every indication that the Pentagon envisages a major confrontation with China in twenty years and intends to possess the means of striking (not necessarily using atomic weapons) without the risk of a devastating nuclear response on American soil.

Let us not forget that the American thalassocracy, despite its official ultra-pacifist and humanitarian language, is an 'imperial-mercantile nation' founded on war and its armed forces. The Untied States needs

---

42 The Strategic Arms Limitation Talks were two agreements between the United States and the Soviet Union to limit the number of nuclear weapons maintained by each side, held in 1973 and 1979. The SALT I treaty included a clause that limited each side to only two ABM installations each.

war ('just war', the crusade against evil, obviously), not only for economic reasons — the arms industry is a locomotive for technology, industry and finance capitalism — but also to maintain its international status as 'protectors and rulers' of the world.

Since 1941, no other country has conducted more military operations and bombardments outside its borders than the United States — and with no fear of an invasion of its territory. Now things are changing. America is not dealing with little countries, Vietnam, Panama, Serbia, etc., but with the enormous country of China, a terrifying challenger that, with its 1.25 billion inhabitants, can survive massive loss of life from nuclear strikes (as Mao noted), and is currently equipped with long-range missiles! This prospect is much worse than a confrontation with the defunct Soviet Union would have been …

Breaking radically with Clinton's policy, President Bush declared in early March 2004, 'China is a competitor and not a strategic partner.'

A war will perhaps have as its theatre and central stake the domination of the Pacific, and eventually bring the United States and China into opposition, perhaps as soon as 2010. What will be the pretext? On the basis of what disagreements will it break out? Right now, no one knows. Unlike, however, the short-sighted and pusillanimous politicians of Europe who 'no longer have enemies', who no longer feel threatened by anyone, who joyously disarm, for whom the military is now nothing but a police force for humanitarian intervention, America's strategists have read Clausewitz; they think about the long term and know that war is always possible, tomorrow, between two major powers even if, today, they do not know the exact pretexts. The question is obviously to know, if such a gigantic conflict took place, what camp would Europe choose, and Russia and India?

***

Despite the new forms that confrontations will take in the course of the Twenty-first century, for example, repeated acts of terrorism, giga-terrorism and civil wars, it is perfectly possible to envisage classic wars between the great powers.

Francis Fukuyama,[43] the American professor of political science at George Mason University in Virginia and consultant to the RAND Corporation, is the author of the bestseller *The End of History and the Last Man*,[44] where he predicts a general pacification of the planet under the reign of liberalism and Western style democracy. Nevertheless, in an interview given to *Le Figaro* (13 January 2000), he admitted that he could not exclude the scenario of a war between the great powers.

Fukuyama said, 'Taiwan could supply the igniting spark between China and the United States. Between Russia and NATO it is not too difficult to find a pretext for war. Therefore it is not yet the end of history.' Now carefully read these words where Fukuyama, more than a year and a half *before* the attacks of 11 September 2001, seems, if not to deny, at least to place severe limits around his theory of the 'end of history': 'Anything could happen. The scale of risks is going to increase because terrorists and rogue states have access to an increasingly murderous technology. But I do not think a sudden strike, even a very bloody one, could change the face of the Earth or the direction of history. I could be mistaken. A terrorist attack that would kill a million people would surely change our attitude on the central question of individual liberties. This would be "History", in my definition. It certainly cannot be excluded.'

---

43 Francis Fukuyama (b. 1952) is an American political philosopher who is best-known for his 1992 book, *The End of History and the Last Man*, which postulated that with the triumph of liberal democracy at the end of the Cold War, humanity had attained the perfect form of government and that the remnants of other ideologies would soon pass away. It was viewed by many as the credo of America's political and economic dominance of the world during the 1990s. Although widely associated with American neoconservatism at that time, he has distanced himself from the movement in recent years.

44 Francis Fukuyama, *The End of History and the Last Man* (New York: Free Press, 1992).

Fukuyama, however, with a flabbergasting naïveté, still believes — with a tone of pure ideological belief — 'History will end in democracy.' On the contrary, however, the Twenty-first century will be the century of the thunderous intensification of history. Fukuyama understands the concept of 'history' in Hegel's sense, that is, 'significant events that produce major social and political changes', like the French Revolution, the Napoleonic wars, the two world wars, the fall of Communism, etc. He seems to think that such events will become increasingly rare, although they will occur with increasing frequency!

The Islamist Iranian revolution, the attacks of 11 September 2001, the civil war in Israel: these shocks are eminently creative of History. We shall see others. It was during the Cold War that History seemed to be fixed, frozen. Now it has resumed its forward course, faster, madder and more uncontrolled than ever. Far from being the kingdom of the end of History, the Twenty-first century will be the century of *Hyperhistory*, if History is understood in Hegel's definition cited above, since we are probably going to witness a general fall of humanity out of modernity, which will end a cycle sketched in the Middle Ages and begun in the Sixteenth century.

When Everyone Has Nuclear Weapons

What will be the consequences of the new American nuclear doctrine? The United States argues: 'Do what I say, not what I do', with all the contradictions that follow. They want to bind the ROW (Rest of the World) to the undiluted free market through the World Trade Organization. They practice protectionism (no one dares to respond with sanctions!), as seen with their tariff on steel imports.

Similarly, the Pentagon wants to overthrow the nuclear doctrine. Casting aside the theory of deterrence, in which nuclear weapons can only be used to answer an attack of the same type, the United States plans to employ miniaturised atomic bombs against the 'rogue states' of the 'Axis of Evil', whether they possess nuclear weapons or not, in a first strike. Such a plan, according to Robert Steuckers,[45] 'betrays the growing frustration of the military-industrial complex and the American leadership at the inability they find themselves in to destroy the terrorists who attacked America.' It also betrays, according to the London *Times* (12 March 2002), the impotence of American ground forces, which are despised by its Afghan 'allies', who, in the course of the recent Operation Anaconda,[46] judged the GIs 'unable to fight and interested only in avoiding casualties'.

One consequence of this new doctrine has been to renew the nuclear proliferation that the United States is trying at all costs to prevent. In fact, many states, feeling themselves threatened by American nuclear strikes, are going to be tempted to acquire the bomb. Madeleine Bunting in *The Guardian*[47] asserts, '[A]s the memory of September 11 inevitably fades, it is not so much Islamist hijackers as US bombs that make the world feel a precarious place', which risks destabilising the world. Ah! The Americans who, along with Francis Fukuyama, thought that after the fall of the Soviet Union they were going to fashion the worldwide *Pax Americana*[48] and the 'end of history', on the contrary, are going to create a generalised *Bellum Americanum*[49] and an acceleration of history.

---

45   Robert Steuckers (b. 1956) was the founder of the Belgian branch of the New Right and is the editor of *Orientations* (Belgium), as well as being a contributor to *Nouvelle École, The Scorpion,* and *Éléments*. He is a certified translator and a specialist in geopolitics and the author of *Dossier géopolitique,* 1980. He maintains the extensive New Right site Euro-Synergies at euro-synergies.hautetfort. com.

46   Operation Anaconda was a joint operation between American, NATO and Afghan forces in March 2002. Although it was hailed as a major victory at the time, the results were inconclusive, and journalists reported that the battle was marked by poor cooperation between the various groups involved.

47   Madeleine Bunting, 'America's Long Shadow' in *The Guardian* (11 March 2002).

48   Latin: 'American Peace', referring to the state of peace that has prevailed in most of Europe since 1945, seen by some as a product of America's ascendancy.

49   Latin: 'American War'.

***

Is Saudi Arabia trying to acquire nuclear weapons? Iran and North Korea may perhaps not be the only thorns in the feet of the United States. As a predictable consequence of the reckless and calamitous invasion of Iraq, Saudi Arabia is trying to preserve itself from American insanity by establishing a nuclear arsenal! This nightmarish scenario, in which the most fundamentalist state on Earth would obtain nuclear warheads, was the object of a secret report uncovered by *Scotland on Sunday*.[50] The report was obviously denied by the Saudis.

It is possible that the report was 'leaked' by the Saudi special services to impress the Americans, who have passed from the status of privileged allies to that of an imperialist threat. According to Daniel Neep, a British expert, Research Director on the Middle East and Africa at the Royal United Services Institute of London, the Saudis envisage the possibility of an American attack, among other possibilities.

This scenario would add another element to the chaos of the Middle East, which is increasingly the world's powder keg. Saudi Arabia probably has the financial wherewithal to buy the bomb, even without the help of Saudi scientists. Judith Yaphe, an expert at the National Defense University of Washington, admits that the Bush administration frightens the Saudis. She explains, 'We have warned that, since we are now the world's only superpower, if someone threatens us, we have the right to a preventive attack. The next question is, after Iraq who will be next? We are giving the impression that we want to remake the Middle East to suit ourselves, beginning with Iraq. Many people are saying that the next target will not be only Iran or Syria, but maybe Saudi Arabia or the Gulf States, even Egypt. All the countries of the region are tormented by this question.' Every day, the evidence accumulates that America's warmongering and destabilising foreign policy is increasingly provoking uncontrolled reactions.

---

50 'Experts Warn of Saudi Arabia Nuclear Threat' in *Scotland on Sunday* (21 September 2003).

***

Sergei Ivanov, the Russian Defence Minister, explains that the American invasion of Iraq is going to increase international military instability: 'As the situation surrounding Iraq was developing, the Pyongyang leadership came to the conclusion that territorial integrity and independence can be guaranteed only through the possession of means of deterrence… Developments have shown that many countries are beginning to act using their own discretion, without caring much about international law. There is nothing good in this scenario.'[51] In other words, the consequences of the American intervention will be that several Third World countries, especially Muslim ones, are going to speed up their clandestine nuclear and chemical weapons programs, in order to deter American 'police' operations.

Israel's Tears

Is apartheid the only solution for Israel? The current policies of the Sharon government and the heating up of the civil war is judged suicidal by an increasingly large number of Israelis who believe that the war will be lost and Israel can never recover from it. Here is the thesis we are defending: since the creation of the Hebrew state and, especially since the 1967 war,[52] Zionist policy in the region has been geo-strategically stupid.

To understand matters, let us begin by examining some public statements. On 5 March 2002, Ariel Sharon announced, 'We ought to concentrate on a single matter, striking the Palestinians as hard as possible. That is what we need, blows. They must understand that they

---

51 'Ivanov: Pyongyang May Ignore UN Resolution on Its Nuclear Plan', in New Europe Online (11 May 2003).

52 The Six-Day War of June 1967 began with a surprise attack on Egypt and ended with Israel seizing large swaths of territory from Egypt, Jordan and Syria, more than doubling its size and giving it a much more secure position against its hostile neighbours.

are defeated.' The celebrated journalist Ze'ev Schiff wrote on the same day in the newspaper *Haaretz*: 'It seems that the day is approaching in the terrible war that is developing here, when anyone who comes to destroy Israeli families, including children and babies, will have to consider that Israel will harm his family, and not only his property.'[53] For the first time, a Jewish Israeli intellectual is theorising in the mainstream press about massacring innocents, in the name of the *lex talionis*, 'an eye for an eye' ...

The Palestinians answered. Marwan Barghouti, head of Fatah in the West Bank, wrote, 'The results of the murderous Israeli incursions in the camps are null. They have only succeeded in killing civilians and destroying houses, without stopping anyone. Sharon's policies are an immense failure.' Abou Leila (one of the leaders of the Palestine Liberation Organisation and the DFLP)[54] said, 'Israeli public opinion realises that Sharon's policy, which is based on a military solution, is a complete illusion. Instead of the security promised by Sharon, insecurity has never stopped growing. In this type of war, neither training nor equipment is really important. What really counts is morale. And the morale of the Israeli army is sinking like a stone.'

The head of the Israeli opposition in the Knesset, Yossi Sarid, responded, 'We have entered a bloody tribal conflict. Now it is an eye for an eye and two teeth for one tooth.' Finally, the latest public statement that summarises by itself the tragic impasse in which the Zionists are going astray: former Prime Minister Benjamin Netanyahu (Sharon's rival who is outbidding him) has just reaffirmed that it is necessary 'to expel Arafat and reject completely the creation of a Palestinian state'. Netanyahu's position is stupid and suicidal for the Jews of Israel.

***

---

53   Ze'ev Schiff, 'Fighting Those Who Are Prepared to Die' in *Haaretz* (5 March 2002).

54   Democratic Front for the Liberation of Palestine. It is a Marxist-Leninist party.

The idea of a Palestinian state has just been proposed, for the first time, by the United States in the United Nations Security Council at the beginning of March 2002, evidence that the Americans, Israel's protectors, are aware of the geostrategic stupidity of their protégés. In fact, the official position of the Hebrew state (increasingly opposed by local public opinion) is the theory of 'Greater Israel', the fanatical founding of colonies on Arab land and the rejection of a Palestinian state with its own borders. This position is based on Israel's unwillingness to lose control of the territories they occupied in 1967. But this position ends in a geopolitical absurdity that will sign the death certificate of the Hebrew state. In fact, the current situation of overlapping — like the Balkans — of 'Palestinian zones', 'zones colonised by Orthodox Jews', and the already misshapen territory given to the Israelis in 1948, without counting the embarrassing presence of Israeli citizens who are Arabs and Muslims, makes this country a *leopard skin* that is totally unmanageable. In the short term, faced with guerrilla war with Palestinians who strike where they want to, the heavy-handed and clumsy military actions of the Tzahal[55] will be just as effective as the GIs were in Vietnam.

***

Israeli governments are therefore choosing, against all logic, to cohabit with Arab Muslims on a territory they control (barely). They dominate by violence a population that is poor, much more prolific demographically, and whose Islamic terrorist partisans will be increasingly aided by the Arab states that encircle Israel! This aberrant colonial scheme can only fail.

Paradoxically, the Palestinian demand to enjoy an independent state separated from Israel is the only chance Israel has to survive. Why? If the Hebrew state were smart, it would follow a policy of *total apartheid*, which can be summarised in three points:

---

55 A Hebrew acronym for the Israel Defence Forces.

1) Dismantling all the Orthodox Jewish colonies in the West Bank and Gaza.

2) Creating an independent Palestinian state in the Gaza Strip and the West Bank (or the eastern part of the West Bank). At the price of displacing Jewish and Muslim populations, the Hebrew and Palestinian states would be both mono-ethnic and airtight: no more mixing, no more promiscuity.

3) There would remain the questions of Israeli Arabs and Jerusalem. Israeli Arabs, now a minority, would no longer pose a problem once 'Israeli oppression' had disappeared. As for Jerusalem, Jews must absolutely renounce making it their new capital out of religious fanaticism. Jerusalem — symbol of the monotheism of the Book — ought to be placed under international administration according to the 'right of enclaves provided with extraterritoriality', proposed by the United Nations in 1949.

Given its overwhelming military superiority, the Hebrew state — with the constant support of the Pentagon — would have nothing to fear from its Palestinian neighbour or from its other Arab Muslim neighbours. It could, on the contrary, guide and dominate them economically. Returned to its 1967 borders, Israel is perfectly viable. Its shrill, expansionist language does nothing but arouse religious fantasies. In addition, Arab leaders have been kind enough to agree to Israel's right to enjoy a territorial state on the land of Judaea and Samaria … It is up to the Israelis to make the next move: a country for Jews, another for Muslims, with borders that are definite, clear and heavily guarded, since total apartheid is the key for peace between different peoples.

***

It is not very likely that this wise solution will prevail, given the fanaticism of the parties involved and the geopolitical ignorance of the current Israeli leaders. In this case, there is no doubt about the result:

Israel will lose the war and the Jews will perhaps experience the fate of the Algerian French. Let us hope not.

In any case, the ethno-religious civil war that has set fire to this part of the Middle East in an epidemic fashion for decades give should cause for reflection in France to intellectuals of Jewish or Arab origin — on the Right or the Left — who sing the praises of ethnic mixing, of 'ethnopluralism',[56] of 'communitarianism'[57] and other dreams. Is not the wisest rule the one formulated by Plato and Aristotle: 'to each his own land on his own territory'?

***

Israel is undermined by its demography. In history, demography is much more important than armies or wealth. In 1950, there were 1.37 million Israelis, of whom 167,000 or 12 % were not Jewish. In 2001, there were 6.5 million Israelis, of whom 1.48 million were not Jewish (Arab Israeli citizens), or 23 %.

Currently, there are 3.5 million Palestinians (Israeli non-citizens), as opposed to 0.95 million in 1967. In total, Muslim Arabs (whether Israeli citizens or not) represent 50 % of the population of the whole area (Israel plus the occupied territories), as opposed to 37 % in 1967. The non-Jewish population of the Hebrew state has more than doubled since 1960, despite massive Jewish immigration, which has now dried up. The number of Palestinians in the occupied territories has quadrupled in 24 years because of Arab demographic dynamism and the low Jewish birth rate.

---

56 Ethnopluralism refers to a social ideology which views the presence of many different ethnicities living together in a state of equality as an ideal.

57 Communitarianism is a social theory which calls for society to be drawn up into separate, but autonomous, communities based on ethnic or religious cohesion to exist side-by-side, with local government taking precedence over central government. It is favoured by Alain de Benoist and his colleagues in the French New Right.

These unbalanced birth rates of the two groups are only accelerating, as happened in Kosovo to the disadvantage of the Serbs, not to mention the Palestinian refugees in nearby countries, who are also proliferating at full speed. In the area of Israel plus the occupied territories, 51 % of Arabs are younger than 20, as opposed to 34 % of Jews. At this pace and if nothing changes, in 2025 the West Bank and Gaza, which now house 3.5 million Arabs, will have 7.4 million.

The Israeli government is fully aware of these statistics and very worried about this demographic time bomb. It knows that in twenty years (if the Jewish birth rate does not sink and there is no mass exodus), 6 million Israeli Jews will be surrounded by more than 100 million Muslims all over the Middle East. In the area of Israel plus the occupied territories, Arabs will then be in the clear majority. Because of the overlapping populations, the 'hedgehog' and 'fortress' military policy will be impossible, and the ultimate recourse to nuclear weapons in the case of open war will be obsolete.

***

So is Israel doomed to disappear? The state of Israel is currently in a very troubling demographic and geopolitical position. Israeli citizens who are Arab Muslims are reproducing at twice the rate of Jewish citizens. Without counting Palestinians, Israeli citizens who are Arab and Muslim (the descendants of the 160,000 Arabs who remained in Israel after the 1948 War) already represent 20 % of Israelis! Immigration of Jews from Russia (and elsewhere) has dried up. A significant number of Israeli Jews emigrate to the United States. In short, the state of Israel, despite the colonisation of Arab territories by Orthodox Jews, is in fact on the defensive.

In the long run, when we take account of the demographic power struggle, and despite the massive foreign aid from the USA (18 billion dollars a year), 'Fortress Israel' cannot hold out against the weight of its Arab neighbours. Among Jews around the world, there exist three irreconcilable schools.

The first position is that of the Lubavitch, Orthodox Jews of the Diaspora who believe that the creation of the state of Israel was a mistake, because it 'despiritualised' the notion of the Promised Land by reducing it to the conquest of a territory and a state like other nations. For them, Judaism has no territory. The Chosen People is at home everywhere and the Israeli state is impious. To be Jewish is to witness to a religion and a people according to *nomadism*.

The second position is that of Orthodox nationalists of the 'extreme Right', a reservation that is rather inappropriate. They want to hold on no matter what the cost, to colonise the 'occupied territories', to reinforce the religious state. This is the anti-Muslim strategy of 'Fortress Israel.' It is based on the expectation that the American protector and sponsor will go along and that the Jewish American community agrees with this policy, which is not clear.

The third position is that of 'modernist Israelis', called Leftists and Labourites. They are the majority of the Jewish Israeli population. They believe that their policy is realistic and goes as follows: Israel must become a secular state and its health lies in the *economic domination* of the neighbouring Arab countries by helping them develop.

If it goes on, the war between Jews and Muslims (despite the American-sponsored 'peace process') will end in a Muslim victory. For demographic reasons in the end Israel is doomed.

***

Why does the state of Israel risk a military defeat? It is not only for demographic reasons, nor because the war would plunge the Israeli economy into recession and the Jews would end up fleeing from a country undermined by terrorism, but also because the Tzahal, the Israeli army, is in no position to win an urban war in the Palestinian areas, despite its enormous budget, technological gadgets and massive striking power. It is the failure of a technology of helicopters and tanks against the primitive weapons of motivated combatants in an urban theatre. This has been shown in detail in a work by a scholar of military history, Jean-Louis Dufour, in *La Guerre, la Ville et le Soldat*.[58] The Tzahal is the victim of what experts call 'asymmetric warfare'. An army trained and equipped to fight another army head-to-head cannot defeat urban partisans with no uniforms. This was Napoleon's experience in Spain.

Every reprisal taken by the Tzahal using tanks, helicopters, F-16s and armoured bulldozers (deplorable in terms of cost-benefit analysis) arouses new vocations among the Palestinians for combat and martyrdom and objectively reinforces them. To win the war, the Israelis could use the technique of carpet-bombing, as the Russians did at Grozny in Chechnya, and massacre the Arabs, but diplomatically this is impossible.

Here is what Dufour wrote in March 2004 on the Web site of *Libération* under the title 'The Tzahal in the Trap of the City': 'The weakest one is not the one you thought. Time does not matter for the Palestinians any more than casualties do. Once upon a time Ho Chi Minh warned the French, "you can kill ten of my men while I kill only one of yours. Even at this ratio, you will lose and I will conquer." The implicit military genius of the Palestinians, or just their dumb luck, is to apply this strategy in urban areas.'

The Israelis have two possible strategies: the massive deportation of Arabs (including Arabs who are Israeli citizens) with the absolute apartheid of the fortress state, or departure *en masse*: The suitcase or the coffin. The compromise solution of 'peace, negotiation and cohabitation', especially between Jews and Muslims, turns out to be basically a stupid utopia.

Two Examples to Make Us Think

The international press does not discuss the issue — it is taboo — but, since the end of apartheid and the establishment of a Black government, South Africa is slowly sinking into barbarism. The first to suffer from

---

58   Jean-Louis Dufour, *La Guerre, la Ville et le Soldat* (War, the City and the Soldier) (Paris: Jacob, 2002).

it are, of course, the Blacks themselves. Some of them (as happened in Rhodesia, Algeria and elsewhere) are beginning to miss 'White Power' … Unemployment has tripled since the abolition of apartheid and crime rates are today the highest in the world: 12,000 murders and 50,000 rapes a year. 95 % of the victims are Black. Heavily guarded by militias, the wealthy Whites live in the cities, surrounded by electrified barbed-wire fences. The situation is paradoxical but explicable. Since the inauguration of black power the difference in the standard of living between Blacks and Whites has increased by 10 % to the advantage of the Whites and *de facto* apartheid has become much more marked than under the old *de jure* apartheid.

***

Is there really a chance that the United States will break apart or be carved up? Charles Truxillo, a Professor of Chicano Studies at the University of New Mexico in the United States, believes that 80 years from now, when several states of the Southwestern United States will have Mexican majorities by immigration, they will secede out of simple electoral pressure to form the Republica del Norte (the Republic of the North — north, that is, of Mexico) that will comprise Texas, New Mexico, Arizona, California and the south of Colorado. The new country will have its capital in Los Angeles and its official language will be Spanish.

'The process is inevitable and, in any case, necessary', Truxillo declares. 'My young students will live the end of their lives, free and sovereign, in their new Hispanic fatherland, the Republic of the North.' This will be the rematch of the Battle of the Alamo, when Texas freed itself from Mexico … The American states have the right of secession from the rest of the union after a referendum. By 2020, Hispanics will constitute the majority in six southern states in the USA, including Florida, which Professor Truxillo could have added to his Republica del Norte.

***

What is the status of the Spanish language in the United States? Its inexorable progress is causing much gnashing of teeth. In Santa Maria, California, in the course of a school district board meeting about policy, one of the board members walked out because the students' parents were asking their questions in Spanish. In San Diego, a high school principal insisted that parents should speak only English to their children, even at home. In one school in Arizona, a new rule requires that only English be spoken in classrooms, the cafeteria and the halls.

However, more and more Americans are learning Spanish — in fact, 50 % of the students in foreign language classes. In some schools in California, Arizona and Massachusetts, instruction in English has practically disappeared! By a Presidential Order from Clinton, school administrations must supply bilingual brochures. In Las Vegas and Phoenix, police who learn Spanish receive a monthly bonus of $100. Spanish is increasingly becoming the language of business. The purchasing power of Hispanics is expected to grow by 315 % from 1990 to 2007. A statistic that is more worrying for English-speakers is that only 4 million of the 35 million Hispanics speak English fluently. They do not need to ... The number of Spanish-language television stations never stops growing, and the same is true of advertisements in Spanish. Some political pressure groups are trying to impose English as the only official language of the United States, like French is in France. It is a battle lost in advance. Domenico Maceri, a professor of languages in California, predicts that in 2020, 'the United States will be bilingual, like Belgium'.

The Return of the Titans

One hundred years ago, Europe was at the height of its power, although it was divided into rival nations. European civilisation dominated the world in every area, as no other had done since the beginning of recorded history. But the Tarpeian Rock is next to the Capitol.[59] Three generations later, domination has become subjection, because of internal conquest by the Third World and Islam, American suzerainty, serious ethical and cultural decadence, global loss of the sovereignty of European nations, which have been diluted into a European Union without coherence or will, etc. Who, at the beginning of the Twentieth century, could have foreseen this fantastic and cataclysmic turnabout?

Some people, although very few, had foreseen it, for the worm was in the apple, and the virus had been introduced. European colonialism was waking up its subjects to political consciousness. Nowadays, the trends toward economic modernity and the demographic vigour of the civilisations of the global South that were asleep or backward are stirring, and they will not fail, if awakened by a shock, to eventually overwhelm us. The chauvinisms of the triumphant European nation-states only succeeded in provoking a suicidal intra-European civil war in two acts (1914–1918 and 1939–1945). Marxist thought, degenerate artistic schools, and ideological poisons opposed to all our traditions began to spread, sapping the foundations of the formidable edifice of European civilisation. The ideal of a large family had already been shaken by bourgeois individualism.

A hundred years later, we are in a situation at once of pre-implosion and pre-explosion. And Europe is clearly not the only party concerned. Let us summarise what we should expect, just around the corner, in the first decades of the Twenty-first century:

1) In Europe, especially France, ethnic civil war will break out, with Islam for its banner. It has already begun in a diffuse but clear fashion, a war of internal conquest that aims quite simply at making

---

59 The Tarpeian Rock was a cliff located near the site of the Roman Forum on Capitoline Hill in ancient Rome. During the days of the Roman Republic and later the Empire, dangerous criminals and the physically or mentally disabled were executed there by being thrown off the cliff.

our continent a new Muslim land (*Dar al-Islam*)[60] where people of European stock are called upon to become subject minorities and the populations that came from the South intend to become the majority. If the initiative succeeds, it will be a case of the pure and simple disappearance of European civilisation, which was born 3,500 years ago.

2) On the world scale, we are going to witness a global Islamic offensive, on the European front (from France to the Balkans) and the African front, but also in Russia, Central Asia, the Indian subcontinent and the Far East.

3) The American superpower can only decline, especially in the face of the formidable rise in Chinese power. Taking account of the atavistic militarism of the USA, a major confrontation between Americans and Chinese cannot be excluded. All the same, we can count on America's clumsy militarism, which starts fires without ever succeeding in eliminating its designated enemies, to multiply hotbeds of war throughout the world.

***

Each one of these conflicts piled one on top of the others (not to mention the return of those movements in Islam bent on conquest in accordance with the doctrines of their ancestors, this simplistic, violent and primitive civilisation, absolutely incompatible with the other great civilisations) will create in the Twenty-first century a general conflagration of the Earth in what will be *globalised* war, and no longer a world war.

The kinds of war we can expect will be total and global, in Europe and everywhere else. They will mix and add on to the classic convulsions between nation-states (India-Pakistan, China-USA, etc.),

---

60 Arabic: 'House of Islam'. In Islamic thought, it refers to those nations in which Muslims can practice their religion freely. For Islamists, it only applies to those nations where Islamic law is in effect.

probably including nuclear strikes, religious wars, civil war and two forms of terrorism, micro-terrorism and macro-terrorism. In a Europe open to the four winds, the increasingly large presence of immigrants from Muslim countries allows us to predict the impossibility of escaping major terrorist attacks in Europe that will be added into the insurrectional climate. The coming economic crisis — provoked by the ageing of the population — will only amplify the gravity of the situation.

***

One novelty is that the most diverse mafias, just like the Islamic terror networks, are going to join in the wild dance of the general criminalisation of the planet.

Paradoxically, just when there is general chatter — with tears in every eye — of the world state, international law, international courts to judge 'crimes against humanity' and other 'war crimes', the rule of human rights and human solidarity, we are entering a century where pacifist ideology has never been stronger, but where war, in all its different forms, will never be so widespread. The overpopulated planet will burn with conflagrations and every kind of conflict is going to increase in number and mingle with one another in the most complete anarchy.

The absolute reign of the rule of law (the domain of the word) is only the failure of every law and the dreamy compensation of the absolute reign of Force — and violence — that will be the law of the Twenty-first century. A general planetary insecurity will result that will overwhelm all the 'forces of order'. It will take place in front of the backdrop of an accelerated destruction of the ecosystem and a global warming that will provoke climatic catastrophes.

This description does not include the intensification of the Israeli-Palestinian conflict that will probably end with the defeat of the Hebrew state.

***

The 'law of war' is going to cease to exist. There will no longer be a clear frontier between war and peace. Everything will be war, from the microcosm to the macrocosm, from each person's daily life to international relations. This situation will be dialectically normal: an overpopulated planet where the ideology of the 'modern' West, clinging stubbornly to its errors, wants to amalgamate all peoples in a pacified and mongrelised world state, will, by inversion, end in a general explosion.

By a dialectical turnabout the ideology of tolerance, well-being, *laissez-faire*[61] and a general cosmopolitanism (two of its masters were Kant and Rousseau, both much more infectious than Marx for broken dreams) will give way to a gigantic law of the jungle. We are quite certainly going to enter an age that will resemble the early Middle Ages, but ten times more violent.

We cannot put the current planetary civilisation back together again. Our children are going to live through a fantastic reshuffling and dealing of the cards. Unheard-of violence awaits them. The Twenty-first will be a century of fire and blood, the end of a cycle. Of course, Parisian intellectual cretins do not suspect for one second what is doing to happen. They do not know the historical weather forecast. They do not know how to see the coming storms.

---

61 *Laissez-faire*, literally 'let them do', is any type of economic system which is free from all but the most minimal of government regulation.

3

TOWARD CHAOS IN EUROPE

In the Eye of the Cyclone

E urope is in the eye of the cyclone. For the moment the storm has not yet really begun, but all the signs show that it is about to be unleashed. All the indicators that concern Europe are flashing red. Every single factor is negative.

The collapse of Europe will be a disaster for the world's economy, of which Europe has always been one of the principal locomotives. Here is a summary of the 'lines of catastrophe' from which Europe is suffering, lines that are at the same time getting worse and converging.

1) First of all, demographic decline. No one seems to be concerned with this fundamental fact. The burden of older people and the lack of young people are automatically going to produce the following phenomena, which are already beginning but are only going to speed up: the impossibility of paying for retirements and social benefits, the brain drain, and a shortage of creators and innovators. Taxes and burdens, like public debt, will keep on growing all the way to a breakdown. The policies of the European states are not taking these facts into account. Bankruptcy looms. Countries

whose population is ageing and declining can no longer be sure of a minimal level of innovation.

2) Economic bankruptcy. For the moment, the system is still working, but this cannot go on for long. The wealth creators will no longer be able to assure the needs of old people and foreigners, who produce little and whose numbers are growing. Unemployment insurance and social security, like healthcare insurance, which is still miraculously working, will collapse for simple mathematical reasons. The 'reforms' that governments are timidly undertaking, slowed down by a short-sighted corporatism, will, of course, fail.

3) Uncontrolled immigration from abroad, which is composed of welfare recipients (many more 'refugees' and illegal immigrants than workers) and not of wealth creators who pay for benefits, constitutes a tidal wave that will not be sustainable in the middle term. The 'integration' or 'assimilation' in which we pretend to believe cannot work because the populations to be integrated and assimilated are too numerous and there is no control over the human deluge. Europe is in the process of undergoing — without the consent of its indigenous peoples — a massive substitution of populations, which is taking place for the first time in its history. The new populations that are settling here are importing a 'Third World culture', that is, they are impoverishing Europe. It is politically incorrect to mention these facts, but we must talk about them all the same.

4) Islam and ethnic civil war. We must also mention the growing presence of Islam in Europe, which is well on its way to becoming the dominant and majority religion in some countries, for demographic reasons and laxity in enforcing immigration. Here again is a situation never seen before. Such a violent civilisational metamorphosis can only produce uncontrollable consequences.

The almost millennium-long war of Islam against the West is already starting to have Europe as its latest battlefield. We are going to see attacks multiply. Some of them will be enormous and devastating, perhaps nuclear, which will add to other destabilising factors.

Let us now add to this balance sheet the explosion of criminal activity, which no government will be able to control and all try to play down. This increased criminal activity is for the most part linked to immigration, a reality that cannot be seriously denied. Everything indicates that an *ethnic civil war* is about to break out in Europe, prefigured by the current face of delinquency.

5) The dissolving of civil society and culture. The crisis of mentalities is deep. The culture diffused everywhere by the media is transmitting a general taste for morbidity and anti-values, what Nietzsche called 'nihilism'. In this perspective, France is particularly affected, although this pathology involves the entire West and strikes observers, for example, Arabs and Muslims, with stupor and amazement. The lowering of public morality (which paradoxically goes hand in hand with a redundant and hypocritical public discourse on 'human rights'), the decline of beauty in the arts, the disappearance of stable families, the privileging of homosexuality over heterosexuality — there is a long list of these symptoms of decline and the rejection of *natural law* that a disoriented intelligentsia interprets as signs of 'progress'.

Let us add the slow shipwreck of the quality of public education that confirms the progress of illiteracy. We are witnessing the breakdown of the transmission of culture to new generations.

As soon as the infrastructure of culture, values and the teaching of heritage is no longer assured, innovation is also no longer assured, and we are struck by *neo-primitivism*.

6) The predictable end of the European Union, which will rapidly become unsustainable. The EU's expansion to the countries of central Europe — and even more to Turkey — will provoke unsolvable problems. The European Union will replace the nation-states in the most total, especially institutional, fog. We are confronting an indescribable mess that will not be able to solve the smallest crisis and will transform the continent of Europe into a space without consistency, politically incoherent, open to the four winds. A collection like this cannot seriously last because no can say what it really is; it is *undetermined*.

The European Union is going to disappear. We must recognise that it was a beautiful dream and worthy of respect. Its unavoidable collapse will provoke a groundswell to add to the other crises.

***

All the intellectuals who have denied these facts were wrong. The question is not to know whether reality is politically correct or not, but to determine whether or not it is the reality. The desire to *politicise* the facts, that is, to disguise them under an ideological grid, condemns us to understand nothing and to be unable to predict anything.

Of course, for the moment these predictions seem wildly exaggerated. We cannot *yet* imagine that the edifice will collapse, since, outwardly, everything is working. However, the interlocking of the disorders will proceed very rapidly. Let us recall the Roman adage: 'The Tarpeian Rock is next to the Capitol'. Europe's current fragility may provoke its violent fall, because we are neglecting all the signs that point to the fall.

Let us stop believing in illusionists and the apparent comfort of a day whose sun is setting.

The Horrible Spectre of Ethnic Civil War

Although the entire political class does not want to know about it, it is more than probable that the constant increase in crime taking place in Europe is a sign of the beginning of an ethnic civil war. It is politically incorrect to say this, but the conclusion is obvious. Most cases of serious crime and routine delinquency are committed by perpetrators who have immigrated from non-European countries. It is absurd to describe as 'racism' a statement of the clear sociological facts.

I maintain the thesis that a number of these acts of delinquency are of an insurrectional and political nature, and not essentially due to the criminal underworld. We see this in the countless cases of the burning of automobiles. I am not trying to judge, but to ascertain the facts. This situation is not at all comparable to what are strictly social riots, but they assume, unfortunately, an ethnic character, in which the idea of the conquest of Europe by Islam plays a role, which at times is unclear, at others quite explicit.

Thus the 'clash of civilisations', which has been noted on the geopolitical level, is found on the European level, according to a logic of civil war, but a civil war of a new type, in which foreign-born populations, who in their demographic dynamism contrast sharply with the anaemic birth rates of the native-born, aim implicitly at taking over the territory. Aristotle foresaw this situation in his *Politics*: the struggle of the foreign-born against the native-born, with the former committing acts of injustice to conquer the latter. This is why Aristotle recommended as the first concern of politics maintaining the ethno-cultural homogeneity of the city-state in order to preserve peace and democracy.

***

Rather than 'immigration', we should be speaking of the massive colonisation for settlement by peoples from Africa, the Maghreb and Asia, and understand that Islam is aiming at the conquest of France and Europe; that 'juvenile delinquency' is only the beginning of an ethnic civil war; that we have been invaded through births as much as through porous frontiers; and that, for demographic reasons, an Islamic power may install itself in France, first at the municipal level and then, perhaps, on the national level.

The public school system is sinking, a prey to violence, especially from 'Beurs' and 'Blacks',[1] the new conquerors. There are more than a thousand zones where the police dare not go. For some years, the number of new immigrants has been exploding, whether they are legal and possess a visa or else are clandestine. The new arrivals are no longer profitable workers, but applicants for public assistance. We are racing to the abyss. If nothing changes, in two generations, France will no longer have a European majority for the first time in its history. Germany, Italy, Spain, Belgium and Holland are following the same gloomy path, though some years behind. Since the fall of the Roman Empire, Europe has never known a similar historic disaster. This is happening with the complicity of a blind and ethnically masochistic political class and the collaboration of the pro-immigration lobbyists.

The ethnic chaos that is getting worse in Europe may abolish our civilisation. It is an event more serious than all the great plagues and wars that Europe has known. Let us not forget that this colonisation as well as this Islamicisation serves the interests of the United States and that integration and assimilation, like multi-ethnic communitarianism, are impossible!

***

The ethnic and cultural identity of Europe, the foundation of its civilisation, has never have been so seriously threatened. Laurent Joffrin[2] could write in *Le Nouvel Observateur* this stupefying sentence: 'The far Right expects to palliate the disorders of the liberal future by a remedy

---

1   In France, these terms refer to North African Arabs and sub-Saharan Blacks.

2   Laurent Joffrin (b. 1952) was the editor of the left-wing daily *Libération*. He left this position in March 2011.

as false as it is murderous, by aggressively opposing ethnic identity to the inevitable mixing of cultures.'

The inevitability of mixing has not been corroborated by the facts. We are not witnessing a 'mixing of cultures' in France, but quite frankly the destruction, eradication and ethnocide of European culture in favour of Americanisation and now Afro-Maghrebisation and Islamicisation.

Under the cover of the ideology of cultural and ethnic mixing, which has never succeeded anywhere in the world, the intention is to abolish our ancestral culture, which has been judged guilty of existing and being intrinsically perverse.

'Ethnic identity' and its defence have been designated as Evil, as the symbol of aggression, according to Laurent Joffrin. In other words, to defend and affirm oneself is racism.

Far from the mingling of a 'worldwide civilisation' as a global village, the Earth is organised today in large blocs that share an ethnic identity and are in competition with one another. The mixing of cultures and the abolition of ethnic identities are not on the schedule of the Twenty-first century. India, China, Black Africa, the Muslim world, whether Arab or Turkish, and so on, are affirming their identities and do not tolerate either a colonising immigration or cultural mixing on their own soil. Only the European pseudo-elites are defending the dogma of a 'multicultural world', which is a chimera.

Europe is forgetting the heritage of its ancestors and the official defence of our cultural 'patrimony' disguises an initiative of museification, but not creation. For a cultural identity, like a biological identity, is fundamentally Archeofuturist[3]: it proceeds by a permanent rebirth of forms and generations, which begins with an original *germen*.[4] Permanent biological and cultural renewal and the constant

---

3   See Guillaume Faye, *Archeofuturism: European Visions of the Post-Catastrophic Age* (London: Arktos, 2010).

4   Latin: 'seed' or 'germ'.

maintenance of the will-to-power is the law of long-lived peoples. Identity cannot be conceived without the complementary notion of continuity.

The war against ethnic and cultural identity is the key watchword of the reigning egalitarian ideology. It is a question of abolishing simultaneously our memory and our origin. The academic curricula bear witness to this. The schools now teach African fairy tales instead of our old French songs.

***

This colonisation for permanent settlement is sinking its roots into the very heart of our own way of thinking. It is the French who will have been the artisans of the destruction of France by invasion by foreigners. If France has been the most affected country, it is because the very notion of ethnic and cultural identity has been rejected in France.

The ill comes from long ago. Since the French Revolution, the new Jacobin France has thought of itself as 'the republic of humanity', 'the fatherland of all men', in imitation of the United States of America that had just acquired its independence. Only in the United States, a country whose very foundation is immigration and the ethnocide of the indigenous Indians, the formula is true, while in France, a land of rooted peoples and ethnicities, this formula is dangerously false. From the time of its origin the French Republic was founded on the dogma of a preference for the man without a country.

After the defeat in the Franco-Prussian War of 1870, the ideologues of the Republic, with Ernest Renan[5] at their head, opposed Germany, a nation 'founded by an original people who speak an original language',

---

5   Ernest Renan (1823–1892) was a prominent French philosopher. Initially sympathetic to the ideals of German philosophy, his views changed drastically following the French defeat in 1871. His opposition to the German concept of nationalism was outlined in his 1882 essay, 'What is a Nation?', in which he contrasted the idea of the nation as a 'daily referendum' rather than being the product of a shared cultural, historical and linguistic heritage.

to France, which they supposed more civilised than Germany because it was founded not on a conquered race, rootedness, and an inherited identity, but on a social contract, a 'will to live together politically'. 1870 was the start of this baleful French ideology that denies the ethnic reality of the peoples of France and imposes the republican half-breed as the model of the ideal citizen.

In 1914 and then in 1940 the German, perceived as a hereditary enemy, was represented as the full-blooded people, the primitive people with an ethnic identity to be defeated. The opposite ideal was the French citizen, republican and without a fatherland (shoulder to shoulder with auxiliaries from across the ocean), detached from every blood tie and bound to other members of society only by a social contract.

By a fantastic historical boomerang effect, the republican ideology, which is opposed to the idea of an ethnic identity, and after having tried to destroy the personality of the regions of France,[6] has failed utterly to integrate, assimilate and brew into a melting pot the identities of millions of immigrants, or let us say rather new settlers, who have conserved their ethnic and cultural identity while the mass of the native-born French has lost theirs. The French ideology is on track to destroy France.

This ideology, based on an incorrigible cosmopolitanism, is anchored deep and integrated in the mentality of the ruling bourgeoisie. This is the source of the almost unanimous vote in favour of the 'antiracist' Pleven[7] and Gayssot[8] laws that instituted a thought police, the

---

6   The present-day departments of France were set up in 1790 during the French Revolution. The departments were purposefully designed to break up the historical regions which had existed previously in an attempt to eliminate local identities in favour of a more universal, national identity.

7   The Pleven Law was passed by the French Parliament in July 1972, making it illegal to incite racial hatred either through speech or writing, or to use language that is perceived as racially defamatory.

8   The Gayssot Act, which was enacted by the French Parliament in July 1990, makes it illegal to deny or question the severity of the Holocaust.

source of the countless pro-immigration measures and renouncing of all border control on the part of governments of the Left and Right. In general the French bourgeois elites, in politics and the media, have no consciousness of ethnic identity.

These elites are complicit in colonisation and invasion by the antiracist criminalisation of opinion and an almost religious ideological faith that 'ethnic identity is evil', just like all political doctrines tainted by ethnic consciousness.

This drive against ethnic identity and obsession with finding racism everywhere — which should really be called 'xenophilia' — that is, a fascination with the other, the foreigner — rather than 'anti-racism', touches the very heart of the political and cultural movements that appeal to French and European identity, but demonise ethnocentrism. This is how deeply the evil, the virus is anchored in the organism.

***

No, it was not Jean-Marie Le Pen[9] who said it; it was the conclusion of a colloquium held in Paris on the theme, 'These Migrants Who Are Changing the Face of Europe', organised by the respectable Institut de géopolitique des populations, and mentioned in the French press only in a (very) brief report in *Le Figaro* (17 October 2003).

According to the experts who attended the colloquium, there are supposedly 40 million immigrants in Europe. 10 million of them live in France and half of them are Muslims. (Other demographers give higher figures.) On the supposition that the birth rate of immigrant women is twice as high as the birth rate of the native-born while the flow of immigrants is not drying up, the Institut's demographic projections are the following: 'By 2030, immigrants and their descendants could represent 24 % of the total French population (15.7 million persons), 23 % of the working population (5.7 million) and 42 % of births

---

9   Jean Marie Le Pen (1928–2025) was the leader of the far-Right Front National from 1972 until 2011.

(or 273,000).' The consequences of this dramatic process are obviously not examined from an ethnic or civilisational point of view (under the pressure of political correctness), but from an economic point of view. Read carefully: the hypothesis, by the due date of 2030, of a 'certain process of economic and social underdevelopment' is envisaged in the case where these populations 'would not attain the degree of skills demanded by a modern developed economy'.

They are not attaining it today and we do not see how they will reach it tomorrow. In other words, the settlement of masses of immigrants is going to provoke in the next twenty years an economic and social collapse of Europe, which will become a 'Third World' country. Things are changing. It is not only the 'dreadful' proponents of ethnic identity or 'xenophobes' who are saying these things, but the Institut de géopolitique des populations.

***

'Immigration: The New Wave' is the title of a paper delivered by Maxime Tandonnet at the 'Sovereignism' summer school at Lamouri (6 September 2003), where he said: 'At a minimum, France will receive each year 300,000 immigrants (a low hypothesis). Now we know that the number of annual births is around 750,000 in our country. The immense majority of migrations into France are settlement migrations. The immigrants never leave and stay permanently in the country of reception. This means that at a due date of about fifty years, in 2050, around a third to a half of the population of France will consist of current immigrants and their descendants. The phenomenon underway today represents a profound modification of the population of France, which is without parallel in history. It corresponds to a scenario outlined by a UN report of 20 March 2000, on "replacement migrations", which foresees the arrival in Europe, from now to 2050, of 700 million new immigrants to replace the current European populations. Today in France, four-fifths of new arrivals come from the Maghreb, Africa and Asia.' It would be interesting to determine the 'point of no return', or rather the 'date of no return' beyond which an inversion of the human flow will no longer be possible ...

***

What are the numbers of immigration? They are continually rising. The annual demographic balance sheet published by the INED (Institut national d'études démographiques) in December 2003 gives the following indications: 145,000 foreigners have obtained the first permission of residence in 1999, 160,000 in 2000, and 183,000 in 2001. This does not include those seeking asylum ... In all, the INED estimates at more than 200,000 the number of first-time arrivals in 2002. Henry de Lesquen, President of the Club de l'Horloge[10] and of the Voix des Français-Renaissance 95,[11] finds these numbers scandalously underestimated. 'According to the media, there are supposed to be 100,000 regular entries in the course of a year. In reality the number is 200,000' (*La voix des Français*, October 2003). He estimates illegal entries at more than 100,000 a year, of which 80,000 have asked for asylum, been rejected but have never been expelled. 'This means 300,000 immigrants more each year, most of them unassimilable, while we have only 750,000 births — of which a fraction, after all, is due to the immigrants themselves. ... A real substitution of the population is taking place.'

***

The number of those seeking asylum has increased by 265 % between 1998 and 2001. In Lyons alone, 1,000 new children from 40 different nationalities must be educated in public schools each year. According to *Le Monde* (October 21, 2003), Corsica has 25,000 Muslims, or 10 %

10   The Club de l'Horloge is a right-wing think tank in France that was founded in 1974. In its early years, it was close to GRECE and the French New Right.

11   Voix des Français-Renaissance, or Voice of the French Renaissance 95, is an anti-immigration association in France that was established in 1993. They also publish a monthly journal.

of its population. What do the nationalists say about this? When will a great mosque be constructed in Ajaccio? Anyhow, 25 % of Marseilles' population is Muslim. According to the Spanish daily newspaper *El Pais*, 2 million foreigners were counted in Spain on 1 January 2002, or 4.7 % of the population, as opposed to 900,000 in 2000. INSEE (Institut national de la statistique et des études économiques)[12] estimates that Spain will be home to a minimum of 4 million foreigners in 2010, or 9 % of its inhabitants. This figure does not take into account illegal immigrants and Spain's very low birth rate ...

***

Let us discuss 'asylum-seekers'. 'At Marseilles, people arrive from everywhere. ... The majority of requests for asylum are not approved because they are not justified. The requests take two years to be dealt with. Meanwhile, the state supplies lodging and financial aid to the asylum seekers and their children are given free schooling. When the request is rejected, the immigrants have the right of appeal. ... No one can say today the exact number of those who are waiting for the decision on their request for asylum or how many have been rejected. Illegal immigration will end by killing legal immigration. Things will reach a level where there will be a revolt against foreigners in general', writes Christian Frémont, Prefect of the department of Bouches-du-Rhône, of the PACA region and the southern zone of defence, in *Metro* (9 January 2004).

With more than 80,000 entries a year by (bogus) asylum-seekers, France has taken first place in Europe. Foreign 'refugees' are treated better than the homeless or the unemployed under French law. In Japan, where there exists no public support for this type of population, there are no 'refugees' or 'clandestine' immigrants. This goes to show the stupidity of the following comment by Prefect Frémont: 'As

---

12 National Institute of Statistics and Economic Studies, which is run by the French Ministry of Finance.

long as there is an enormous gap in wealth between different nations, the struggle against clandestine immigration will be a problem.' The problem is not 'economic'; it is mental and moral. All it would take would be to turn off the suction pump of welfare to refugees to stop the flow of immigration. But the ideology of 'human rights' is firmly opposed to that ...

***

What is the birth rate of foreigners in France? A report published by INSEE, *La fécondité des étrangères en France* (May 2003), reveals that in 1999 women of non-European origin had an average of 3 babies as opposed to 1.7 for French women. The prediction of the 1980s that the birth rate of immigrant families was going to decline and align itself with those of native families has turned out to be wrong. African women, three times more numerous today than in 1980, have 4 babies on average; Turkish women have 3.35; and women from the Maghreb have 3.25, with no sign of birth rates going down since 1990. Granted, the older the families who immigrated from the Maghreb become, the more their birth rate goes down and comes to resemble European birth rates. The problem is that new families are arriving non-stop from North Africa and they maintain the very high birth rate.

In addition, INSEE has noticed that the birth rates of the Turks, Moroccans and Tunisians living in France is higher than the birth rates of their compatriots who have stayed in their own country, thanks to the recrudescence of 'arranged marriages' with young women who come from these countries because of the policy of family reunification and all kinds of public aid not found in their own countries. Let us add that talk about the birth rate of 'French' women (1.7) is a highly administrative definition, since it does not distinguish between native-born and naturalised women. The birth rate of women of French stock must obviously be much lower.

***

The real numbers of immigrants from Africa are unknown. Jean-Paul Gourévitch, an expert on Africa and author of a recent book, *La France africaine*,[13] gives the following statistics in the journal *Géostratégiques* (February 2001), which have been ignored by the French media. The High Council for Integration (Haut Conseil à l'Integration) reports for France 96,500 legal immigrants from Africa in 2000, an increase of 55 % compared to 1999. As for illegal immigration, the range is estimated from 30,000 to 150,000 a year. The IOM (International Office for Migration) estimates at between 400,000 and 500,000 the number of illegals who penetrate each year into the European Schengen space.[14] Only about 7,735 illegal immigrants a year are deported, or about 17.3 % of the judicial decisions, and the majority of the deportees will return. The birth rate of women of sub-Saharan origin who have settled in France oscillates between 4.8 and 6.9 against 1.7 for French women. Unless things change, according to the opinion of Jean-Paul Gourévitch (who calls this fact *unavoidable*, just the opposite of the opinion of the *JTC*!), the population of African origin will represent half of the inhabitants of France by the middle of the Twenty-first century. Finally, do you know the number of the historically French who leave their country yearly, most of them with university diplomas, and principally to Anglo-Saxon countries? The IOM reports 40,000 to 50,000.

***

And now, here are some basic statistics on Islam and immigration. Roger Caritini, in *Le génie de l'islamisme*,[15] wrote, 'There are about 1.2

---

13 Jean-Paul Gourévitch, *La France africaine: Islam, intégration, insécurité* (African France: Islam, Integration, Insecurity) (Paris: Pré aux clercs, 2000).

14 This refers to an agreement that was signed between 25 European nations in 1985 in Schengen, Luxemburg, which allows for the free passage of citizens from one country to another. It was absorbed into the EU in 1999.

15 Roger Caritini, *Le génie de l'islamisme* (The Genius of Islamism) (Paris: M. Lafon, 1992).

billion Muslims in the world and this population will have probably doubled in 30 years.'[16] One estimate reckons six to ten million Muslims in the USA,[17] but Oriana Fallaci in *The Rage and the Pride* counts 24 million. Christopher Caldwell, 'Allah Mode: France's Islam Problem' in *Weekly Standard* (15 July 2002), and Alexandre Del Valle in 'Islam, avenir de l'Europe' which appeared in *Valeurs actuelles* (July 2002), report 20 million Muslims in Europe, excluding Russia, but Patrick Poivre d'Avor has talked about 30 million on TF1[18] (14 October 2002), as has Aymeric Chauprade (École de Guerre Économique, report, December 2002).

Jean-Paul Gourévitch estimated 12 million Black and multiracial inhabitants in France in *La France africaine*. There are no accurate statistics for the number of Muslims. 4.1 million according to Documentation française (*Notes et études documentaires*, August 2001), 5 million according to *Télérama* (as cited in the previous paragraph) and the discussions of PPDA on TF1 (14 October 2002), and 8 million in 2000, according to Christopher Caldwell and Alexandre Del Valle (cited above), a figure also given by the Institut du monde arabe. Aymeric Chauprade (cited above) suggested the figure of 12 million Muslims in 2001 and predicted 15 million in 2005! The number of Algerians who have immigrated into France has gone from 805,000 to 2 million between 1982 and 2002, according to Ali Laïdi and Ahmed Salam, *Le Jihad en Europe*[19] (Seuil, 2002), p. 265. They estimate the number of mosques at more than 1,500. Documentation française suggests 1,600 mosques, a number repeated by France 2[20] (11 October 2002).

---

16 Roger Caritini, *Le génie de l'islamisme*, p. 692.

17 Catherine Portevin, *Comprendre l'Islam: si loin, si proche* (Paris: Télérama), p.74.

18 A private national French television channel.

19 Ali Laïdi and Ahmed Salam, *Le jihad en Europe: les filiáeres du terrorisme is-lamiste* (Paris: Seuil, 2002).

20 A public national French television channel.

500,000 illegal immigrants may have settled in France in 2001, according to Daniel Duglery in a speech to the Gaullist UMP[21] for the legislative campaign, reported on France 2 (June 11, 2002). Thierry Desjardins estimated that the number of clandestine immigrants in France will have passed from 350,000 in 1991 (figure from ILO — International Labour Organization) to 800,000 in 1996 in *Lettre au president à propos de l'immigration.*[22] INSEE estimates the net migratory balance — the number of additional immigrants — from 1992 to 2002 at more than 100,000 a year in its *Rapport sur la population* (March 2002). Benoît Duquesne gives an estimate of 50,000 for the number of new illegal immigrants each year in his *Contre-enquête* on France 2 (14 October 2002).

Philippe de Villiers suggests the following, even higher figures in *Le Figaro* (12–13 September 2002): 'The number of clandestine immigrants grew from about 140,000 persons a year and in 2001 80,000 persons requested political asylum. ... More than 200,000 visas were given to Algerians in 2002 as opposed to 60,000 in 1996, etc.'

On the basis of these figures and others, all contradicting one another because of the silence of official statistics, but nevertheless colossal, a statistician has privately written, 'Beginning with a low evaluation of 1.8 million clandestine immigrants and "political refugees" in 2002 in France, I estimate at 9.5 million the regular and irregular immigrants in France, or 16 % of the population, without taking account of naturalised French or French of foreign origin.'

If we take these last into consideration, imagine the number of non-European inhabitants that France must contain: perhaps 15 million, or

---

21 Union pour un Mouvement Populaire, or Union for a Popular Movement, is a centre-Right party which is one of the two largest political parties in France today.

22 Thierry Desjardins, *Lettre au Président à propos de l'immigration: et de quelques autres sujets tabous qu'il faudra bien finir par aborder* (Letter to the President about Immigration: and Some Other Taboo Subjects That Will Be Addressed) (Paris: le Grand livre du mois, 1996), pp. 96–97.

more than 20 % of the population, growing constantly (through new arrivals and a higher birth rate). These considerations may perhaps explain the fact that the number of those who believe that 'There are too many Arabs in France' has dropped from 76 % in 1990 to 63 % in 2000 (poll by the Commission des droits de l'homme).

***

A very optimistic article was published in the *International Herald Tribune*, written by Jonathan Power, an American sociologist 'of the Right', under the title, 'Europe's Fake Crisis Over Immigration and Aging'.[23] We shall summarise it for you. First of all, Power recognises the calamity of the low European birth rate and massive immigration from the Third World, 'factors leading to economic and cultural impoverishment'. He ridicules the UN vulgate, repeated by the *Financial Times*, according to which Europe should accept '170 million immigrants to renew its working population'. For Power, it is not too late, however. His solution lies in increasing the native European birth rate, which he sees dawning in Sweden and France, and by natalist policies. He tells us, and we would like to believe him, that 'in the healthiest parts of the European middle classes, large families are much more popular than in the previous generation.' To take up the slack of the generations with a weak workforce, he suggests the abolition of the age limit for retirement. One can always dream.

***

Let us mention the illusion of helping to create jobs in the Third World. The following appeared on the Polémia Web site (www.polemia.com): 'About fifty international financial leaders met quietly in early July in Athens. The European Central Bank (ECB), the World Bank and the European Investment Bank (EIB) were represented. The bankers

---

23 Jonathan Power, 'Europe's Fake Crisis Over Immigration and Aging: Don't Believe the Hype', in the *International Herald Tribune* (31 July 2003).

concluded: if, over the next ten years, 40 million jobs are not created in the Arab countries south of the Mediterranean, Europe will be confronted by a wave of immigration without parallel in everything Europe has known up to the present.' To accomplish this job growth, the European Investment Bank envisages financing 'large-scale projects of economic development' in Arab countries.

Where is the money for this project going to come from? What was not possible yesterday when Europe was growing will be even less possible tomorrow in a Europe in probable recession. Creating 40 million jobs in ten years is a pure and simple utopia. It is necessary to stop taking seriously this worn-out idea that it is possible to keep immigrants in their own country by massive financial aid to the local job market. The only solution for Europe is hermetically sealed borders, massive deportations and turning off the suction pump of financial aid to first-time arrivals. These policies cost less and work much better.

***

An Algerian official has deplored the 'invasion of Europe' by Africa. Tamanrasset in southern Algeria is the disembarkation point for thousands of illegal immigrants (30,000 a year) from Black Africa, who are trying to reach the European 'El Dorado'.[24] The mayor of Tamanrasset, Moktar Zounga, reacted in *Le Figaro* (1 April 2002): 'There are organised networks coming from Mali and Niger in truckloads. We do not have the means to stop them. We turn back at the borders those who commit crimes or traffic in drugs at public expense. But when ten leave, twenty arrive. ... This is a problem for the whole world and especially Europe. The situation is serious. After us, it is Europe's turn! Europe is being invaded! They are determined and they have nothing to lose. It is your bread they come to eat. Today there are thousands. How many will it be tomorrow?' Heavens! Would not this language be

---

24 El Dorado was a mythical city made of gold which was sought, through great sacrifice, by Spanish Conquistadors in Sixteenth-century South America. No evidence for its existence has ever been found.

illegal under the provisions of the Pleven law? To stop the haemorrhaging, Moktar Zounga is inclined to 'keep Africans at home, by making their villages agriculturally self-sufficient.' He explains, 'The problems of a village can be fixed with an auto-pump costing 300 euros [$400].' Unfortunately, the global mechanisms for 'aid to the Third World' are completely indifferent to local subsistence agriculture. Loans and gifts from the nations of the global North and international organisations end up in the rulers' pockets. The result is pressure on the peasant masses of Mali and Niger, who are not being helped effectively, to spread out over Europe.

***

An ideological reversal is occurring in the French Jewish community because of the rise of a very strong North African anti-Judaism in France. The article 'Eurabia: A New Civilisation' in *Israel Magazine* (April 2003) opines: 'Europe has abandoned the Christians of Lebanon to Palestinian massacres and the Christians of the Islamic world to persecutions by Islamists. ... On the European demographic level, the immigration policies of the European Union have encouraged the Islamist desire to Islamicise Europe. The real numbers of this immigration has been kept from the public. For the only time in the history of immigration, exporting the culture of immigrants into the countries that welcomed them was written into the accords between the EU and the Arab League[25] as an unalienable right of immigrants. ... The European Saint-Justs[26] of anti-racism have succeeded in eliminating all discussion concerning the danger, criminal activity and fanaticism of a population that refuses to integrate.'

---

25 The Arab League was founded in 1945 to provide grounds for cooperation between the various Arab states. It currently has 22 member nations.

26 Louis Antoine de Saint-Just (1767–1794) was a French revolutionary who was closely associated with Robespierre and the Reign of Terror. He was executed at the same time as Robespierre.

The author, Bat Yeʾor,[27] who also writes for the influential *Observatoire du monde juif*, defends the thesis of the coherent solidarity of Jews and Europe, an alliance of Israel and Europe, deplores Europeans' pro-Arab policies and blames them in the following terms for Arab Islamism that she calls the principal enemy: 'The contempt for "infidel" Judaeo-Christian culture is expressed in the affirmation of the superiority of Islamic civilisation, from which European scholars have humbly drawn. This absurdity, repeated obsequiously by our European ministers, constitutes in fact a religious principle of the Arab world, which recognises no superiority in the civilisation of the "infidels." … Veneration of the myth of Andalusia[28] replaces scholarly knowledge of the devastating Muslim invasions.' Bat Yeʾor goes even further: 'Since the 1970s, immigration policies, integrated in the economic and political conception of EAD (Euro-Arab Dialogue), has been planning a homogeneous implantation into the secular European tissue of foreign communities numbered in the millions, who have come, not to assimilate, but to impose their own civilisation by right in the countries that welcome them. … From the beginning of immigration, assimilation was excluded, even while EAD was demanding for Arab immigrants rights conferred by European institutions, which the immigrants rejected since they privileged their own Arab Islamic culture founded on *shariah*.'

An analysis like this denotes a nearly complete reversal in the opinion of the Jewish community on the subject of Arab Islamic

---

27 Bat Yeʾor (b. 1933) is the pen name of Giséle Littman, a British historian who writes about Jews and Christians living under Muslim rule. She coined the term *dhimmitude* to describe what she believes is a permanent state of fear and anxiety in non-Muslim populations who have been forced to live under Islamic rule or in Muslim-majority areas, brought on by the Muslim doctrine of *jihad*.

28 Al-Andalusia was a region in southern Spain which was ruled by the Muslims between 711 and 1492 CE, being the only part of Europe that was successfully conquered by them. As there were many Christians and Jews living under Muslim rule, some historians have depicted it as a generally benevolent reign under which all three traditions cooperated and flourished.

immigration-colonisation. Ideologies and customs always collapse under the pressure of facts. It will be important to analyse very seriously this radical change of opinion.

***

The prelude to civil war is extending the domain of the struggle. Everywhere in France the areas of criminal activity of 'ethnic bands' are spreading, dominating the countryside and formerly peaceful quarters of cities and no longer limited to 'sensitive quarters'. We are dealing with a strategy that operates by expanding the areas of criminal activity in a carefully thought-out strategy of civil war.

In Marseilles, for example, cars are burning in the southern quarters, which had been spared up to now. The regional press, on 19 January 2004, reveals that four vehicles were set on fire without provocation in the sixth and seventh *arrondissements*[29] and two others in the eighth. Dominique Tain, Deputy Mayor of the sixth and seventh *arrondissements*, deplores 'a rise in violence, of violent deeds, an increase in delinquency, mob activities in front of schools … in the southern quarters.' On 29 December 2003, a merchant was mugged in broad daylight on rue W. Puget. More interesting: on 4 January 2004, the large wooden crucifix that rises above the monument to the dead of Saint-Giniez was burned. On 9 February, a 57-year-old retired teacher, who took care of the church of Saint-Cannat without pay, was found stabbed to death near the baptismal font. And that's not all. In the same vein: on January 18, on the rue Fort-du-Sanctuaire, which leads to the church of Notre-Dame-de-la-Garde, tourists and pilgrims were greeted with the sight of two vehicles that had just been set on fire. When will they set fire to Notre-Dame-de-la-Garde? We could make

---

29   The administrative districts of Paris.

certain suppositions about the identity of those who ordered these acts of 'uncivil disobedience' and the ones who perpetrated them.[30]

***

What is this kind of vandalism? There is little public discussion of it, but vandalism is an increasingly serious scourge, as damaging as violent crime. Let us not talk only of the countless vehicles set on fire, but also of the destruction of gymnasiums and public swimming pools, acts of arson against public buildings, the massive theft of materials, the damage inflicted on public buildings, and so on. These acts have multiplied significantly over the past three years and so has their cost. Let us take the example of Marseilles: according to *La Provence* (7 October 2003): 'The bill has arrived for the municipality: about 1.86 million euros a year, or 12.5 million francs', drawn from the local taxpayers, without counting the expenses of guards and security of 140,000 euros. The local press obviously does not bother to mention the ethnic origin of these 'vandals' other than with the expression 'urban youth'. This criminal activity, which is increasing all over France, represents a growing burden for the French economy.

***

The slums are arming themselves. The authorities have stopped counting the muggings, hold-ups, and riots that increasingly involve military weapons: hand grenades, rocket launchers, assault rifles, and so on. Criminologist Xavier Raufer[31] declared in *La Provence* (30 December 2001), 'Arms trafficking never stops growing, especially particularly

---

30   This text was written before the mass rioting that took place in France in October and November 2005, when primarily immigrant youths, in which nearly 9,000 vehicles were burned and an estimated 200 million euros in damages took place. Rioting on a smaller scale also took place in November 2007.

31   Xavier Raufer (b. 1946) has been active in various far-Right groups in France since the mid-1960s. He supported Alain de Benoist and GRECE during the 1980s. He is also a noted criminologist and has written about terrorism.

from the Balkans. The hot slums have been teeming with heavy weapons for about two years. These military weapons are conveyed into France by criminal elements from Serbia and Croatia or the Albanian mafia. But gun trafficking only exists because it is answering a growing demand, especially on the part of criminal "start-ups", groups of urban delinquents on the way to organised crime.' This arsenal is not only useful for attacking armoured cars; it is a preparation for civil war. It is not at all certain that the local police are prepared, or the state police or even the army ...

***

First cars are set on fire, then apartment buildings. In Chalon-sur-Saône, on the night of 8 to 9 February 2002, 'youths' innovated. After a night of rioting — provoked in the classic scenario by the (failed) arrest of hoodlums who attacked the Vox cinema to rob the box office — an apartment house was burnt to the ground, along with a brush factory. More seriously, in the Fontaine-au-Loup quarter, apartment houses were threatened by burning garbage cans that had been doused with petrol and set on fire. People living on the waterfront succeeded in putting the fires out without help, because the firemen were pelted with stones and could not get to the buildings. Naturally, the Chalon public prosecutor's office released the ten rioters who had been arrested.

During the night of 2–3 March, in addition to burning a dozen cars, rioters set fire to the entryway and a staircase of an apartment in the 'inner city' of Strasbourg, Arago Square. The apartment's inhabitants had to move to new dwellings. At 9:40 PM, rue Augustin-Fresnel in Cronenbourg, the fire from burning cars spread to the lower floors of apartment houses. On rue Becquerel, the riot police (CRS)[32] managed to put out several fires set in apartment basements.

---

32   The Compagnies Républicaines de Sécurité (Republican Security Companies) is the French riot police force.

In the village of Pujaut in the Gard department in southern France, on 4 March 2004, a retired couple's farmhouse in the scrubland was attacked by a band of 'youths' whose origin there is no need to mention. The couple were 'tied up like sausages' and beaten, their credit cards stolen after they revealed the passwords under duress, and their house was pillaged and devastated before their eyes. The perpetrators then burned the farmhouse and nearby tenant's house and sadistically forced the retired couple to watch their property going up in smoke, threw their dog into the burning coals and then shut the couple up in the pigpen. They barely survived the ordeal.

One more step has been taken on the road to a future ethnic civil war. There can be no mistake. We are soon going to see massive attacks on the downtowns of large cities, towns and isolated properties with the burning of buildings, and all this even in the 'nice parts' of town.

***

The slums are suffering from 'amateur' terrorist attacks. Naturally the media do not talk much about them. We are witnessing a rise in attacks with explosives for which no one claims credit, especially in France. Three cases took place at the end of December 2003 and January 2004 involving homemade bombs: 1) At Belfort, a bomb exploded in front of the Maison de l'information sur la formation et l'emploi in the 'problem area' of les Résidences, following two criminal incendiary acts against public buildings with significant damage; 2) The Youth Culture Centre (MJC) of Mulhouse — again in a problem area — was attacked by a bomb (using a fire extinguisher filled with explosives), probably because it had been closed following incidents between 'youths' and educators; 3) In Montgeron (in the south of the Parisian slums) the façade of a high school gymnasium was completely levelled by a bomb. The school's administration expressed its 'surprise' and explained, 'no recent incident could explain an act of vengeance or of reprisals.'

In reality, this is the beginning of guerrilla warfare. For the time being, there have been no human victims, but that will come ... These apprentice terrorists (in fact, who are they imitating?) are increasingly proficient in the use of explosives. It is going to get worse ...

***

France is not the only country where firemen are stoned and attacked. In Great Britain, in 2001, there were reports of 161 attacks against firemen, when they came to fight car fires that had been deliberately lit. On 19 September 2003, in the Blackhill neighbourhood of Glasgow, a group of firemen were attacked with knives and incendiary devices. Many firemen were seriously wounded. In the suburb of Maryhill, ten-year-old children threw Molotov cocktails at fire trucks. The local captain of the firefighters responded, 'I am flabbergasted. There are more and more of these attacks. Why?' 'Political Correctness' will never supply an answer.

Firemen (like the police) symbolise a 'native-born uniformed authority'. The British communitarian model does not work better than French-style compulsory assimilation. This is obviously anti-European racist activity. The highbrow sociologists do not see it, but ordinary people do, perhaps ...

***

Let us recall the affair of the attack on the 'supercops' of the GIPN.[33] In Briançon, on Tuesday, 25 November 2003, a squad of elite police from the GIPN arrived from Nice to subdue a madman who was shooting wildly. The operation was successful. The madman was brought to the psychiatric hospital of Laragne-Montéglin. When the operation was finished, about fifteen policemen, still in uniform, headed for a restaurant. They were then insulted and attacked for no particular reason by what was called 'a band of youths'. It ended in a general brawl and various injuries. No one was arrested, despite the help of police from

33   The *Groupes d'Intervention de la Police Nationale* or National Police Intervention Groups is the counter-terrorism unit of the French police.

the local commissariat. The self-righteous newspaper *La Provence* (27 November 2003) suggests, 'It was the GIPN members who caused the skirmish.' Of course, no doubt about it! It was the police who provoked the 'youths' by walking around in uniform. This business, which Maurice Fortoul of *La Provence* called 'a rather surprising incident', will surprise only the blind.

***

A confidential report (28 July 2003) of the DCRG[34] was devoted to the alarming increase in attacks on off-duty police. The national origin of these attackers is never mentioned, but may be suspected. The report says, 'Attacks on off-duty police, beyond the symbolic challenge to public institutions, expresses a true hatred of authority and civil servants become the victims. Sometime the explanation may be a desire for revenge of the part of the delinquents who meet an official who participated in their arrest or in court proceedings that involved them.'

The report mentions an increase in the following: 1) very violent ambushes against police who are returning home; 2) attempted vehicular homicide of police both in uniform and plain clothes, even if the attacker was never involved with the victim; 3) brutal attacks on the family or relatives of police (including sexual assaults on policemen's wives) when it is learned that 'so-and-so is a policeman'; 4) attacks on young ADS[35] or beat cops 'coming from the projects' (that is, from immigrants). These events are accompanied by racist comments and graffiti. They are typically the first steps to civil war.

The report also points out 'the uneasiness of communities in the face of summer violence. They have become the theatre for clashes between rival gangs ... which tarnish the celebrations of the end of the summer season. Since they cannot assure security at the events,

---

34 The Direction Centrale des renseignements Généraux was the intelligence unit of the French police. It was merged into another department in 2008.

35 *Adjoints de sécurité*, or security officers, is the lowest grade of officer in the French police force, designating those with only short-term service contracts.

elected officials and organisers have cancelled certain celebrations.' In fact, a number of long established traditional festivals have one after another been suppressed. Was this not the goal of the violence?

The report also notes the spoiling of popular French vacation areas (this, of course, is not true of stylish areas, which are heavily protected): 'Commonly, with the large crowds of vacationers that go to the seaside, combined with the arrival of youths from problem areas encouraged by the operation "Ville Vie Vacances", which promotes seaside vocations for urban youth, seaside areas that were once peaceful and crowded with families now experience "significant acts of street crime."' VVV is a lovely initiative, where small-time drug lords, supervised well or ill, are rewarded with vacations at taxpayers' expense ... When will the French people finally have enough?

***

It is often said that in the 'problem developments' the young burglars and punks are 'only a handful, a minority', implying that with a few more arrests and tougher laws the police could immediately restore order and that the threat is basically minimal. Uneasy at the multiplication of large and violent gangs, sociologist Bjarne Melkevik notes the unstoppable growth of a 'subculture of violence', that is increasingly widespread among young Africans from the Maghreb in *Violence et délinquance des jeunes*.[36] Demonstrating that the phenomenon is not at all marginal, sociologists Sophie Body-Gendrot and Nicole Le Guennec, in a report on urban violence submitted to the government in May 2001, explain, 'In a housing project (ZUP) of 28,000 inhabitants like Le Val-Fourré or Mantes de Jolie, 11,000 youths are all potential rioters.' In other words, in a 'normal' situation the police should confront fewer than 100 hoodlums. These 100, however, will be 'officers' who are training several thousand assailants. Then, if for

---

36 Catherine Samet (ed.), *Violence et délinquance des jeunes* (Paris: La Documentation française, 2001).

each ZUP we count 11,000 'combatants', in France as a whole, if a riot breaks out, there must be many more than a million potential rioters! The urban police, the CRS and the state police would be unable to deal with them. It is no longer a *police situation* of maintaining order, but a *military situation* of open war. The government knows this. This is why it is doing everything possible to 'buy' peace in the slums and towns. They are moving back to jump farther. The preventive measures they are taking will not stop a spark from provoking a simultaneous and generalised insurrection in developments that will look just like a civil war.

***

In Belgium, the Islamists form a state within the state. A report of the Belgian parliamentary commission that specialises in education observes the following facts: the secret services have discovered that the 'hardcore' Islamist network Salafi, based in Saudi Arabia, 'has created a virtual secret religious state inside the Kingdom of Belgium', with an 'Islamic police' that enforces respect for Islamic laws and punishes drug dealers, pimps and Arab merchants of alcohol. Among its other activities are the diffusion of cassettes of Bin Laden and pro-terrorist preachers, and paramilitary training and parachute jumps in the Ardennes forest. The 350,000 Muslims of Belgium are the target of this organisation that aims at fanaticising them. The good deputies and senators of Belgium fear that these Islamists 'are destroying the work of assimilation achieved by the government' and that 'this fifth column may perform dangerous acts if the conflict in the Middle East gets worse.' The report concludes, 'Belgium has become a central logistical base for terrorist groups like Al Qaeda, the Algerian GIA, Wahabi Tabligh, the Palestinian Hamas and the Egyptian Muslim Brotherhood.' Armand de Decker, President of the Belgian Senate, declared, 'Many of these groups are in the process of trying to re-Islamicise the Muslim population of Belgium in the most radical direction.'

Similarly, the 'Arab-European League' directed from Saudi Arabia (its Pakistani terrorist section is Rabita Trust), threatens the Belgian government on the Internet with establishing Islamic power structures in Belgium and Europe. Islamist residents have understood perfectly that Belgium, a weak state that is the home to European Union institutions, is an ideal entry door to conquer Europe. What does the Islamophile Louis Michel[37] think of all this?

***

Mathematicians know that there are certain equations that cannot be solved, that there are problems without a solution, 'all things being equal', that is, in the setting of current parameters. As soon, however, as we change the system of assumptions, the 'set', *set theory* to be precise, like *catastrophe theory*, shows that equations that cannot be solved in the old system A, become solvable in an eventual new system B.

Let us apply this *mathematical philosophy* to the apparently unsolvable problem of immigration.

A first solution was that of assimilation: 'People born abroad will all become good French and good Europeans.' Let us move on. It is not working. This was the fad of the 1970s and 1980s. This solution disappeared when faced with mass immigration and the growing power of Islam. Only a few obstinate 'republicans' still defend it. On the contrary, it is the native-born French who are threatened with having to 'assimilate'!

The second solution is communitarianism, also baptised assimilation. It is a question of a compromise, inspired by the United States and rather unclear theories of intellectual 'ethnopluralism', right-wing and left-wing. People born abroad keep their 'culture', but adhere to

---

37   Louis Michel (b. 1947) is a Belgian politician who served as Minister of Foreign Affairs from 1999 until 2004. He then served as European Commissioner—first for Research, then for Development and Humanitarian Aid—from 2004 to 2009, and was a Member of the European Parliament from 2009 until 2019 . He has been known for actively supporting causes in various Islamic nations.

a common 'minimum', a global Social Contract.[38] Society becomes a pacific kaleidoscope, united by a soft and pacifying *deus ex machina*.[39] This utopian vision, Rousseauian and adolescent, still defended by learned old fogies, who flirt just a little with apartheid (whence its partisans on the extreme Right) has been tried by all the European states. The result has been total failure. There has been no 'assimilation' of 'ethnic communities' cohabiting peacefully. On the contrary, ethnic civil war is just around the corner.

The third solution is control (checking and limiting the entry of immigrants, security policies, etc.), the solution favoured by the 'extreme Right', as they have been baptised, mistakenly by the way. This solution is impossible in the current state of affairs — system A. For twenty years its advocates have been offering programs and policies everywhere in Europe without ever winning more than 15 % of the vote. This is a problem. Meanwhile, the leak is not plugged.

The solution to this problem is mathematical. We must change the referential. The 'point of no return' in system A has been reached. Moving to system B will allow the discovery of an *acceptable solution*.

In mathematics, leaving one set (as in physics, by the way), means entering another, where the algebraic parameters are no longer all the same. In this new set, the equations can finally be solved.

The question of immigration can therefore find its solution only in the framework of a new normative system, in which incomprehensible equations will become comprehensible and where what was not envisaged will be. What, however, will be able to make us change the reference system, to move from system A to system B? *Catastrophe theory*

---

38   The Social Contract is an idea first developed by Jean-Jacques Rousseau to illustrate the universal doctrine of citizens giving up a certain amount of their freedom to a group of leaders with the understanding that the leadership will use their power for the benefit of the entire society, and to maintain law and order.

39   Latin: 'god from the machine'. This is a term originally taken from the theater, which refers to a difficult problem that is suddenly solved by an unlikely and unexpected occurrence.

gives us the answer: a violent change of situation, a 'tipping over' into chaos, starting from which a 'new system' (system B), formerly unthinkable, will, however, become real. And the unsolvable equation will be solved.

Economy: Tomorrow, the Great European Depression

The European economy is heading for serious structural reasons towards an *unprecedented recession*.

An economy experiences long cycles of expansion and contraction that, unlike short cycles, are not due to psychological factors of confidence, but to objective elements of infrastructure, called 'structural fundamentals', which include technical progress or decline, demography, migration, peace or conflict, the nature of economic and monetary institutions, but also government policies, level of education, and, finally, the quality of the workforce, even climate.

To give an outline, since 1850, apart from passing crises (1929–1937), the European economy has experienced a continuous expansion never seen in its history (as has the rest of the 'West') that the world wars did not interrupt. It can be predicted that this long period of material 'progress' and growing wealth is going to stop and reverse its course during the first decade of the Twenty-first century and that we are going to enter a *very long recession* that could last for a hundred years. This situation has already happened several times in history, where entire civilisations have passed from prosperity to lasting poverty.

In fact, for the first time the 'structural fundamentals' of the economy are all profoundly destabilised. All the warning lights are red. Remember, in the last analysis an economy's health does not rest on currency manipulation or banking or financial speculation, but on human work.

The serious destabilising structural factors, which are all converging, are the following:

1) A dramatic ageing of the population. Its effects will start being felt in 2005 (from the retirement of numerous groups). Since the government did not foresee and reform the retirement system paid out of each year's taxes, we know it is already too late. There will not be sufficient funds to furnish allocations and healthcare to seniors and ever higher taxes will be levied on those who are working. The result will necessarily be a generalised lowering of purchasing power and therefore of economic growth based on consumption. The ageing of the population will also rapidly lead — it is already happening — to another frightening effect: a loss of technological skills. There are not enough young minds.

2) The massive immigration of new battalions from the Third World to palliate these gaps, so desired by the UN, is an imposture. These migrants are unskilled and need social services themselves. They are mouths to feed, not the brains needed in a post-industrial society. Germany wanted to import more than 30,000 engineers that it needs (already), but got only 9,000 Indians. The immigration-colonisation (of which the entire cost is already more than 122 billion euros a year), which will not stop growing, added to the steadily increasing birth rate of the foreigners — most of them, as everyone knows, are not able to earn a good education — will be one more brake on economic prosperity. The current masses of 'youths' from Africa and North Africa will for the most part have a choice only between unemployment supported by welfare payments or participation in the parallel and criminal economy. The professional value of the workforce is going to experience a dramatic decline as soon as 2010.

3) These factors are aggravated by the net lowering of the quality of education, which is getting worse in every area, even science. Add to this phenomenon the brain drain. 50,000 French research scholars have emigrated to Silicon Valley and have been replaced by crowds of sub-Saharan immigrants, who are unskilled and

need social subvention. Currently half of the graduates of French business and scientific schools want to emigrate from France, especially to Anglo-Saxon countries. The reasons are higher salaries, lower taxes and the assurance of a better quality of life (security).

4) Another destabilising element is the fact that the economic institutions of the European Union are getting worse, because of the regulatory burden, the absence of leadership and big projects and the increase of entitlements. The economic policy that consists of opening the borders to the world market, while weighing down and handicapping European businesses under the burden of a bureaucratic socialism, is suicidal. I have already said, in agreement with Maurice Allais,[40] that in order to function, the European economy has to practice autarchy in relation with the outside world (a quota system for goods and migrants) and neo-Keynesian liberalism for the domestic market. In Europe we practice the reverse, a globalised but bureaucratic ultra-liberalism.

5) To these woes must be added the calamitous handling of the new common currency, the euro. The euro has not dethroned the dollar. Far from that, it has made it stronger! The unpardonable mistake was to depoliticise the currency, to put into the hands of an irresponsible central bank, that is, in the hands of international financial speculation. There can be no confidence in a currency that is not directed by the monetary policy of a clearly territorial sovereign government, as is the case with the dollar.

***

We are witnessing the first signs of Europe's economy descending to Third World status. The artificial 'jobs for youth' (*emplois-jeunes*)

---

40 Maurice Allais (1911–2010) won the Nobel Prize in Economic Sciences in 1988. In his later years, he often criticized the economic and legal foundations of the European Union.

are giving us a first taste of this. Does anyone seriously imagine that France and Europe will be able to preserve its current standard of living in the Twenty-first century? In ten, twenty, or thirty years, they will be increasingly encumbered with immigrant-colonists from the Third World, increasingly Africanised and Islamicised, prey to increasingly serious problems of security and maintaining law and order. Their native-born will be increasingly older; their educated young people will be fleeing their own countries *en masse*, while the need to provide subvention for the unproductive will be increasingly severe. There is surely no hope at all! And because of the 'snowball effect' the collapse may well occur suddenly, even by the middle of this decade.

A prosperous economy rests on a high level of research and investment in order to preserve the environment, develop tourism and state of the art industries, maintain the national patrimony, transmit its cultural traditions and identity, innovate, and so on. Especially in France, the trend is quite the opposite. Productive investment is continually smaller in proportion to the size of the national debt, the burden of subventions and social services, and the creation of superfluous and unqualified public positions. For example, all the great military and nuclear programs have been revised downwards, although these are the most valuable investments in technological spin-offs and the creation of high-level jobs — not to mention the dependence such a resignation entails *vis-à-vis* the United States, our principal technological and economic rival. The United States devotes, as a share of GDP, 50 % more than the European Union to investments in research and development. It is not Wall Street that is behind this policy, but rather the executive branch of the government and Congress, who support with a determined and nationalist consistency all cutting edge industries, whether we are talking about cinema, computers, outer space, aeronautics, and so on.

François Perroux[41] used to repeat in his courses at the Collège de France, which I attended in the 1970s, 'The United States extols free market liberalism without protection or utopian socialism for other countries, in order to weaken them, but for themselves they apply the recipe of planned and directed state capitalism, according to the good old recipes of Keynes[42] and Schacht.'[43]

***

European societies are completely subject to the short-term dictatorship of the market, speculation, high taxation and public subvention, but also of socialist and bureaucratic habits. They privilege money over work and the 'structural fundamentals'. The paradox of these societies is that, by surrendering themselves, bound hand and foot, to economism, they are very bad at running an economy! When the market alone directs the economy, the economy goes blind and soon falls into a permanent crisis with poverty for the people.

All respected economists know that long periods of prosperity have never been assured by markets, but by political leaders who guarantee a high-quality education, spur a dynamic demography by pro-natal policies, encourage investments by great national programs, keep taxes low, limit imports, assure a free and transparent domestic market, support national entrepreneurs, develop research and control migration severely.

---

41 François Perroux (1903–1987) was a French economist who was best-known for his criticisms of economic policies involving the Third World, which he felt were too centred on Western interests and concepts.

42 John Maynard Keynes (1883–1946) was a British economist whose ideas on the possibilities of the free market and business cycles have been extraordinarily influential.

43 Hjalmar Schacht (1877–1970) was a German liberal economist who opposed socialism, leading him to briefly support the National Socialists in Germany during the 1930s, although he parted ways with them and joined the resistance movement against Hitler.

This is exactly the opposite of what we doing today. Our government gives support to Gay Pride and Techno-parades, hires environmental agents in the departments, multiplies teaching positions by encouraging electives in a national education system with results that are increasingly wretched, cancels the debts of African countries, wastes taxpayers' money on totally useless 'urban renewal' projects or on billions for subventions to pseudo-humanitarian associations. It also dismantles the Super-Phénix nuclear power plant, cancels the Rhine-Rhône canal, balks at investing in the new French-German EPR nuclear reactor, scuttles expenses on military hardware, continually reduces the size of the rail system, and on and on.

***

We have eaten our white bread. The good days are over. My predictions are very dark, but I do not see anyone who could contradict me, except incompetents like Alain Lipietz.[44] All the economists with whom I have discussed them, especially Maurice Allais, the only Frenchman to win the Nobel Prize in Economics, but also successful businessmen, fear a deep and prolonged recession of the European economies. Anyway, in this society founded on short-sightedness, only a shock can be healthy. A *giant economic crisis*, such as we have never seen before, which will probably be amplified by the extraordinary fragility and volatility of current economic mechanisms, which are 'networked' and absolutely interdependent, will perhaps be the only means of settling certain problems, which have reached an acute stage …

***

The brain drain is accompanied by the arrival of masses of unskilled immigrants. While looking through my files, I came across this

---

44 Alain Lipietz (b. 1947) is a French engineer, economist and Green Party politician who served as a Member of the European Parliament from 1999 to 2009 and is also a noted author. He is part of the Regulation school of economics, which holds that economic crises are the result of problems in regulation.

comment by Christian Saint-Étienne, an economics professor at Paris-Dauphine, which was published in an interview in *Le Figaro Magazine* (28 February 1998), on the subject of the departure of young French college graduates: 'The phenomenon is extremely alarming in terms of the demographic balance sheet. We are witnessing simultaneously the emigration of 40,000 to 50,000 highly skilled persons a year, while France attracts to her territory each year 100,000 foreigners, of whom 80 % to 90 % are absolutely unskilled.' What do they want? 'To take advantage of our social security system and not to produce in an efficient manner.' More precisely, 'If the phenomenon continues, in ten years, our country will have accepted a million unskilled immigrants while a half-million educated French will have left!'

Saint-Étienne estimates that (adding the cost of education to value added lost) the emigration of each young college graduate equals '10 million francs of value added lost by the French economy in ten years'. He explains, 'On the opposite side, a typical family of immigrants entering France costs on the order of a million francs a year (housing subvention, free health care for all, free schooling, unemployment assistance …). Multiply this cost by 100,000 immigrants a year and you will see that the barn is on fire. We must act now!'

The reasons why people leave France include high taxation due to the retirement system paid out of current taxes and paying for unemployment and social services (especially for immigrants) and an anti-work ideology (retirement at 55, 35-hour workweek, etc.) Remember that in the USA people work 30 % longer than in France. To the loss of college graduates should be added the expatriation of capital and investments, which earn more and are taxed at a lower rate abroad — see the case of Vivendi. Saint-Étienne concludes, 'I urgently call for the creation of a parliamentary commission to establish the "balance sheet of skills" of immigration. … If this phenomenon were to continue for five or ten years, France would soon become the only major industrialised country "on the path to underdevelopment."' He concludes, 'Refusing to look facts in the face will bring the country to suicide.'

***

The European Commission is worried about the size of the brain drain to the USA. Philippe Busquin, commissioner of research for the EC, comments in the Agence France-Presse, '75 % of Europeans who are awarded a doctorate in the United States plan to stay there rather than return to work in Europe. It is a vicious circle. We have the grey matter, we lose part of it and European businesses go looking for it where it is, for example, in Boston.' In addition, 50 % of the graduates of the great French business schools are planning to leave France. One cause of this haemorrhaging is the flexibility and dynamism of American businesses and the USA's low taxation. At the same time we are importing masses of humans without professional skills, mouths to feed from the Third World.

***

Creative French are emigrating in increasing numbers (50,000 French in Silicon Valley near San Francisco, 40,000 in London, etc.). Innovative businesses are moving their headquarters to London, Amsterdam, New York, and other places. Rémi Godeau writes in *Le Figaro Économie* (13 July 2001): 'How long will French companies like Vivendi Universal keep its headquarters and Aventis its anti-cancer research centres in France? EADS, Euronext and Dexia have made their choice: they have left.' A poll by Ernst & Young reveals that 44 % of CEOs living in France would like to move part of their activities abroad! The report (December 2000) by inspector of finances Frédéric Lavenir — which of course never had any effect — denounced 'the disastrous image of France' held by industrial decision-makers and the 'catastrophic fate reserved for creative young people'. A Senate report (June 2001) worries about the 'expatriation of educated people, capital and businesses and the government's wrongheaded decisions'. The cause of these very serious facts has been analysed in an alarmist report by the Socialist Michel Charzat, which was submitted to Lionel Jospin[45] (July 2000): discouraging levels of taxation, social and union rigidities, the 35-hour workweek, fussy bureaucratic burdens, new charges and obligations imposed on businesses (the law of 'social modernisation'), and so on. Even within the Left, people are getting upset with this dogmatic and suicidal policy of socialist-Trotskyite power and Marxist dogmatism. The state prefers to finance the unproductive 'youth' of the slums, hire voters as superfluous bureaucrats and run a 'social' politics for short-term electoral reasons (which are basically totally anti-democratic) and tax away the vital forces in society, the only real creators of wealth, who end up by leaving the country. Admittedly, since 1793, the true inspirers of Jospin's Socialist government have known that 'the Republic does not need scientists'.[46] It is the old hatred of elites in favour of the 'masses' … In those days, they were guillotined, like Lavoisier; now they emigrate to the United States. 857 French scientists with distinguished reputations have left France since 1997! The result will be poverty and our economy and society will be reduced to Third World status. The 'fourth ranked world economic power' (*dixit* Laurent Fabius) stands a good chance of losing that position before long …

***

Cutting our military budgets compromises employment and high technology. Although the threats against Europe have not lessened at all since the end of the 'Cold War' — rather the opposite — Europeans are cutting their military budgets (the United States is doing the opposite). These budgets are being strangled by the pressure of social and

---

45 Lionel Jospin (b. 1937) is a member of the Socialist Party and was Prime Minister of France from 1997 until 2002.

46 This quotation is attributed to various officials of the Revolutionary Tribunal during the French Revolution, which sent many people to the guillotine. The occasion was the sentencing of the chemist Antoine Lavoisier, often called the 'father of modern chemistry', to death in 1794.

medical expenses, which are caused by immigration and the ageing of the population. Cutting defence expenditures is not only a strategic mistake; it is a major economic mistake, because more than anything else military technology is the source of breakthroughs in science and jobs.

The new, multinational European group for aeronautics and defence, EADS (formed by an alliance of Matra, Alena Marconi Systems, British Aerospace, Deutsche Aerospace, Aérospatiale, Finmeccanica and Belgian, Spanish and Dutch companies), has fired 1,500 persons in 2001 (highly trained engineers who will leave for North America), because European defence markets are stagnating or shrinking. Germany, Belgium, France, Italy, etc., are reducing their military purchases. In 2000, 1,500 regular troops have already left the defence division. Thomas Enders, the director of this division, stated in the *Financial Times* (15 December 2000), 'Military budgets are not a waste of money, but an irreplaceable locomotive for civilian technological breakthroughs and good jobs.' Let us recall that the Internet, cell phones, telecommunication satellites, civil aeronautics, etc., are direct spin-offs of military technology.

The social consequences of cutting military budgets are disastrous. For example, the DCN (Direction des constructions navales) is firing workers in the dockyards of Toulon and Cherbourg. This is suicidal. 'Jobs for youth', unskilled youth, are replacing highly skilled technological and military jobs.

***

Is the reform of retirement benefits just dust thrown in our eyes? The Raffarin government boasts that it has courageously tackled the problem of retirements and has solved the question of financing them, while shaking up Leftist corporatism. This is not the opinion of Marie-Laure Dufrêche, general delegate of the 'Sauvegarde Retraits' association, as she says in the journal, *Renaissance des hommes et des idées*

(December 2003). She concedes that the Fillon law[47] (21 August 2003) has made three positive, if timid, improvements: making the indexing of pensions uniform between private and public entities; equalising the extent of assessments (only from 2008); and flexibility in the administration of pensions for surviving spouses. These are marginal measures, however, that do not touch the essential.

First of all, out of fear of strikes by the civil servants' unions, this 'reform' does not attack the special, privileged administration of civil servants, especially of the French national rail system (SNCF), which is extremely costly, since it employs 180,000 active agents for 350,000 retired ones, who are essentially remunerated by taxpayers. The average retirement age of conductors is 50; office agents retire at 55. Only in France ... Finally, SNCF maintains the same absurd fashion of calculating pensions for retired agents: 'The base salary that serves to determine the increase of the pension remains based on the last six months for public employees, while it is a function of the 25 best years for private workers.' Last of all, this small-scale reform is not financed or financeable: 'The deficit foreseen in 2020 rises to 43 billion euros. Thanks to the new measures, it could be held to 18 billion. This last estimate rests on a hypothesis of economic growth — a very optimistic one — of 2.5 % a year and an equally hypothetical unemployment rate of 6 % ... The time is not far off when the 3.5 million public retirements will cost taxpayers more than the 8.5 million private retirements.'

It is necessary to remember that the majority of the political class and the deputies, of both Right and Left, are composed of 'unattached' bureaucrats. It is evident that the next 'reform' of social security will be just as timorous and ineffective and the famous 'gap' between public and private will continue to grow. The whole affair is an optical illusion, dust in our eyes. If we put off the solution of the problem, we will

---

47   François Fillon (b. 1954) was the French Minister of Labour in 2002. The Fillon law refers to reforms he made to the 35-hour workweek and pension laws. He later served as Prime Minister from 2007 until 2012.

go straight to the wall. Only a shock, a real one, in every area, will be able to provoke real *reforms*.

***

France is a corporatist country, a stalled society[48] incapable of the slightest reform and any perception of the future. It is the opposite of Germany, which is willing to take the serious problem of retirement by the horns. The legal age of retirement in Germany is 65 for men and 60 for women. Gerhard Schröder wants to raise it to 67 in 2011, despite the opposition within his party,[49] the SPD.[50] Katrin Goering-Eckhardt, president of the parliamentary group of the Greens, believes 'one can take seriously a reduction of the level of retirement payments' of well-off retirees. In France, such measures and discussions are unthinkable ... Despite these drastic and courageous measures, however, the finance minister, Hans Eichel, has just recognised, 'the proportion of retirement expenses has moved in the past three decades from 14 % to 29 % of the budget. If this continues without slowing down, the proportion will be 80 % in 2050. This cannot go on' (*Süddeutsche Zeitung* and *Leipziger Volkszeitung*, 30 May 2003). In other words, it would mean the collapse of the entire economy.

***

What are the real causes for the overwhelming deficit of health insurance? The report of the Court of Accounts on 18 September 2003 (which no one will ever take account of, we must admit) explains this gap of 29 billion euros — a 90 billion francs deficit accumulated from

---

48 This term was first coined by French sociologist Michel Crozier in a 1970 book, translated as *The Stalled Society* (New York: Viking Press, 1973). He used it to describe France's tendency to have too much bureaucracy which stifles social change, leading to problems that can only be resolved in times of crisis.

49 To date, this has not been done.

50 The *Sozialdemokratische Partei Deutschlands*, or the Social Democratic Party of Germany, is socialist and is one of the two major parties of Germany today.

1997 to 2003 — by the incompetence and incoherence of every government that allows expenses to grow.

This uncontrolled inflation is not at all the consequences of a
'perfect storm' or a lack of income, nor even of a better medical management (just the opposite!), but of continual laxity and wastefulness
of governments from Jospin to Raffarin.[51] The Court enumerates the
absurdities of the administration of incompetents who, by demagogy
and unwillingness to change because of cold feet, are drawing us inexorably ever closer to bankruptcy: 1) an uncontrolled rise in medical
prescriptions, ignoring and twisting past agreements; 2) lax increase of
daily indemnities for sick leave; 3) application of the 35-hour workweek
in hospitals (with a cost of 3.4 billion euros annually); 4) Raffarin's rais-
ing honoraria for general practitioners (690 million euros); 5) lack of
prescription 'generic medicines'; 6) increase in 2001 by 900,000 persons (5.7 million in total) with 'long-term care', reimbursed at 100 %,
plus increasing the costs for house calls; 7) continual ignoring of 'price
controls' and agreements signed by doctors, who refuse the 'evaluation of practices' — 180 out of 130,000 have signed on to it; 8) inability
of Martine Aubry and Élisabeth Guigou, and then of Jean-François
Mattei to suppress reimbursements for medicines that do not work
(insufficient for 'medical service rendered') and therapeutic activities
'for comfort'; and 9) refusing to abolish privileged care in numerous
categories for bureaucrats, which are perfectly unjustified.

We now know that the weak Raffarin government will no more solve
the problem of health insurance and the reform of Social Security than
it has that of retirement. The objective of the calamitous Mattei[52] was
not at all to take the bull by the horns (as other European countries are
doing) and end the deficit, but simply to try to bring the deficit of 2004

---

51   Jean-Pierre Raffarin (b. 1948) is a French conservative politician and was Prime
     Minister from 2002 until 2005.

52   Jean-François Mattei (b. 1943) was Minister of Health in 2003, and presented a
     plan in September 2003 to curb spending in France's national health insurance
     system, which was operating at an enormous loss.

(17 billion to take care of health insurance) back to the level of 2003 (12 billion). Lamentable ... Did I forget to say that all these cumulative deficits are nothing but loans, and so debts contracted, that taxpayers will pay one day, plus interest?

The problem is no longer to know *if* the system is going to collapse, but *when*. This will not be a pretty sight to see, with the imminent ageing of the population.

***

What is the situation of the French debt? It is flabbergasting and every French government for thirty years has let it grow, abandoning any discipline in public finances. Remember that the European Social Forum,[53] consisting of Trotskyite globalists, was in part financed by the Prime Minister's office ... The national debt (borrowed to fill the budgetary deficit) has grown since the 1980s from 20 % of the GDP to more than 60 % and will reach 70 % in 2005. The French state's expenditures rose in 2003 to 280 billion euros with only 220 billion euros of income. No household or business can support expenses higher than its income by 27 %. This indebtedness is among the worst in the developed world and contributes to our country's slow descent to Third World status.

For each active worker, the debt is 38,000 euros. To reimburse this debt and its interest, each French household pays 2,000 euros a year — and the sum grows every year. Without this debt, there would be supplementary revenues that could be reinjected into the economy. Servicing the debt has assumed the number two position in the budget after the 'Mammoth', national education. The Court of Accounts knows it, it storms against it, but without legal power it protests in vain.

---

53 The European Social Forum is a series of conferences that has been held since 2002 by the alter-globalisation movement, which seeks to allow trade unions, anti-racist groups, social movements, and so on to unite and make their voices heard through the process of economic globalisation.

In addition, we must wonder if the enormous cost of immigration is not a significant factor in this impending bankruptcy. And then let us not forget that the state's financial bankruptcy has often been the factor that unleashed revolutions.

***

France cannot deal with work. It is the industrial country where people work the least, what with a 35-hour workweek, holidays, 'bridges',[54] long paid vacations and, of course, systematic strikes of public workers or excessive public enterprises. It is the country where there has been the most theorising about the right to be lazy,[55] where old-fashioned Marxists demand in their platforms a 'citizenship income', which is equivalent to an indexed minimum wage (*salaire minimum interprofessionel de croissance*, or SMIC) for every person who has chosen not to work. (Such a measure, in addition to increasing irresponsibility, would have the disadvantage of reinforcing immigration's suction pump.) It is the country where people retire at the earliest age and still there are calls to lower the retirement age even further, despite the ageing population. It is the country where intellectuals out of touch with reality explain that work is a form of alienation and the future will be a society of leisure.

Compared with its neighbours, France is moving in slow motion. Vacations are the centre of every conversation. Productivity per capita is 40 % higher in the United States than in Europe, which is the principal cause of Europe's stagnation in terms of power and wealth.

---

54 'Bridges' are long weekends, in which the days between a single-day holiday and the weekend are also included as a part of a holiday period. They are very common in France.

55 *The Right to be Lazy* is the title of a book by Paul Lafargue (1842–1911), who was a French socialist activist and was Karl Marx's son-in-law. In it, he argued that all forms of work are slavery and that laziness, if used effectively, can be a great source of human innovation.

Then — the opposite of the common opinion — this refusing to work, this laziness, to call it by its name, leads like all sloth to clinical depression. France is one of the European countries with the highest youth suicide rate and the greatest use of tranquillisers. In fact, degrading the value of work and despising productivity strips people, especially those of modest means, of reasons to feel useful and enjoy self-respect, and leads them to depression. Reducing the quantity of work aggravates social friction and generalises ennui. In addition to the enormous social problems they provoke (see the hospital sector), the disastrous 35-hour workweek further upsets the balance between work and leisure and causes the population to lose, little by little, their taste for activity and hard work and lures them to the temptation of loafing.

What about leisure activities? For most people, these activities are rarely active and creative. The middle classes, who are increasingly impoverished, cannot allow themselves to take advantage of excessive leisure travel. For them, leisure is not an occasion to learn or create. They experience leisure as 'dead time', which they mostly spend staring at the television screen or playing video games, an occasion to realise one's social uselessness. Only work, even humble work, allows them to occupy their minds. 'Production is the basis of morale', L. Ron Hubbard[56] wrote in *The Way to Happiness*.[57] In other words, work, not leisure, creates quality of life.

Silly intellectuals are always criticising 'work as a value'. They want us to believe that gains in productivity, which they expect to increase to infinity, are going to make up for the shrinking of time spent working. The argument is absurd. France is working less and less compared to Great Britain and the United States, where the gains in productivity are the same. Well, when you work less with the same productivity

---

56 L. Ron Hubbard (1911–1986) was a science fiction and self-help author who is best remembered as having been the founder of the Church of Scientology.

57 L. Ron Hubbard, *The Way to Happiness: A Common Sense Guide to Better Living* (Los Angeles: Bridge Publications, 1984).

(in the best case), you grow poorer compared with everybody else. The stupid slogan, 'work less to work better' is irrelevant, since the French are not encouraged to work better than their competition. I remember reading in the *Financial Times* when we voted on the 35-hour workweek, 'The French are geniuses: they work less in order to earn more.' Intellectuals always imagine that workers experience work as degrading and disagreeable, which is totally mistaken. It never occurs to them for a second that nurses, roofers, vintners, engineers, and so on, could find their work fulfilling and that this is noble. Intellectuals share the old mentality, the product of the decadent urban nobility and bureaucratic bourgeoisie, according to which 'work dirties your hands'.

It is not difficult to understand that, in a world of generalised competition, as soon as one country shortens its workweek, it grows poor and becomes proletarian, especially when this minimum wage is accompanied by (and at the same time causes) growing tax burdens and payroll withholding. The situation is aggravated by the masses of people on public relief and mouths to feed with no skills that are pouring out of the Third World.

The result is that French businesses are the ones in Europe that invest most heavily abroad. This is not a victory, but a defeat. They are moving away from their local communities; they are fleeing France (just as foreign investors do), where the cost of labour grows (because of the cost of entitlements) in proportion to the shrinking of its productivity. At the same time, business executives and young college graduates are leaving France *en masse* — the elites, those who want to work and love to work — replaced by unskilled immigrants. France's outstanding trump card, the legendary quality of its workforce, is rapidly degrading.

***

There is also a significant correlation between the unemployment rate and the reduced workweek. This is quite logical: the work of one group creates jobs for others. The less a country — or a business — works, the less it 'sends orders' to neighbouring suppliers. If the French worked a 45-hour workweek, like the Americans, instead of 35 hours a week, their businesses would create that many more jobs in France itself. Work creates work. By augmenting the objective cost of work in France, the reduced workweek obliges businesses that take orders, both from French and foreign, to turn away from French suppliers. Recently, a large publishing house drove a French printer into bankruptcy when the printer raised its prices because of the 35-hour workweek. The publisher chose a Spanish printer. Hospitals, similarly, have been obliged either to hire supplementary personnel — thereby increasing costs and leading to two-tier medicine where the wealthy receive better care — or to cut back on the quality of healthcare.

Since the French mind is always marked by the old faith in 'the providential character of wealth' (money comes, miraculously, from the state), it is hard for it to understand that money has only *one* source: work and the production that ensues. The only exception involves some Arab states that live off oil revenues without the need to work themselves. The economic culture in France, however, is very low and always marked by ideological dogmatism. The French want both a welfare state and a society with a short workweek. But where does the manna of this state come from, in socialist reality? From income taxes and the value added tax (VAT). Where do *they* come from? From the incomes of taxpayers and consumers. How do they get their incomes? From the fruit of their labour sold on the market.

The dominant French intelligentsia has never understood that pragmatism is worth more than idealism; that quantity is not the enemy of quality, but its condition; that the more you work, the better you work; that prosperity and happiness are not possible without a vocation, which is both difficult and yet attractive. In France we look upon work as a kind of serfdom or slavery.

***

A society with a short workweek, the paradise of the theoreticians of the 'right to be lazy', who are as ignorant as babies of economics, is possible only in the framework of a strictly autarchic system, which maintains no trade with an outside world much more productive than itself. This system can be indifferently Communist or mercantile, but its level of consumption, wealth, health care, etc., will necessarily be low. In short, it will be a neo-primitive economy. Why not? This is the dream of 'radical environmentalism'.

The problem with intellectuals (like Alain Lipietz) who extol the no-work model and 'radical environmentalists' who demand an economy with little energy consumption is that they are absolutely unprepared to take personal responsibility for the consequences of the radical lowering of their 'standard of living', an expression execrated by the 'anti-quantitative' theoreticians, who, however, all turn out to be bourgeois super-consumers.

The second possible facet of an economy with little work is that of the Gulf States, the states living off their incomes, of whom we just spoke. This income could dry up any day. The third model is the late Roman Empire, whose citizens lived in sloth, maintained by a bureaucratic welfare state that took booty from conquered provinces. We know how that model ended.

***

From a strictly mathematical point of view, if France were to reinstate the 40-hour workweek (minimum), limit holidays and 'bridges', reduce paid vacations for everyone to four weeks a year, abolish all mandatory retirement ages and suppress 50 % of subventions to non-workers, the unemployment rate would be significantly reduced. French public opinion would never accept such measures, however, and no government would have the courage to take them.

'Put France back to work', according to the consecrated formula, is not possible today, with the current mentality, which has been long encouraged to boast of the lack of bad consequences of the welfare state, the cult of rights and acquired advantages, the ideology of the lack of connection between production and wealth, the detestation of hard work and personal discipline maintained by public education, without speaking of the weakness of a state without authority. Work will return to popular taste, like the return of a pendulum, only under the heavy and painful constraint of a giant crisis, a catastrophe, matters predictable and unavoidable.

***

The 35-hour workweek is an economic injustice and a social imposture. According to Maurice Thévenet, who teaches at the Conservatoire national des arts et métiers (CNAM) and the prestigious business school ESSEC (École Supérieure des Sciences Économiques et Commerciales), and wrote *Le Plaisir de Travailler*[58] (*The Pleasure of Working*) (Éd. L'Organisation), the law on the 35-hour workweek is not responsible for the slight drop in unemployment, which is essentially due to an ephemeral and accidental economic recovery, independent of the government's intentions. On the contrary, without this intrusive law limiting economic activity, the economic recovery would have been much stronger.

Thévenet also notes that the law on the 35-hour workweek does not penalise large capitalist businesses, especially the multinationals, but handicaps mainly small and medium-sized French businesses. Once we recognise the Trotskyite origins (a cosmopolitan and international ideology) of the inspirers of the Aubry laws,[59] we begin to understand.

He then asserts that this law was inspired by a hatred of work. He writes, criticising the decisions 'made from above' by technocrats and rule-makers, that, 'Some people take pleasure in the activities that

---

58 Maurice Thévenet, *Le plaisir de travailler: favoriser l'implication des personnes* (The Pleasure of Working: Encouraging the Involvement of People) (Paris: Editions d'Organisation, 2000).

59 The Aubry laws, introduced by socialist Minister of Labour Martine Aubry in 2000, reduced the legal limit to the French workweek from 39 to 35 hours.

deep thinkers judge as "part-time jobs" and they deserve to be heard, before being criticised, neglected or despised.' He adds, judging that the workplace is not necessarily a hell, 'It is necessary to leave behind this permanent denunciation of work and abandon the idea of making people happy in spite of themselves.' For the dominant ideology on 'the Left', the ideal of the unemployed person, the welfare recipient, the person living off investments or public assistance has replaced the ideal of the *worker*.

But limiting the hours of work is just as much a social injustice in the middle term. Whether you like it or not, the 35-hour workweek has a price, in terms of payments by the state (that is, the taxpayers) and new costs for businesses. As soon as the current economic growth slows down (which will happen before long), businesses will start looking to move from France to find a workforce that works longer for the same salary. In general, by making the cost of labour in France more expensive and in reducing its productivity, the 35-hour work-week represents a competitive advantage for the salaried workers of other countries and will therefore eventually contribute to job loss, the inverse of the law's intended goal. Like the PACs,[60] this is a question of ideological demagogy taken by the most reactionary Left in Europe, who always sees the economy through the spectacles of the socialist old fogies of the Nineteenth century.

***

Let us now discuss the sociological aspect of this question. This discussion will inform us about the relations between the French and work, relations marked by the syndrome of sloth.

According to the most recent report of BIT (Bureau international du travail), published on 16 December 2000, the French work 33 % less

---

60 PACS, or *pacte civil de solidarité*, is a type of civil union in France which is available to same-sex couples as well as traditional couples, although it gives fewer rights than does marriage.

in real time than Americans, 37 % less than the Japanese, 17 % less than Germans, and 20 % less than the Dutch. Stop the applause!

The 35-hour workweek only aggravates an old phenomenon: multiplying holidays, the sacrosanct 'bridges', the five-week paid vacations, augmented by falsely claimed sick leave, repeated strikes by protected professions, and so on.

All of this ends by weighing down productivity and reducing collective wealth. One can be an old hand in a society of sloth, like the Situationists[61] of yore, California eco-freaks, left-wingers or 'anti-utilitarian' dreamers (Guy Debord,[62] Raoul Vaneigem,[63] Guy Hocquenghem,[64] etc.). Today their ideology influences the politics of the 'plural Left'. Why not? In this case, however, you must choose. It is not possible at the same time to insist on driving a 4 X 4 with bullbars, claim 20,000 francs a month of minimum income, benefit from cradle to grave healthcare insurance and also enjoy the standard of living of Luxembourg or Switzerland.

For, in the end, who is going to pay? Who is going to work? For the foundation of the economy and prosperity — this is what neither the Left-socialists nor the adepts of global finance have understood — is

---

61 The Situationist International was an international group of anarchists in Europe that was founded in 1957. The foundation of their philosophy was the attempt to create situations that allow the fulfilment of desires that could not be expressed under the prevailing reality of capitalism.

62 Guy Debord (1931–1994) was a French Marxist philosopher and the founder of the Situationist International, and whose ideas have become influential on both the radical Left and Right. The spectacle, as described in his principal work, *The Society of the Spectacle,* is one of the means by which the capitalist establishment maintains its authority in the modern world — namely, by reducing all genuine human experiences to representational images in the mass media, thus allowing the powers-that-be to determine how individuals experience reality.

63 Raoul Vaneigem (b. 1934) is a Belgian philosopher who has written many books on anarchist themes. He is best-known for being part of Debord's Situationist International during the 1960s.

64 Guy Hocquenghem (1946–1988) was a French Marxist who was very active in homosexual causes, and wrote many books on sexuality.

work, in quantity and quality. The money (of the unemployed, those on welfare, the retired, speculators on the stock exchange, etc.), this money that everyone needs, even the 'anti-productivists', is only the price you have to pay, the concrete result of production. And we really need someone to do it!

The current pathology of vacations and leisure as an ideal of life indicates one more serious social malady: work is perceived as *punishment*, a work gang, and no longer as an act of self-accomplishment, a vocation, a creation, a means of participating in society. For work is not only a material production of goods and services, but a communitarian cement for a family, a group, a nation. The modern West has promoted passive sloth (one of the symptoms is the non-stop audiovisual spectacle) to the rank of civic virtue. A people whose dream is that of an independently wealthy spectator (the syndrome of Rome's decline and the dying aristocracy of the Seventeenth and Eighteenth centuries) can ask questions about its future. For who is going to work in its place?

***

Why is the French economy getting poorer? In ten years, the French standard of living (GDP per capita) has passed from third to twelfth place in Europe, according to Eurostat. The Trotskyite socialists deserve much of the credit. The 35-hour workweek ('working less to earn more'), the neo-Marxist Law of 'Social Modernisation',[65] the expensive jobs programs for unskilled youths, the massive arrival of welfare parasites from the global South, the brain drain to the Anglo-Saxon world (200,000 creative French living abroad in America), the lowest employment rates in Europe in the competitive sector and the largest in the overprotected and swollen public sector, the dogmatic refusal to plan retirement by capitalisation instead of funding it from each year's

---

65   The Social Modernization Law, which was passed in December 2001, regulates 'moral harassment' in the workplace, referring to acts of harassment of a non-physical nature.

taxes, scuttling high-level research budgets (military, nuclear, biological, etc.), the corporatism of unrepresentative unions and the culture of strikes, and so on. There is a very long list of the pathologies that augur that France is going to become poorer and poorer.

Here are some brute facts that are symptoms that speak for themselves of the spreading evil. 1) A study published by APEC (Association pour l'emploi des cadres) in early February 2004 anticipates, from 2004, a lack of 40,000 managers a year. We are not going to find replacements for them in Africa. 2) Six million persons (10 % of the population) are below the poverty level (Insec). 3) The cost of construction is 30 % higher in France compared with our partners in the European Union (Eurostat). 4) Despite the burden of the *Mezzogiorno* (the south of the peninsula), Italy has a real standard of living 10 % higher than that of France. 5) According to the IMD[66] in Lausanne and the World Economic Forum of Davos, France is ranked twenty-fifth in the world in business competitiveness, because the French state, instead of helping them as in the USA, taxes them and is bent on constructing for them a legally and economically unfavourable environment. 6) France is the world champion in foreign investment — hurray! ahead of the USA — quite simply because its businesses move away from France and prefer to create jobs outside the Hexagon.[67] The annual net French investments abroad were 900 billion francs in 2001, or 10 % of the GDP, representing a fantastic haemorrhaging of capital and know-how. Jean-Pierre Robin in *Le Figaro Économie* (17 January 2002) wrote, 'By what miracle would a country that holds the European record for unemployment among its population of working age claim to be more prosperous than other countries?' France is quite simply undermined with laziness. The awakening will be brutal. So much the better!

***

---

66   The International Institute for Management Development in Switzerland is one of the top-rated business schools in the world.

67   France is often described as a Hexagon due to its geographical shape.

France is losing its entrepreneurs and its economic patrimony. 50 % of each class in the top business schools (HEC)[68] plans to emigrate to Anglo-Saxon countries. 40,000 creative young French managers have left for Silicon Valley and even more for Great Britain. They are driven away by high taxes and bureaucratic paralysis. These elites, creators of added value, are replaced by masses of immigrants from overseas, of whom only 5 % are 'workers' in search of a job (and even they are unskilled). The rest are looking for a handout. In four years 800 billion francs of capital investors have left. Because of confiscatory taxation, 200 MEP (*moyennes entreprises patrimoniales*, or medium-sized family businesses) with strong technological value were in four years sold to foreign groups who moved them out of France. Educated French workers are fewer and fewer. There is a lack of skilled workers (the brain drain has become a brain haemorrhage) and a plethora of the unskilled, due to the growing mass of a working-age population that is unskilled or receiving social services, coming largely from immigration. The economy will end up as a Third World economy, the final stage of all this. This is good news for the United States.

***

The French economy is becoming a Third World one. The recent law of 'social modernisation', of wholly Marxist inspiration, which, like the 35-hour workweek, makes the Anglo-Saxon press laugh — even the Russian press! — is going to end with a hiring freeze, the ebbing of foreign investments and the movement abroad of French businesses. The phenomenon has already started. France is the Western country that invests the most abroad and whose managers leave in the greatest numbers. Is this good news? No! This is flight, not conquest. The

---

68 The Hautes Études Commerciales refers to a number of prestigious business schools in France.

Vivendi-Messier affair[69] attests to it. The vital forces of France are fleeing to the Anglo-Saxons.

200,000 French managers have left or are in the process of leaving.
Who will replace them? Battalions of unskilled welfare recipients who
have come from rural cultures in the global South.

The burden of bureaucrats gets heavier; the competitiveness of
businesses shrinks because of the 35-hour workweek. 'Let us work less
to earn more!' is the slogan of the plural majority.

French industry, which was one of the most productive in the world,
is losing ground, because instead of supporting it, the French state is
puncturing it — the old Marxist culture. In the USA the state helps national industry instead of sponging off of it. A report published in early
January 2004 by the Groupe des fédérations industrielles (GFI), which
represents 85 % of industrial businesses, expresses fears of a decline of
French industry on the world scene in the next few years.

What are the concrete threats that weigh on French industry?

1)   Financial investment is jeopardised by bureaucracy and high taxes,
     but also by the belief in a 'post-industrial service economy' without
     factories. Now industry is vital for the French and European econ-
     omy, first so as not to depend too much on foreigners to supply
     material goods, and finally because factories and manufacturing is
     still very important. This insight is the opposite of the myths spread
     by the bards of the 'new economy'. French industrial production
     of the secondary sector represents 170,000 businesses, 4.1 million
     salaried jobs and 760 billion euros (4,985 billion francs) in sales, of
     which 35 % is in exports. The heralds of the 'new economy', which
     is centred on service, the Internet, information and computers,
     soon forget that there will always be a need for factories to make
     computers, televisions, and smart cards!

---

69   Jean-Marie Messier (b. 1956) is a French businessman who was Chief Executive
     Officer of Vivendi SA until he was forced to resign in July 2002, after which the
     company suffered an almost 14-billion-euro loss in 2001.

2) If French big businesses are massively influential abroad, they are fleeing France, whose competitiveness is affected by bureaucracy, legislative dictatorship (the 35-hour workweek, etc.), continually rising labour costs, insufficient research funding, excessive obligatory taxation, and so on. In 2000, France was in first place in the world, ahead of the United States, in foreign investments! French industries prefer to do business abroad.

3) Because of this fact, importation of capital is drying up and industrial investment in the Hexagon is stagnating. From 1996 to 2000 France moved from sixteenth place to twenty-fifth place worldwide in terms of competitiveness.

4) Professional education in technology is managed very poorly. The professional tax paralyses productive investment. Industry is insufficiently connected with technological instruction (another Marxistoid knee-jerk reaction) and is left to the vagaries of 'national education'. It is well known what a fantastic job public education is doing.

The 'Colbertist'[70] and later 'Gaullist'[71] tradition of the French state was to support national industry — exactly as in the USA, which ignores the 'liberal' and 'free trade' image it presents to the world. The system worked rather well during the 1960s and 1970s: nuclear energy, high speed trains (TGV), support for aeronautics and space industry were inspired by the 'Gaullo-Colbertist' model. On the other hand, with computers and biotechnologies, the model has been a complete failure. Today, the worst of cocktails is prevailing: at home a reactionary

---

70 This refers to the economic policies of Jean-Baptiste Colbert (1619–1683), who was the French Minister of Finance under King Louis XIV from 1665 to 1683. His doctrine, which has come to be known as Colbertism, was built on the premises that the wealth of a nation should primarily serve the interests of the state, and that state intervention should be used to ensure this.

71 The policies of Charles de Gaulle.

and paralysing bureaucratic socialism (of Left or Right), with ultra-liberalism abroad.

The Demographic Coma

The most recent UN population report indicates that the world's population has grown from 2.52 billion in 1950 to 6.06 billion in 2001, and is predicted to rise to 9.32 billion in 2050. The number of Europeans (including Russians) is going to decrease: 548 million in 1950, 727 million today and 603 million in 2050. According to these projections, Africa will grow from 794 million today to 2 billion in 2050. These raw statistics do not explain what 'Europe' will mean if a growing number of people of non-European origin continue to immigrate here to settle permanently, as in North America. If these statistics do not change, the estimates are that Whites (including all countries), who represented 1 out of every 2 humans in 1950 and are presently 1 out of 5, will be only 1 out of 8 in 2050.

***

Wolfgang Lutz and Brian O'Neill of the Vienna Institute of Demography issue a warning cry that points out an unprecedented cataclysm: 'This has never happened before. Waiting to confront it will amount to swimming upstream against an inexorable phenomenon of economic compression and an ageing population.' Fatalist ...

Europe's birth rate, the lowest in the world, is 1.5 babies per woman. (A birth rate of 2.1 is necessary just to replace each generation.) If this birth rate continues up to 2020, Europe will lose 88 million inhabitants in 2100 (and if the mortality rates stay the same). In addition, late pregnancies are going to increase the deficit of active workers. The proportion of active to retired is about to pass from 4 to 1 in 2000 to 3 to 1 in twenty years. Those who oppose revising the retirement system seem not to realise what this will mean.

The consequences include risks of the collapse of economic productivity, the end of the social security systems and widespread poverty. The authors of the UN report, obviously, do not recommend a serious pro-natal policy, but, on the contrary, extol immigration as the best solution. Being politically correct is more important than facing an emergency, even a life or death one.

***

The French media recently celebrated a victory dance. French demography, along with Ireland's, is the strongest in Europe since 2000: 1.9 babies per woman. The French population (60.1 million) has passed the population of the United Kingdom.

The media forgot to mention three considerations: 1) An increase in population does not prevent its ageing. 2) This birth rate of 1.9 — which is below replacement level — is due to foreigners, most of whom live on welfare. The birth rate of European couples does not exceed 1.6. 3) France's neighbours are experiencing lower birth rates than ours. We are only the one-eyed in the kingdom of the blind. Despite large-scale immigration, Germany, Italy, Spain, etc., have lost population every year since 1995.

Here are the facts for Russia, reported by the *Russian Observer*. Since 1992, Russia has lost 2.8 million inhabitants, which led to a policy devoted to repatriate Russians from the colonies of the former USSR. The Russian Academy of Sciences fears that in 2050 Russia's population will fall below 100 million. It would require 3 million births a year to stabilise the population. In 2000, there were 1.3 million births, not even twice that of France, with only a third of the population.

If nothing changes, according to the Académie des sciences morales et politiques (ASMP), the population of Europe and Russia (including immigrants) is going to shrink from 727 to 606 million by 2050 (a reduction of 17 %), while the population of Africa will grow from 591 to 1.697 million (an increase of 187 %), in spite of infant mortality, wars and epidemics. European women have a birth rate of 1.4 — replacement

level requires 2.1 — and African women have a birth rate of 5.9. These
statistics are serious and they foretell catastrophe.

***

According to a confidential report from the section on demographic
studies of the United Nations, in 2050, if birth rates do not rise, Europe
will have 40 million fewer inhabitants than today, a decline of 10 %,
despite the massive immigration from which it is suffering. Right now,
Europe is losing 157,000 inhabitants a year, and the phenomenon will
probably only get worse. The countries most affected today are Italy,
Spain and Germany, whose populations in 1999 started to decline for
the first time in their histories. To the colonising immigration aimed at
permanent settlement is added an ageing population and the depopulation of native Europeans. The governments of our continent display
only total indifference to these developments.

***

German demographer Herwig Birg presented conclusions and predictions in *Die Welt* (8 June 2002), which are relevant for all Europe. If
nothing changes, Germany's population will shrink from 82 million
today to 68 million in 2050, in spite of immigration. Birg does not
believe that this immigration will be able to fill the gaps in qualified
jobs (because of the lack of skills, education and industrial culture),
nor will immigrants be able to pay the retirement benefits of the ageing
Europeans. There is another fact about Europe worth emphasising that
never gets mentioned: 40 % of immigrants' children born in Europe
never graduate from high school and are not ready to participate in a
modern society. The European economy needs educated workers. We
are witnessing a change to a Third World economy.

Birg predicts an ethnic change in Europe's population that will
make any 'assimilation' impossible, as the minorities become majorities. 'Society will no longer be majority "German." In big cities, the
proportion of Germans and immigrants is going to be reversed by 2010

for those under 40. "Assimilation" will then mean: how, as a German, am I going to assimilate into a society with an immigrant majority? We never hear a word on this topic in all the reports on immigration.' Finally his lucid pessimism breaks out: 'Many immigrants do not see much point in education. Virtues like a taste for hard work or a sense of duty, mocked for so long, virtues that are necessary to maintain a functioning society, often have little value in their eyes.'

Birg demolishes the myth in which Asia will pour out 'skilled experts' for us to import. India, with a billion inhabitants, has fewer Internet connections and computer scientists than Germany. He denounces the idea of Europe's 'sharing' prosperity with the overpopulated Third World and extols the idea of Fortress Europe in his analysis, which is very politically incorrect and ethnocentric: 'Far from experiencing a wave of immigration, Europe is going to transform itself into a fortress. This concept is going to assume a positive sense, because it assures a certain level of prosperity to those who live here. ... We have no choice but to exclude millions of persons from our prosperity, for prosperity cannot be shared by an act of will. In 2035, Germany will see deaths exceed births by 16 million persons [!]. By the end of the century, there will be 1.8 billion Indians. In these circumstances what sense does it make to speak of sharing with the 50 million Germans who will remain?'

Even if immigration and the colossal changes it represents are halted, Birg foresees that the decline in the number of active (and, even more, skilled) workers will unavoidably and soon provoke economic stagnation, since expenses for health care and retirement benefits will replace consumption and investment. The brilliant society of consumption and leisure is behind us, despite what everybody thinks.

***

According to the German Institute of Demographic Studies, the population of Germany is going to decline by 20 % by 2050, shrinking from 82 to 67 million, despite the annual arrival of 100,000 to 200,000 migrants. The German birth rate is 1.4. (The replacement rate is 2.1.) If nothing changes, mathematically Germany, just like France, by 2050 will be an ageing country, half of the population of which will be foreigners, in general of non-European origin.

The same situation holds in Great Britain. *The Guardian* (3 September 2000) claims that native English will be a minority in England by 2100, if immigration and native births remain at present rates. By 2010, Whites will be a minority in London. Official English statistics, which are probably underestimated, indicate that since 1991, the foreign-born population grew from 3 to 6 million! (This means an increase of 185,000 each year of entries and births.) In 2020, in the United Kingdom, foreigners born outside Europe will contribute one-half of the births.

In France, the demographer Jean-Paul Gourévitch, author of *La France Africaine*, predicts that, if nothing changes, by 2050 half of the French population will be of African origin, and more than 50 % of the younger generation.

Russia is in the same bad situation, except that she is spared colonising immigration. From the collapse of its medical system and birth rates, its population is predicted to shrink from now to 2020 from 145 to 125 million inhabitants. Since 1988, Russia's birth rate has fallen 50 % with infant morality at 10 %, the highest rate in Europe.

The United States, in order to weaken Europe, encourages a multi-racial society, which objectively helps the Islamic penetration of Europe. This sets the example of the 'superiority' of their model, not necessarily to please conservative circles, since they, too, are experiencing this phenomenon.

According to a report by Current Population Survey,[72] the population of California (16.5 million inhabitants) is today 49.9 % White, 31.6 % Mexican, 11.4 % Asian, 6.7 % Black, and 0.5 % Indians. In 2025,

---

72 The Current Population Survey is a statistical study undertaken by the U.S. Census Bureau for the Department of Labor to maintain estimates of employment.

Whites will be a minority at 33 % with Latinos 42 %. In the entire United States in 2050, Whites will represent only 45 % of the population. Without counting births in the USA, the immigrant population has tripled since 1970, growing from 9.6 million to 26.3 million. Since 1990 the non-White population has represented, by immigration or birth, 70 % of US population growth. (The American administration used the expression, 'non-White people'.)

What conclusions should we draw from all these statistics? Let us notice, first of all, that even if the general human birth rate is undergoing a gradual decline (experts predict a stabilisation at 10 billion in 2050), only the White race has passed below the fateful threshold of 2.1 babies per woman. There are, therefore, fewer and fewer Whites on the Earth every day. This dramatic decrease was predicted in the 1970s by Pierre Chaunu and Georges Suffert in a work that would probably be rejected today by publishers, *La Peste blanche*.[73] Finally, if things remain the same and if nothing happens to avert this sinister demographic trend, some Latin American countries like Argentina, Chile, or Columbia, will have an anthropological composition more 'Europoid' than Europe itself! This is a veritable historical *maelstrom*, never seen before. For the first time in their long history, the people of European origin are declining numerically and are about to be surpassed by other peoples on their own soil.

The causes of this change are strictly ideological and moral (and not military or the result of epidemics) since it is White people themselves who are responsible for their decline, by refusing to reproduce and organising the arrival on their own soil of immigrants from abroad. They are paralysed not by superior physical force but by ideologies.

***

---

73 Pierre Chaunu and Georges Suffert, *La peste blanche: comment éviter le suicide de l'Occident* (The White Plague: How to Prevent the Suicide of the West) (Paris: Gallimard, 1976).

When we talk of France, Germany, Russia, Europe, and other nations, we treat these nations as *eternal essences*. When geopoliticians draw up plans for the Twenty-first century, they start from the principle that these entities, these countries, will always exist, say in 2030, as they did in 1930.

Well, not necessarily. A nation is totally dependent on its demography and can disappear very quickly in the joint case of a collapse in the native birth rate and massive foreign immigration. A civilisation rests on a *people*, an ethnic *germen*.[74] (Let us take the case of Germany, presented as the leading European economic power, as described by Alain R. Arbez in *Le Lien Diaspora* (10 September 2003) and *Idea Spektrum 2000, Kirche und Politik*.

The birth rate has imploded, from 2.3 in 1960 to 1.2 and 0.9 in the East today. Germany is committing suicide. In 1999 the government registered 800,000 births (including those to foreigners) for 300,000 abortions. Without abortion the German birth rate would be 35 % higher. In the 1960s, no one imagined these dramatic problems of depopulation. Today, certain quarters have lost their residents and schools and nurseries have disappeared. The totally oblivious baby boom generation, protesters and hyper-bourgeois consumerists, took full advantage of their Glorious Thirties,[75] but they did not have children. On the contrary, they welcomed the arrival of masses of immigrants. They prepared for themselves terrible old days.

At Dortmund (600,000 inhabitants) only 5,000 German babies were born in 2002. The loss of one-fifth of the population, which migrants are not replacing, will mean that in 2010 Dortmund will be only 60 % German and most of them will be old. The youth of Dortmund will be 70 % Turks, Africans, Asians, etc. Frankfurt and Stuttgart will no longer be majority German by 2030. In 2012 foreigners aged 20 to

---

74 Latin: 'seed' or 'germ.

75 This refers to a 30-year period from the end of the Second World War until 1974, when the French economy was marked by great prosperity, ending with the oil crisis.

40 will represent 46 % of the population of Duisburg and a greater percent of those under 20. At Berlin the proportion of foreigners under 20 will be 52 % in 2013. By the end of the Twenty-first century, traditional Germans will fall from 75 million to 22 million. In these conditions Germany will obviously have become a Third World country.

Sociologists Meinhard Miegel and Stefanie Wahl predict that German cultural, religious and linguistic identity will be totally eliminated in the course of the century. This 'programmed disappearance' of Germany is proudly ignored by politicians and prelates, who behave like crazed sleepwalkers. To avoid depopulation and economic chaos, the UN recommends 500,000 immigrants a year and the blind *Frankfurter Allgemeine Zeitung* approves!

Integration and assimilation have turned out to be complete failures. Only minorities can be assimilated, not mobs. The German people are disappearing before our very eyes. There is a *change of people*. You just have to take a stroll through Germany's big cities. 75 % of Turks (naturalised or not, from first generation to the third) consider Germany only as an 'economic fatherland'; they still feel that they are Turks and Muslims and watch only Turkish TV. Out of 800,000 annual births, only 278,000 births of Christian babies are recorded (1998 statistics), a terrifying 35 % of births.

According to demographer Rainer Münz, Germany will have 14.2 million foreigners in 2030, without mentioning those who are naturalised and hold dual citizenship. Even if immigration were to end today — and without massive deportations — Muslims, because of their higher birth rate, will be a majority by then. This same situation exists in France, Belgium, and elsewhere.

A 1997 study of Muslim youths by sociologist Wilhelm Heitmeyer reveals that 1) a third wants to expand the presence of Islam in Germany; 2) 36 % of them call themselves militants and are ready to use violence against 'infidels'.

When people cross the Rhine in 2030, will they pass from North Africa to Turkey? To avoid despair, let us cite a passage from an editorial by Dominique Venner,[76] 'L'histoire n'est jamais finie', in *La Nouvelle Revue d'Histoire* (September-October 2003): 'The unthinkable, despite every expectation, could happen. As late as 1960 and even later, the unthinkable was the expulsion of the million French *pieds-noirs*[77] from Algeria. … The unthinkable, in the decades that followed independence, was the arrival of several million Algerians in France. The unthinkable today is, for example, the repatriation of these Algerians and other African immigrants. Let us learn from the past that the unthinkable can, one day, become reality.'

***

What is the condition of Russia's demography? It is in terrible shape and this is perhaps why Vladimir Putin, who is aware that his country is threatened by a 'demographic coma', which is also a healthcare coma, has taken anti-abortion measures by abolishing the Leninist laws on abortion. (The abortion rate in 2001 was 60 women in 1,000, while in France the rate is 13 out of 1,000.) Here are the statistics published by the DER (Demografitsceskil Ejegodnik Rossü (the equivalent of the French INED, the Institut national d'études démographiques), which end in early 2002. Read them carefully. Since 1992, the Russian population shrunk by 3 million inhabitants. (Today the population of Russia is 145 million.) If the decline continues to accelerate, in 2050 Russia

---

76 Dominique Venner (1935–2013) was a French historian. In his youth, he was a radical nationalist, and fought as a paratrooper in the Algerian War. He was also jailed for his involvement in the anti-Gaullist Organisation de l'Armée Secrète. He began working with Alain de Benoist in the 1960s and was a supporter of the French New Right in its early years. Venner took his own life in Notre-Dame Cathedral in Paris as a symbolic act of protest against mass immigration and cultural decay. Arktos has published English translations of two of Venner's works: *The Shock of History: Religion, Memory, Identity* (2015) and *For a Positive Critique* (2017).

77 Literally 'black foot', this term refers to those of European origin who lived in Algeria during the period of French colonisation (1830–1962). The original meaning of the term has been lost and is still debated today.

will have fewer than 100 million inhabitants in a territory that is 35 times the size of France. Life expectancy in Russia is only 58 years (it is 80 in the West). 25 % of women of childbearing age are HIV-positive, while the prison population has reached a million!

The DER fears that by 2075 Russia will have only 55 million inhabitants, if things keep up this way. In 2002, 65 regions out of 89 were in demographic coma with three times more deaths than births. Certain territories are losing population at full speed: from 2001 to 2002, the district of Murmansk shrank from 1,300,000 to 900,000 inhabitants. The number of divorces equals the number of marriages (7.5 per 1,000 inhabitants). The Far East of Russia (Magadan, Kamchatka, eastern Siberia, Sakhalin) is becoming a desert. The pressure of Chinese immigration — really, an invasion — is growing. In addition, 1.1 million Russians left the country from 1991 to 2002. 6.7 million people inhabit the Far East (36 % of Russian territory), while the three neighbouring Chinese provinces contain 100 million people. It is easy to guess how this film will end.

These facts help us to understand that demography (basically *family morale*) constitutes the basis of a people's ability to survive. Words like 'Russia', 'Europe', 'France', and 'Germany' will mean nothing in fifty years, despite the learned theories of the geo-politicians, if their peoples disappear and are replaced by other peoples living on their soil. History has often seen similar cases …

***

The government of Mr. Putin — this subtle chess player — does not stop, of course, taking interesting measures, not only against the 'oligarchs', but also against the shrinking Russian birth rate, although our press does not talk about the latter. Russian law has reduced the legal grounds for abortion from thirteen to three, abolishing the very lax (or 'progressive') provisions of Soviet legislation, which authorised abortion on demand. The 'democratic' leagues and the Russian feminists accuse Putin of yielding to pressure from the Orthodox Church, an unlikely explanation for this old KGB bureaucrat, whose temperament is more nationalist than religious.

Abortion was the scourge of Russia: 4.5 million a year, four times the number in the USA, with thirteen abortions for ten births! The new law forbids abortion after 12 weeks of pregnancy, with exceptions permitted up to 22 weeks in extreme cases, including rape, genetic defects or the mother's health. This is the reaction of the Russian government to the catastrophic demographic situation. Russia loses a million of its 144.5 million inhabitants every year because of low birth rates and early death. Deputy Alexander Chuyev, a supporter of the new law, declared, 'Abortion increases the ranks of women who become sterile.'

***

Are there *physiological* causes for Europeans' low birth rates? Low birth rates among rich peoples have causes, it is known, that are partially *sociological*. A large family with many children does not represent wealth, but a burden, in a society dominated by the hedonist imperative of immediate satisfaction. On the other hand, contraception and abortion, which necessarily limit births, are promoted. There exists, however, perhaps a third cause of a prosaically *physiological* nature. Here is one sexologist's hypothesis: 'The Japanese competition with Viagra arrived in Europe in July 2001, with sales of 190 million euros in the European Union (1.246 billion francs) alone. Selling the cure for masculine impotence affects 36 million potential consumers! We need to face seriously, I believe, one of the causes of Europe's low birth rate: masculine impotence, quite simply. Is this problem growing among European males? I would not be surprised, if it were increasing. After all, we live in a hyper-sexualised environment that arouses fantasies of every sort, but inhibits passing to the act. It is equally necessary to point out masculine infertility: the proportion of fertile sperm of Europeans, that is, the number and germinal quality of spermatozoids, no longer reaches half of what it was in 1900. There are many reasons, pollution of food and atmosphere, a permanent state of stress, and so on.' Our correspondent also raises the issue of growing female infertility: 'Our women smoke like locomotives, and they start smoking at increasingly early ages. I have seen girls of 13 to 14 with a cigarette in their mouth at 7:45 AM before going to class. Female addiction to smoking will sooner or later create very serious problems of public health. How can we imagine that babies born to women who are inveterate smokers will themselves be healthy and strong?' We could add growing drug use. Drugs harm both sperm production and ovulation. Spiritual and ideological devirilisation works hand-in-hand with physiological sterilisation.

The Cancer of Decadence

We are living through an 'involution', that is, the regression of a civilisation towards maladapted forms, which entail a decline in vital force.

Today we are seriously threatened by involution, especially cultural involution. It is not only because of the expansion of a mass commercial culture, of which America is one of the centres of diffusion, but also by the Africanisation of European culture and the Islamic invasion. Cultural involution is encouraged by the decline of national public education (40 % of adolescents are completely or partially illiterate), the regression of knowledge, the collapse of social codes, the immersion of youth in electronic pseudo-games, the constant growth of neo-primitivism, the loss of all instinctive reactions of self-defence, and so on.

Involution also has biological roots: devirilisation caused by ideologies, but also by the urban ways of life of a market society and the ideologies of guilt, low birth rates, anti-selection, and so on.

Of course, optimists will say that they do not observe involution. It is *not yet observable*, since involution is still growing, like a virus, which is not yet massively and clearly noticeable. For anyone who observes daily reality, however, it is in full progress. Involution begins with minds and behaviour, before progressively infecting social and economic institutions.

***

'Neo-primitivism' is an observable process of cultural involution today that consists of a return to the behaviour of primitive masses, a decline of cultural memory and the appearance of social savagery. There are countless signs of this new primitivism: the rise of illiteracy in schools, the explosion of drug use, the Afro-Americanisation of popular music, the collapse of social codes, the retreat of general culture, mastery of knowledge and historical memory among young people, the dilution of contemporary art into the nihilist brutality of less-than-nothing, brutalising the masses and stripping them of culture by audiovisual media (the 'cathode religion'),[78] the increase in criminal activity and barbarous behaviour (social savagery), the disappearance of a civic sense, the accelerated crumbling of homogeneous social norms and collective disciplines, the impoverishment of language, the reduction of social codes, and so on.

The generation of young *Beurs-Blacks* offers a remarkable example of this neo-primitivism, but they are not the only ones to be affected by it, far from it.

The paradox of this new primitivism, a real process of 'decivilisation', is its association with a dominant devirilised ideology that extols civility, the rule of law, altruism, humanitarianism, citizenship, 'culture'. It is, however, a question of a banal *phenomenon of compensation*. This neo-primitivism is perfectly consistent with a tightening of social controls, domestication by consumerism, and a collective loss of intellect and of all critical thinking. It is manifested as the pendant of neo-totalitarianism. It serves the short-term goals of the strategies of domination of the political class, the intellectual-media class and, especially, the transnational financial and economic complex. In a

---

78 As opposed to the Catholic religion.

dialectical style of reasoning, this neo-primitivism could well turn against the contemporary civilisation that gave birth to it, to the degree that the present young generation of new barbarians will no longer be capable, very simply, of making this civilisation function technically.

This generation will oppose only little resistance to the work of purging and brainwashing carried out by active minorities, whoever they may be. What can a mass of slaves, the 'last men' Nietzsche talked of,[79] do in the face of real and resolute aristocracies?

***

More than ever, society is 'stalled' and suffers from sclerosis, because of the enormous advantages acquired by stonewalling public bureaucrats that are hostile to any reform and the impotence of governments in the face of union minorities, pressure groups and street mobs. All this indicates the appearance of a new class struggle. It is the voters on the Left who find themselves objectively on the side of the exploiters. Here is what we are facing:

1) Those with 'guaranteed salaries' (all those public and quasi-public bureaucrats who enjoy a job for life, with complete social coverage and countless privileges); immigrants who, more than native-born citizens, have become overprotected welfare recipients practicing parasitism with impunity; the traditional and relatively small class of the wealthy grand bourgeoisie (allied with the sphere of intellectuals and the media), now joined by a new class of speculators.

---

79 'Alas, the time is coming when man will no longer give birth to a star. Alas, the time of the most despicable man is coming, he that is no longer able to despise himself. Behold, I show you the last man. "What is love? What is creation? What is longing? What is a star?" thus asks the last man, and he blinks. The earth has become small, and on it hops the last man, who makes everything small. His race is as ineradicable as the flea-beetle; the last man lives longest.' From Friedrich Nietzsche, *Thus Spoke Zarathustra* (New York: Penguin Books, 1978), p. 5.

2) The middle class, which is less and less protected by guaranteed lifetime employment, is in full decline because of limited-term contracts (CDD), social plans, downsizing, etc., and placed in a precarious position, although the totality of economic growth and the creation of wealth rests upon them.

3) A growing native-born proletariat, unemployed and underemployed, lives in a state of poverty and insecurity. We should note that the famous 'exclusion' affects principally native-born Europeans, since colonising immigrants benefit from the privileges of public aid and communitarian solidarity.

The result is that the protected class lives at the expense of working, unprotected classes that they exploit. The members of the legislature and the executive branch who make the rules belong obviously to the protected class.

As a result, we are witnessing the very serious phenomenon of the flight of the elites, the prelude to a process of descent into Third World status. Fleeing this stalled and overtaxed society, where the state burdens creative forces rather than helps them, millions of young brains move abroad every year. Who is replacing them? Unskilled and unproductive immigrants, who are extremely expensive, since they are for the most part takers and not givers.

Democracy, already diminished by the oligarchic careerism of professional politicians, sees itself disfigured by a judicial republic and an aggravated censorship of the 'politically incorrect', where 'thought crimes' are viewed as antithetical to the rule of law. Abstention from voting has reached unheard-of proportions. Governments are based on minorities, that of the class of intellectuals and media. When you realise the Greens and Communists, who represent only a small part of public opinion, succeed in imposing the laws they favour, you understand everything.

In reality, everything is happening as if this Western 'democracy' is slowly aligning itself with the Stalinist model, itself inspired by the despotism of the masters of the French Revolution. The ruling class of intellectuals and media, openly hostile to populism and demagogy, opposes all direct democracy, and, especially on the Left, has sunk to cultivating contempt, suspicion and phobia of the people. Western pseudo-democracy is really an oligarchic, neo-totalitarian system.

For a process of soft totalitarianism has been put in place, legitimised of course by 'democracy'. The political circle of political parties in power in Europe (bogus majorities and bogus oppositions) really resembles a single party that subscribes as a whole, with nuances, to the same ideology. Direct democracy, like Switzerland's, is perceived as illegitimate, and popular opinion as immature and dangerous. One party, the Austrian Freedom Party,[80] is officially considered illegitimate, even though its candidates are duly elected.

Paradoxically, the institutional weakness toward morals, crime and immigration is accompanied by a strengthened political repression, of surveillance and heavy taxation of native-born citizens. Big Brother has become Ubu Roi[81] and *vice versa*. The dissolution of the vital forces of society, the muscles, in favour of an ossification and strengthening of the skeleton is taking place.

In our economy, we have piled up the disadvantages of capitalism and socialism without receiving any of the advantages of either system. From capitalism, we receive only the free market system and

---

80 The *Freiheitliche Partei Österreichs* (FPÖ), or Freedom Party of Austria, is a right-wing nationalist party. It remains active and influential in Austrian politics. In 2005, prominent members — led by Jörg Haider — split from the FPÖ to form a new party, the Alliance for the Future of Austria (*Bündnis Zukunft Österreich*, BZÖ), though the BZÖ has since declined in significance. As of 2025, the FPÖ has regained considerable political strength and remains a central force in Austrian opposition politics, often polling at or near the top nationally.

81 *Ubu Roi* is a well-known play by Alfred Jarry written in 1896, and which is regarded as one of the primary precursors of the Theatre of the Absurd. Ubu, the main character, is depicted as the culmination of all of the flaws of modern man, being selfish, cruel, vulgar and dishonest, and manages to become King by murdering his predecessor.

the irresponsible open border policy without being helped by the advantages of the freedom to create business; from socialism, we receive only centralisation, union corporatism, high taxes and bureaucracy, with no advantages from social justice, real social solidarity and the right to a job.

Theoreticians of the Left and Right, who lack economic knowledge and business experience, are wrong to affirm that 'liberalism is the chief enemy' and that we living in a society of savage ultra-liberalism. This recycling of Leftist analyses misunderstands the reality.

First of all, it is quite right to combat an unbridled global free-market system, but not the play of the market in a protected European continental interior space. Demonising the 'market' comes to the same thing as playing the game of a sclerotic and Communist-like corporatism. Finally, criticism of the 'market society' and the 'almighty dollar' should not cause us to forget that the principal motor of performance, economic energy and innovation is *competition*. The initial cause of the dynamism of competition has been and always will be, deplore it or not, maximising gains (and not virtue).

Criticising the 'market society' does not mean criticising the market and its liberal principle, but opposing an eventual *dictatorship* of the market and the forces of speculation. It also means demanding, above the market, the presence of a sovereign function and political leadership, and, below the market, corrective mechanisms of social solidarity for citizens who cannot subsist by their work.

What causes problems for our society is not too much liberalism, but too much socialism; and the worst sort of socialism, not the socialism of Proudhon[82] and Blanqui,[83] but one inspired by Communism,

---

82 Pierre-Joseph Proudhon (1809–1865) was a French politician and philosopher who opposed capitalism and did not believe in state ownership of property, instead believing that property should belong to workers' groups.

83 Louis Auguste Blanqui (1805–1881) was a revolutionary activist. His version of socialism, however, differed greatly from Marx's, especially in that he believed that a socialist revolution would not be brought about through a mass movement

bureaucratic corporatism, acquired privileges and colossal mandatory taxes. This is very far from the idea of social justice, proclaimed all the louder as it has never been applied.

Slowly the great institutions of the public sphere, the very foundations of all civilisation, are crumbling: school, hospital, army, police, and with them the founding principles of a living society—security and public health, the transmission of knowledge, and so on.

Still society remains on its feet, like a scarecrow in a field ravaged by crows. It is the 'new society' of the 'new modernity', which keeps growing larger (on the Internet, of course) while it is rotting away inside like a colossal dead tree that is held up by its bark and will fall with a loud crash when the hurricane arrives.

As society exhausts its inner sap, its moral values and biological energy, the dried-up mechanism of the state responds by becoming even stronger. Administrations grow harder and swell, but there is no heart, the blood no longer flows, enthusiasm and liberty die out. A bogus civilisation is built up while a true culture collapses.

**

What are the real statistics of semi-literacy and illiteracy in France? They are mind-blowing and mark the failure of the lax and 'educationalist' methods of public education, which have been dogmatically imposed since 1968. Semi-literacy is a very poor mastery of the written language; illiteracy betokens total ignorance. 25 % of college graduates are currently 'semi-literate' in the definition given in 1901 by Louis de Sours, 'eccentric orthography, non-existent syntax, slow reading', in *Les progrès de l'éducation républicaine* (The Progress of Republican Education) (Éd. Fasquelle, 1901). It is a reasonable guess that the proportion of young semi-literates is today higher among teenagers and young adults than in 1910. When one takes account of

---

of the workers, but rather by a small elite who would enact the revolution by imposing a temporary dictatorship.

mass immigration, 20 % of the adult population is estimated to be illiterate (not knowing how to read or write). This brings us back to
the statistics of about 1830. It has been established that the 'capacity to
write' and 'to read a simple text' by today's student (high school gradu-
ation) is inferior to the competence of a Third Form student (holding
a 'diploma') at the beginning of the Twentieth century. Testing done by
the Ministry of Defence on draftees and enrolled soldiers from 1970
to 1999 shows mastery of written French shrank by 35 % during this
period. One could respond cynically that in the age of multimedia and
audiovisual hype it is no longer necessary for people to know how to
read and write …

***

The rule of law is dying. The state is proving to be increasingly incapable
of making people respect the law and its 'monopoly of public power',
the symbol of the *jus publicum europeanum*[84] since the Fourteenth
century. Many examples confirm this hypothesis in very different
areas: private security companies are replacing the police; 85 % of
crimes are not prosecuted (Europol statistics, June 2001) because of a
lack of means or will; illegal immigrants are not deported, even when
they commit other crimes, despite the law; illegal 'rave parties' and the
traffic in drugs that they entail are tolerated; the atrocities of the partisans of the Trotskyite José Bové[85] (the pseudo-anti-globalist) remain
totally unpunished; obviously there is no need to speak of Corsica,
where hoodlums, who call themselves 'autonomists', parade armed as
if for war under the eyes of the mocked and impotent police. The only
people punished are reckless drivers who drive faster than the speed
limit authorised by the law. It all fits perfectly.

---

84 Latin: 'European public law'.

85 José Bové (b. 1953) politician who has been an activist in agricultural causes
    such as organic farming, and has also opposed globalisation and Israel's occupa-
    tion of Palestine. He served as a Member of the European Parliament from 2009
    to 2019

This decline in law and order is accompanied, quite logically, by legislative inflation. Over the past twenty years, 7,500 laws have been passed and the immense majority remain a dead letter. The *Journal officiel*[86] is 17,000 pages long. Too many laws kill the law. Power no longer has the means to make people respect an excess of often surreal texts. Add to this the legislation of the EC, also worthy of Ubu Roi. The collapse of the rule of law in Europe corresponds precisely to the rise to power of a judicial ideology best described as the 'dictatorship of judges'.

In the tradition of ancient Greece (reread Solon[87] and Plato), the law was supposed to be 'brief, imperative and solemn', and above all it was not to tolerate any transgression.

Nature has a horror of the void. What happened at the end of the Roman Empire could very well happen again. The law of a failing state run by incompetents — who are, however, filled with the certainty of their competence — is replaced by another law, that is, a new type of relation of force. Our leaders should reread the history of Rome at the end of the Third century …

The European Union: The Shattered Dream

The expansion of Europe is a fool's bargain. Here are extracts from an interview in *Le Figaro* (7 October 2003) with Christian Saint-Étienne, author of *La puissance ou la mort: L'Europe face à l'empire américain*:[88] 'Over the next twenty years, the strategic problem is not knowing

---

86 The *Journal Officiel de la République Française* (Official Journal of the French Republic) publishes all the major legal information of the French government.

87 Solon was an Athenian lawmaker in the Sixth century BCE who drafted a constitution to make the state more resistant to tyranny. He also enacted many new laws which were an attempt to prevent what he saw as Athens sliding into degeneracy and decadence.

88 Christian Saint-Étienne, *La puissance ou la mort: L'Europe face à l'empire américain* (Power or Death: Europe Faced with the American Empire) (Paris: Seuil, 2003).

whether the United States is going to collapse or not, but if Europe is going to disappear or not.' Predicting that when a federal Europe will be 30 or 40 years old, it will probably be totally powerless, Saint-Étienne reaffirms that the nationalist principle and not 'world government' will rule the Twenty-first century — under the giant states of the USA, India, China, and others — and that the idolatry of 'international law', which belongs to the past (Twentieth century), is only a pretext hypocritically defended by the weak — like contemporary France. Similarly, the American Robert Kagan[89] notes, against the dogmas, 'The globalisation of civil societies and governments is not credible over the next generation.'

Saint-Étienne continues, 'In the short term, the arrival of the Ten,[90] and especially Poland, to play the role of the fifty-first American state in Europe — or the fifty-second if Great Britain is reckoned as already the fifty-first — is naturally going to confuse European strategic choices... Europe would do better to concentrate its efforts on civil and military technology, not the entry of new members... Europe should fight against three major scourges, colossal demographic decline, extreme weakness in research and development and lack of productive investment.' The last two factors are largely due to the brain drain and the gigantic socio-economic cost of uncontrolled immigration.

**

European institutions are working against Europe. The authority of the unelected European Commission is once more about to overstep its

---

89   Robert Kagan (b. 1958) is a historian and foreign policy commentator at the Brookings Institution. He was one of the founders of the neoconservative Project for the New American Century, although rejects the label of neoconservative for himself. He has been influential upon both Democrats and Republicans, including John McCain, Hillary Clinton and Barack Obama.

90   The Ten refers to the ten former Communist nations which were or are seeking membership to the European Union.

role and in a very important area: the diversity of Europe's national languages.

In 1994, France decided to proscribe the use of English (and any other foreign language) in publicity campaigns and advertising products. The Eurocrats agreed with the decision, but now they have changed their mind. In a justified ruling, the European Commission insisted that France no longer impose the use of French on food labels; a picture of the product would suffice. The result was foreseeable. For obvious reasons of economy, the farming and food firms (waiting for the rest) are going to label their products in English, the best-known European language.

This anecdote summarises by itself the following situation: European institutions, and especially the European Commission, are not defending Europe, but are destroying it to the advantage of the Americans and the masses of immigrant-colonisers. Here are some points that underline this perverse trend:

1) The European Commission by its 'directives' arrogates to itself the powers of the Council of Ministers completely illegally. Manipulated by 'committees of experts', it systematically corrodes and undermines state sovereignties without replacing them with a federal political sovereignty and without being checked by the rump Parliament in Strasbourg. The 'Convention' with Giscard d'Estaing[91] as its President will probably make things worse. The European Commission represents a technocratic despotism in a chemically pure state that exists nowhere else in the world.

2) European institutions flout the principle of subsidiarity[92] and de-centralisation and practice, on the contrary, a fussy and aggravated

---

91 Valéry Giscard d'Estaing (1926–2020) was President of France from 1974 until 1981. He made a famous speech in September 1991 in which he referred to immigration as an invasion and called for tougher standards for aspiring citizens

92 Subsidiarity is a principle which emphasises the importance of the people having as much decision-making power as possible in regard to the issues which

Jacobin centralism. What business does Brussels have with the labelling of products in France or Italy, the procedures for making cheese in Normandy, or the maturing of oysters in Charental? Have the 'regionalists' who support the current European Union not understood that the EU is in fact totally opposed to all regional autonomy? In the USA, the states have great latitude in legislating in relevant areas — more so than European states! Recently, several German *Länder* (regions) have noticed that the EU is eliminating the powers accorded them by the German federal state.

3) In all matters, the European Commission and the Parliament in Strasbourg are following a political and ideological line totally contrary to the interests of Europe: dogmatic global free trade, a low profile in the face of American commercial injunctions, encouraging the use of English, open borders immigrationism and militant Islamophilia and Holy Roller humanitarianism, matched by a total lack of political or geopolitical vision for Europe, which is replaced by the religious vulgate of human rights.

4) The expansion of the EU without any preparation into central Europe (indeed into Turkey) will make whatever results unmanageable. And it will cost a lot of money. The countries that have applied for entry are first of all looking for subventions. It is absurd to make countries participate in the same economic and monetary unit when the ratio of their standard of living is sometimes 1 to 5. On 1 January 2004, the EU will grow from 15 to 25 members. No one agrees on the size of the subventions to offer them. A two-tier Europe will be established, and we shall see the unemployed of ten new countries pour into the West. The 'Convention' with Giscard d'Estaing for its President has not made and will not make any proposal to revise the EU's institutions to accommodate these new countries.

---

affect them, while decisions regarding the welfare of the larger community are left to the central government.

5) The initial project of the Treaty of Rome[93] to construct an economy that was to be self-centred and protected over its large territory has been scandalously turned from its objective and has generated a Europe open to the four winds by migration and markets, whose currency is managed by no political authority. The European Central Bank of Frankfort lets the euro fluctuate at the will of the markets. The result is that the European Union, stripped not only of its internal national boundaries, but of its external frontiers as well, cannot claim that it is becoming a 'federal state'.

We have the worst alliance that can exist, combining ultra-liberalism and a subventionist[94] and dirigist[95] bureaucracy, quite the reverse of what should have been done. Anyhow, if the USA has not been opposed to the ambition of the European Union, there is a reason. This submissive, emasculated, headless Europe, which scores goals against its own side, suits the USA perfectly. When asked the question, 'Are you for or against the construction of the European Union?' a high American functionary answered, 'In favour, as long as it does not work.'

---

93 The Treaty of Rome, which was signed in 1958, established the European Economic Community, the forerunner of the European Union.

94 The providing of financial assistance.

95 Dirigism refers to a form of capitalism that is also subject to strong regulation by the government.

4

TOWARD A GIANT
ECONOMIC CRISIS

The End of the Paradigm of
'Economic Development'

There has been a revolution in the way people think. They have just noticed, without daring to say it, that the old paradigm, 'the fate of humanity, individual and collective, is getting better every day, thanks to science, democratisation, and egalitarian emancipation', is false.

The age that believed it is over. This illusion has fallen. This progress (debatable anyhow according to people like Ivan Illich)[1] lasted probably less than a century. Today, the unintended consequences of mass technology are beginning to be felt: new resistant viruses, the toxicity of processed food, the exhaustion of the soil and the shrinking of the world's agricultural production, the general and rapid degradation of the environment, the threat of the invention of new weapons of mass destruction to add to nuclear weapons, and so on. In addition,

---

1   Ivan Illich (1926–2002) was an Austrian philosopher and Catholic priest. In his books, he accused many of the major pillars of modern society, such as education, medicine and industry, of what he termed 'counterproductivity', which is when institutions end up impeding the very goals they were meant to attain.

technology is entering its baroque age. The fundamental inventions were discovered by the end of the 1950s. The improvements to them made in later decades have contributed fewer and fewer concrete ameliorations, like so many useless decorative motifs added to the superstructure of a monument. The Internet has probably had fewer revolutionary effects than the telegraph or the telephone. The Internet is a significant improvement applied to a pan-communication that was already substantially realised. Techno-science is following the '80–20' power law. At the beginning it takes 20 units of energy to obtain 60 units of force. Later it takes 80 units of energy to realise only 20 units of force.

A possible objection is raised: is it not an excessive pessimism that causes some people to exaggerate the negative consequences of progress and world growth?

The answer is, no. Contrary to the comments made by French intellectual Jacques Attali and repeated everywhere, humanity as a whole has nothing to gain — for example — from the economic rise of Asia. The bill to pay in terms of the exacerbation of competition with the old industrial countries, and so forth, will be very expensive. Anyhow, this economic growth is not going to continue. It is going to become unsustainable, will run up against ecological limits and will provoke massive socio-political and even military problems. Catastrophe by itself, not the will of governments, will cause the change of the current macroeconomic model.

The various positive effects of global economic growth are in reality ephemeral and fragile and they will bring serious consequences.

The universalisation of techno-science has made us pay for each of its advances with a step backward. Life expectancy is increasing (although even now it is starting to stagnate and even regress in many countries), but are people living more harmoniously and with less anxiety? There are always more atomic, biological and chemical weapons of mass destruction. Agriculture is getting better, but renewed famines are threatening an overcrowded humanity, who have been duped by falling mortality rates and confronted by the exhaustion of the soil, tropical deforestation, the shrinking of arable land and the exhaustion of oceanic fauna.

The negative effects took twenty or thirty years to arise, but after an illusory phase when people's lives got better (which is over today), they always show up in the end. The intensified volume of production and trade encourages cooperation, but multiplies the reasons for conflicts and national chauvinisms, and arouses everywhere the backfires of ethnic and religious fanaticisms. Easy communication spreads over the entire planet, but loneliness strikes the individual and communities are in despair.

The urban technological way of life affects 70 % of humanity, but in many places, especially in the global South, it is necessary to put up with hellish cities, cesspools of violence and human chaos. Do people realise that, proportionally to the increased population, humans living in poverty and job insecurity are more numerous than before the Industrial Revolution? Medical science is progressing, but this has provoked a demographic explosion and increased the resistance of new viruses that are then spread by migration. The level of energy consumption is rising, but the environment is deteriorating and the danger of ecological collapse is becoming clearer. African and Brazilian peasants have access to machines for clearing land, but by destroying the forests, they increase desertification and prepare future famines. In brief, after an incubation period, progress, growth, and the uncontrolled expansion of techno-science see their goals reversed. A world is being born harsher than the one we want to transform and improve.

The Impending Death of World Economic Development

We must now confront a serious objection. We can never prevent poor countries or those 'on the path to industrialisation' from trying to industrialise, get rich by every means, or follow the West's path and the 'global religion of the growing GDP'. What a terrible injustice, if we did …

Of course, but historic dreams and hopes are not determined by *moral* motives, but by the *thresholds of physical impossibility*. This is the logic of catastrophe that will limit the ambitions for 'development' of countries of the global South, who, especially in Asia, have not yet become disenchanted with progress. Developing later than the West, they are still positivist, attached to the egalitarian universalism they are just discovering. They want to do what the West has done to obtain their piece of the pie. Unfortunately, it is too late. The Asian financial crisis was a harbinger. The Earth will never be able to sustain — and so neither will humanity — a technological and industrial development of all Asia and Africa at the present level of belief in miracles typical of universalism. Massive industrialisation of 'emerging countries' is likely to be physically impossible because it will exhaust scarce resources and destroy the ecosystems. The Cassandra cry of the Club of Rome will perhaps turn out to be right fifty years too early.

But there were Africans in the 1960s, like the South African Credo Mutwa,[2] who were already saying that pre-colonial tribal societies, which were not very populous, scattered and demographically stable, were much pleasanter to live in than contemporary African societies, which are complete failures, the results of botched imitation, a badly performed transplant of the European model totally foreign to them. After all, why should the entire human species desire to go to Mars, travel 500 kilometres per hour on high speed trains, fly on supersonic airplanes, eat ice cream in summer, live a hundred years thanks to transplants and antibiotics, write blogs on the Internet, watch television

2   Vusamazulu Credo Mutwa (1921–2020) was a South African Zulu diviner and author who advocated the idea that Africans should return to their native traditions rather than attempt to imitate Western civilisation. He also collaborated with conspiracy theorist David Icke. Mutwa passed away in 2020, but his books and teachings continue to influence discussions around African identity, mythology, and esotericism.

shows, and so on? This *fever* belongs only to certain people and certain groups.

This fever cannot be transmitted to the whole human species. This technological and industrial way of life can no longer be applied to the entire population, even in Europe and the United States, in the eventual case of structural collapse. Here a new objection arises, advanced from technocratic circles. Technology can counter the unintended consequences of technology. It can reduce pollute and discover new resources, if there is a real willingness to work together.

Optimism is a beautiful thing, but all these hopeful statement are only words. Anyhow, it is not happening. This system is coherent in its global logic and it cannot reform itself. It is, in the true sense of the term, incorrigible. It has to be changed.

Anyhow, the new system will impose itself in the coming chaos. We need to be concrete and stop daydreaming about the masturbations of the pseudo-experts. None of the resolutions of the Rio and Tokyo conferences have been put into effect, and they were, after all, nowhere near strong enough. Nature, which we wanted to conquer and put under our control, is as a consequence reacting violently, after a period of silence, in its bacterial, viral and other, more visible, forms. The collective certitudes are giving way to doubt and confusion. A new nihilism is appearing, which is very serious because it is hopeless, and has nothing in common with the philosophies of decline and the reactionary prophets of decadence that was only the dogma of progress stood on its head, of an ideological attachment to the past. Now it is the *philosophies of catastrophe* that are going to impose themselves. Uncertainty confronts us and its disturbing hulk casts a shadow on the techno-science that was believed to be predictable and controllable, which it is not. Heidegger turned out to be right, not Husserl[3] and the rationalists. The Jewish allegory of the Golem saw the truth.

---

3   Edmund Husserl (1859–1938) was the founder of the phenomenological school of philosophy, which was the predecessor of existentialism. Phenomenology has been defined as an attempt to apply the objective methods of science to the

Toward a 'Civilisational Break-Up'

But what new ideologies or types of social, political and economic organisation could replace those of the pursuit of progress and individualism? Must we return to theocracies, to which some Islamist countries are pointing the way? Let us remark first of all that an ideology that is non-progressive and rejects egalitarianism is not necessarily unjust, cynical or tyrannical. Egalitarians, aware of the failure of their projects of justice and humanity, paint their opponents in these demonising terms. A new non-egalitarian vision of the world will have to present itself as *concretely philanthropic*, where egalitarianism is only *ideally humanitarian*. The end of progressivism is obviously also the end of Hegelian rationalist idealism. Already, spontaneously, disordered and irrationalist ideologies are advancing all over the world. They are anti-scientific and anti-industrial, which is what worried the signers of the Heidelberg Appeal.[4]

But hold on: it is not necessary either to believe or hope that science and civilisation are going to disappear and be replaced by cultures based on magical beliefs.

Techno-science will continue to exist and develop, but *it will change its meaning and will no long be supported by the same ideal*. Global economic growth is soon going to shrink because of physical barriers. It is physically impossible to realise the ideal of progressivism: a techno-scientific consumer society for ten billion people. When the dream collapses, another world will arise. Scenarios for this new world are

---

study of consciousness, which is viewed as the basis of existence. Heidegger, however, although he was Husserl's student, came to believe that consciousness is only a by-product of existence, which is the actual ground of being.

4   In 1992 a statement signed by many scientists was released to coincide with the environmental Earth Summit. It was a plea for world leaders to avoid advice from irrational or pseudoscientific circles, especially those upholding a call for a return to nature, and other groups hostile to the aims of science and technological progress. It further stated that science, technology and industry are the best means for the 'indispensable tools of a future shaped by Humanity'.

obviously uncertain in detail, but they are much less unrealistic than the program of infinite global economic development under a world government parcelled out under UN supervision. The new scenario envisages the coexistence of *globalisation*, the end of state control of the economy and a *civilisational* break-up of the Earth that will be endured and not chosen. In this scenario, the Earth would not be divided into states that are politically independent and economically interdependent, but between *types of civilisation*. States that preserve the techno-scientific and industrial mode of existence (but animated by different values) would coexist with traditional societies, which may be magical and irrational, religious, rural and neo-archaic, expending relatively little energy on hunting, polluting and consuming.

There Is No Reason to Believe that Traditional Economies Are 'Underdeveloped'

Progressivist advocates will reply that this scenario will mean organising a sort of voluntary underdevelopment, with the gifted above who consume and the ungifted below who vegetate. This concept of underdevelopment is unfair and stupid. It is an invention of progressivism to signify that only the industrial way of life is humane and valid. A traditional rural non-technomorphic society is in no way barbarous and 'underdeveloped'.

In the non-egalitarian and organic vision of the world, there is not a single axis of 'development', but several. Real 'underdevelopment', more exactly real barbarism, is the result of progressivism: it is all the cast-offs of the industrial way of life, who have abandoned for a mirage traditional societies with small populations to cram themselves into the overpopulated metropolises of the countries of the global South, which have become human hells. Furthermore, members of a traditional society without much cash are not 'poorer' or unhappier than the inhabitants of New York or Paris weighed down by too many gadgets, even if their medical standards and life expectancy are lower. Lastly, we can point out that this likely socio-economic division of humanity in the course of the Twenty-first century will not result from a voluntary plan, but will be imposed on people by catastrophe, by the present system's collapse into chaos.

But what will make different types of society coexist? Will not those on the bottom again want to imitate those on top and 'develop themselves?' Not necessarily, because, on the one hand, the memory of the failure of the botched universalism of industrial society and techno-science will appear as a Dark Age (as Communism does today) and, on the other hand, because these neo-traditional communities will sanctify their way of life. Societies that preserve the techno-scientific way of life will be perfectly able to live in a globalised planetary economy, but one much less burdened than today's economy by the volume of trade and production and therefore much less polluting, because it will involve only a minority of humans. This minority will then no longer be animated by the eschatology of progress, but by the demands of the *will*.

Is the Techno-Scientific Economy Viable?

After the inevitable catastrophe that will mark the beginning of the Twenty-first century, once the stupid celebrations of the year 2000 have passed away, it will be necessary to pragmatically construct a new global economy with a spirit free of every utopia and unsustainable ideal, and without the spirit of oppression and neo-colonialism toward the part of humanity that will have returned to neo-traditional societies. History will no longer be conceived as progressivist idealism, but a *realistic, concrete and contingent* vision of reality, nature and man. Voluntarism, thinking about the concrete and the possible, is opposed to the idealism of today's global civilisation, which is founded on the abstraction of unrealisable ends. The techno-scientific spheres share with the neo-archaic a non-egalitarian and naturalist worldview, the one based on rationality, the other on irrationality.

Obviously, many people fear that the death of the idea of progress and the new organisation of the Earth will put an end to all rationality and destroy science and industrial production. Will this mean a general regression of humanity?

A contemporary prejudice holds that techno-science rests naturally on a progressivist and egalitarian pedestal that is the necessary condition for its existence. This is a mistake. The end of progress and the dream of universalising the society of industrial consumption do not signify abolishing techno-science and condemning the scientific spirit. Techno-science has been perverted by the egalitarian universalism of the Nineteenth and Twentieth centuries, which has tried to extend its sphere excessively.

Those who continue to maintain a techno-scientific civilisation, globalised but numerically restricted, will base it on other intellectual foundations than frenzied consumption and the generalised hedonism of the universalised progress of consumerism.

This will be easier because the true foundation of science and technology is fundamentally non-egalitarian (the life sciences), poetic and undetermined. Real scientists know that their thinking progresses only by destroying certainties. Their rationality is only a means and not an end. They know it never ends in automatic qualitative improvements that are the consequences of their discoveries. They know that technological experimentation is an opening to the unexpected: risks taken, enlarging the field of the contingent and the opacity of the future. On the contrary, in traditional societies, the future is predictable, because History is experienced cyclically. So linear progressivism will be replaced in neo-traditionalist areas by a cyclical vision of History, and in techno-scientific zones by *a belief in chance and a 'landscapist' vision of history* (Giorgio Locchi's[5] 'spherical' and Nietzschean conception,[6] which I mentioned earlier). History will unfold like a landscape, an unpredictable succession of plains, mountains, and forests, with no way to 'read it' rationally.

This vision of History and destiny increases the liberty, responsibility and lucidity of the people who share it. They analyse rigorously the true nature of reality and time, without utopian dreams, conscious of the risks. They deploy their will to realise their projects, to *order* human society in the most conformable way possible for *justice*, for recognising man as he is and not as some people want him to be.

The Neo-Global Economy of the Post-Catastrophe Age

A question arises: according to the hypothesis that the future two-tier world economy will be 'globalised', how can we define this concept of 'globalisation' in relation to universalism? Are they really opposites? Yes.

---

5   Giorgio Locchi (1923–1992) was an Italian journalist who was a founding member of GRECE and an occasional collaborator with Alain de Benoist. He also wrote on Wagner and Nietzsche. He remains untranslated.

6   In *Why We Fight*, Faye defines this as follows: 'The "spherical" conception of history, formulated by Nietzsche and developed by Giorgio Locchi, is this tragic, surhuman, and Faustian philosophy whose dynamic is no longer based on an eternally recurring cycle or a predetermined linear movement ('the meaning of history'), but by the 'eternal return of the identical' (not the 'same'). The past can be reappropriated, even transformed, at any moment by a project of renewal. This position is spherical, like a ball that rolls across a flat surface, with its different points touching the same phases of ascension, decadence, war, peace, crisis, etc., that constantly return, but in different situations and modalities. The present in this way fuses the immemorial past with a desired future. Tradition and futurism become here the same willed energy. The future remains open, unlike archaic pagan cyclicalism or Judaeo-Christian linearity — both of which are deterministic.' From Guillaume Faye, *Why We Fight: Manifesto for the European Resistance* (London: Arktos, 2011), pp. 161–162.

Universalism is an infantile concept, founded on the cosmopolitan illusion. Globalism is a practical idea. How many planetary networks for computers and exchanges exist, but do not in any way involve all humans! Universalisation is the ambition to extend mechanically and quantitatively to all humans a single way of life which is comprised of industrial consumption and urban life. Universalism is perfectly compatible with government control of the economy and egalitarianism drives it. All the billions of living human atoms have to be converted to the same rule of life, the kingdom of the market. Globalisation, on the contrary, describes a process of spreading markets and firms across the planet, internationalising economic decisions and major actors, but it does not need to be universalist and can easily tolerate billions of humans readopting traditional ways of life. On the other hand — and this is a very important point — globalisation is equally compatible with the construction on a continental scale of semi-autarchic blocs (the autarchy of large spaces), which practice different economic systems.

After the failure of economic progressivism and consumerist universalism, there could well be a planetary global economy (it could even get stronger) with no ambition to draw all humans into its order, since it would involve only an international minority. This is a very possible scenario for the post-catastrophe world, since techno-science and the industrial market economy cannot be neglected; they are too deeply rooted and are already well on the way to globalisation. Universalising industrial society to all humans cannot be attempted, since it is impossible from energy, health and ecological perspectives. The 'neo-global' economy that will follow the catastrophe will certainly be *planetary* in its networks, but in no way *universal*. The inequality intrinsic to it will permit, by the general decline in energy consumption, ending the destruction of the ecosystem and its reconstitution and so the improvement of every people's way of life.

Of course, the GDP of the world economy will shrink considerably, like a deflating balloon. Some will object that the shrinking of the world's GDP will dry up financial resources and make investments impossible because of 'loss of scale', since industrial society will involve only a fraction of humanity and therefore markets and demands will shrink proportionally. This objection ignores the fact that this economy will be freed from two considerable burdens. Lower pollution will reduce the enormous volume of external diseconomies and costs now experienced. The expense of loans to 'developing' nations will disappear along with the goal of development. The costs of the welfare state will collapse since the massive social service budgets will disappear, because they will be rendered useless in the context of a return to economies of solidarity and proximity of a neo-medieval type.

Obviously, there could be another solution: keeping universalism and persuading rich countries to accept a lower standard of living and energy consumption in order to preserve the environment, share with poor countries, and pay for the industrialisation of 'emerging countries'. In this clever and logical perspective of the ecologists the solution would be more equality and not less.

This hypothesis, however, turns out to be totally idealistic and unworkable. Rationality has never had the upper hand in history. Can you imagine Americans voluntarily giving up their cars and agreeing to double their taxes to help the countries of the global South? In the scenario of the economic division of the Earth, large areas and fractions of the population *in the heart of the industrial countries of the global North* could well return to traditional economic ways of life with a low level of energy use and centred on a diversified rural subsistence economy.

A Non-Egalitarian Economy

We need to understand that, although techno-science has had devastating effects, this is because it is directed by egalitarian universalist progressivism and not because of faults that are intrinsic to it — quite the opposite of what traditionalists of the Right or dogmatic ecologists believe. Because the techno-scientific method has been extended beyond due measure and people have attributed to it an imaginary gift of miraculously bringing a crowd of benefits, some people today are disenchanted with it. *In reality, techno-science is, by nature, suited to concern only a minority of humanity.* It devours too much energy to be generalised.

Of course, there are good-hearted souls who will reproach these theses for extolling a generalised *exclusion*. This is yet another quasi-religious concept, born from reductionist ways of thinking, convinced that the present model of development is the morally legitimate one for everyone.

In reality, the 'exclusion' of neo-traditional societies from the techno-scientific sphere is part and parcel of the exclusion of the latter from the neo-traditional world. We need to abandon the prejudice that techno-scientific societies are 'developed' in comparison with traditional societies. This is the myth of the savage that is based on an implicit racism.

Neo-traditional communities would be, in the hypothesis of the preceding scenario, in no way seen as inferior or underdeveloped. They would live according to the rhythm of another civilisation and perhaps live better than today. The entire Western intelligentsia is characterised by an inability to rid itself of progressivist and egalitarian dogmas and paradigms, of even imagining other socio-economic solutions.

Pascal Bruckner,[7] for example, in an article in *Le Monde*, begins by recognising the disenchantment with and failures of technology and then admits the unintended consequences of extending technology to the entire Earth. He adds naïvely: 'Despite the hopes of the Eighteenth century, technological progress is never synonymous with moral progress. At least we have a guide for action, the democratic values inherited from the Enlightenment, values that are themselves

---

7   Pascal Bruckner (b. 1948) is a French writer who has been critical of multi-culturalism, and has accused Western Leftists of glorifying the Third World unjustly at the expense of their own civilization. Several of his books have been translated, such as *The Tyranny of Guilt: An Essay on Western Masochism* (2010).

secularised translations of the messianic beliefs of the Gospels and the
Bible.'

This pitiful recitation of talking points amounts to saying: to
oppose the bad consequences of technological progressivism, a
legacy of the Enlightenment, let us return … to the philosophy of
the Enlightenment! What ideological imbecility! He does not grasp
that it is precisely the egalitarian progressivist universalism of the
Gospels, reinforced by the Protestant ethic and the philosophy of the
Enlightenment, which has expanded techno-science excessively and
massively with an unsustainable momentum like a runaway engine to
the entire Earth, instead of limiting it to certain areas.

Techno-Science as Esoteric Alchemy

Question: By predicting and extolling this socio-economic model, are
we not trying to make science and technology confidential, like al-
chemical formulas, restricted to a minority of humans who know how
to control them? Yes, exactly. *It is a question of removing techno-science
from the rationalist mentality* … and liberating it from the egalitarian
utopia that claims that it is suitable for all humanity.

In one scenario of the post-catastrophe era, when people will have
taken the measure of the dangers of the indefinite extension of science, technology and the industrial economy and the harmfulness of
uncontrolled exchange of information (excessive communication),
it would not be surprising if there were a return to an *initiatory and
almost esoteric vision* of techno-science, in order to preserve humanity
from the dangers of its viral, massive and uncontrolled excesses. This
techno-scientific civilisation is eminently risky, but intrinsically linked
to the spirit of certain peoples and human groups who are a minority
scattered over the Earth. The ideal would be for it to be attempted by
only a few and remain esoteric. Techno-science cannot be a mass or
'open' phenomenon. The planet rejects the hypothesis. Only 10 % to
20 % of humanity can lead this way of life. For some people there is

wisdom and the natural certainty of reproducing the species, cyclical time and the agrarian or tribal welfare of stable traditional societies. For others there are the temptations of a global and historicised world: for some, René Guénon;[8] for others, Nietzsche.

When the Worst Is Probable

Economic growth continues, in appearance, but it has a sickly hue. The world economic system is not sustainable, because it is based on the short-term and the myth of the unlimited maximisation of individual consumption. The economy of the Earth, which has now become a homogeneous and interdependent whole ('globalisation'), is experiencing an immense fragility and its collapse is predictable, because of several factors:

1) The exhaustion of fossil fuels, especially petroleum, but also natural gas, without speaking of the decline in agricultural and fishing resources. The world economy is still growing and using up the planet's natural resources at a rhythm four times higher than its capacities. We know the analogy: it would take four Earths to satisfy the frenzy of our current needs!

Developing nations, with their vast and continually multiplying populations, aspire to the economic level of the West, an aspiration that is politically comprehensible but physically impossible. We shall inevitably reach the breaking point.

2) The globalised economy has become purely speculative (the casino economy), having abandoned any idea of planning — even in Communist China, and that says it all! This lack of planning

---

8   René Guénon (1886–1951) was a French writer who founded what has come to be known as the traditionalist school of religious thought. Traditionalism calls for a rejection of the modern world and its philosophies in favour of a return to the spirituality and ways of living of the past (Guénon himself ended up living as a Sufi Muslim in Cairo). He outlines his attitude toward modernity in *The Crisis of theModern World*, which is available in English.

makes the economy fragile and dependent on the volatility and pusillanimity of the financial markets. Add to this the very dangerous phenomenon of the indebtedness of most of the world's states, which has become like a house of cards that is always being built higher with no realisation that it rests on nothing but a virtual reality. The bankruptcy that struck Argentina in 2003 will occur again, but on a gigantic scale. The factors that precipitated the crisis of 1929 are all present, but in a much more acute state.

3) As we have seen, a massive recession in the European economy is very likely from 2010. Because Europe is a central economic player in the world economy, this catastrophic event will have consequences that will worsen other factors contributing to the coming collapse.

4) One can also foresee a generalised economic war provoked by the exhaustion of resources. There could soon be wars for petroleum, water, agricultural and fishing resources; conflicts over access to the markets of the developed world; incompatibility between the economic egoisms of the global North and the needs (or dreams) of the South, and so on. The present myth of generalised growth is incompatible with conflicts where politics interferes with the economy. Commercial competition is positive if it does not pass a certain threshold of hysteria and stress. Beyond that, confidence erodes and markets and investors back off, when the situation becomes too hostile. This situation awaits us.

***

Let us also mention the paralysing effects on the world economy of the catastrophes described earlier, as for example the conflicts involving Islam, the rise of giga-terrorism, the explosion of mafias that intrude into every sphere, and so forth. It is known that stock exchanges and investment levels are extremely sensitive to the slightest quiver in the economic or political situation. The attacks of 11 September 2001 — which was only a pinprick in the edifice of the Western system — caused global growth to lose several points. Imagine what would have happened if an event one hundred times worse had occurred, and that could well take place ...

This globalised economy, on which the entire framework of the present worldwide civilisation rests, is a giant with feet of clay. Its fragility comes from the fact that it no longer recognises any partition, any frontier. By choosing the paradigm of a single economic space — according to free trade dogma — that stretches over the entire Earth, it has made a serious mistake. It should have opted for a general model of *economic spaces* that are relatively watertight, semi-autarchic, according to a continental logic, each of which develops at its own rhythm.

For interdependence is synonymous with fragility. But ideology has obscured and neglected the facts (the ideology of 'development', of 'progress' interpreted in a quantitative and material sense, the ideology of international free trade present in liberal capitalism as well as Communism). The fault lies with this aberrant notion of a *unified humanity* that informs all the ideologies, from ultra-liberal to anti-globalist.

The End of 'Growth'

'Growth' today is very superficial and will be ephemeral for the following reasons, which portend the possibility of a general collapse. What are they?

1) The fragility of the stock market economy. The present globalised economy is based, even more than in the 1920s, on the speculative fragility of international stock market frenzy, which is completely unreal. The Dow Jones, the Nikkei and the CAC 40[9] direct the

---

9   The Nikkei is the Japanese stock market index; the CAC 40 is the French one.

world economy with an extremely short-term vision, in a day-to-day speculative spiral (because of the lure of immediate gain from sudden panic or euphoria), while politicians have abdicated their economic responsibilities and long-term realities are neglected.

At the slightest bad rumour, speculative investment, business' motor, can collapse. We have already had a warning shot with the 'Asian crisis' of the 1990s.[10] Frédérique Leroux writes in *Le Figaro Économie* (20 March 2004): 'With the least grain of sand in the cogs the virtuous machine stops and goes into reverse.' It is the 'butterfly effect', as in meteorology: a chain of minor events provoking panic in investors. A speculative and globalised economy is a giant with feed of clay. Leroux writes, 'In the ephemeral nirvanas of the economy and the stock markets, the smallest change of fashion turns irrational exuberance into anorexic depression. … We are today at the same critical point of the long economic cycle where the securities market, that versatile entity we have abandoned ourselves to, is in charge of the economy.'

'Growth' or control over the economic fundamentals totally escapes governments and the political sector. This growth is in the hands of the pure psychological chance of speculation, which depends on euphoric states or irrational depressions. It is significant, however, that Europe (unlike the USA) no longer has a monetary policy, which depends now formally on the European Central Bank in Frankfort, that is, in reality on the caprices of the short-term market, a situation unknown in history. Based completely on speculation, the so-called 'new economy' is only an exaggerated form of finance capitalism, made still more fluid by the Internet.

---

10 The Asian Financial Crisis began in July 1997 in Thailand when the government, faced with bankruptcy due to its massive foreign debt, switched the national currency from a fixed to a floating exchange rate, causing its collapse. The crisis then spread throughout Asia, resulting in massive inflation which continued to affect many nations until the end of 1998. Indonesia was particularly impacted, culminating in widespread rioting and the resignation of President Suharto.

2) The exponential growth of world indebtedness, public and private. All the world's countries, rich and poor, are in debt. There is talk of cancelling the debt of the Third World. Who is going to pay for this, at the end of the day? The world's economy resembles a business on the edge of bankruptcy but still maintained, in euphoria, by a virtual banker. The bulletin of the Prigest society of investment banking (July 2000), which can hardly be suspected of anticapitalism, notes: 'Private debt is increasing at an uncontrolled rate. It has become the transmission belt of a "vertical" circularity between the increase in stocks and economic inactivity. It makes the system fragile while giving the impression of strengthening it by the increase in growth that it still permits.' The report also speaks of the 'irrational exuberance' of this 'new economy', which is surfing on the edge of the abyss. A world economy cannot last very long when it is based on indebtedness (monetarist dogma) and no longer on work and the estimates of serious extra-economic parameters (demography, ecology, energy, etc.).

3) The demographic ageing of Europe and other leading industrial countries is multiplied by the economic burden of immigration. For the time being, we can still hold out, but this will not last. The lack of active workers, the burden of retirees and the expenses of healthcare will end, from 2005–2010, with burdening European economies with debt. Gains in productivity and technological advances (the famous 'primitive accumulation of fixed capital', the economists' magic cure) will never be able to match the external demographic costs. Lastly, far from compensating for the losses of the working-age native-born population, the colonising immigration Europe is experiencing involves first of all welfare recipients and unskilled workers. In addition, this immigration represents a growing expense (insecurity, the criminal economy, urban policies, etc.). An economic collapse of Europe, the world's leading commercial power, would drag down with it the United States and the entire Western economy.

4) Contempt for ecological limits. The planetary development of the mass industrial economy (which ecologists do nothing to fight against, impostors in fealty to the kings of petroleum) has generated enormous pollution that is already beginning to make its effects felt and is only going to get worse: climate catastrophes (which have increased 290 % between 1970 and 1999 according to the insurance companies), exhaustion of reserves of ocean fish, increase of desert areas and shrinking of fresh water reserves, destruction of forest cover and the marine phytoplankton that renews oxygen. And so on.

To summarise, in spite of the infantile euphoria provoked by the 'new economy', the expansion of the Internet and the purely situational short-term and fleeting acceleration observed for some years, the fundamentals of the world economy are flashing warning signals and we are probably headed towards an enormous planetary economic crisis at the start of the Twenty-first century. This civilisation, entirely based on exalting the market society, affirming financial values as the only true ones and privileging absolutely the economy (under its socialist and capitalist forms), may well perish because of the crisis of the activity it has installed in the heart of the world. The economy will collapse precisely because it was placed in the centre of everything, because everything has to rest on it before crushing it.

This society will perish exactly as a society based on strict militarism perishes, as a result of the unnecessary wars it provokes and then ends up losing. It is always those who know the economy well (Maurice Allais, François Perroux) who warn against the idolatry of the economy, and military men who warn enthusiastic civilians against militarism.

The structural factors (especially demography and ecology) are never taken into account in a world fascinated by immediate results that can be computed in the very short term. The apostles of the 'new economy' are only infants disguised as experts. The new world economic order these pusillanimous false prophets hope for is only the swan song of the old order.

Economism Is Condemned

For the first time since the beginning of its history, humanity is using more resources and energy on the Earth's surface than the Earth can provide. The Earth's 'capital' is being whittled away, like a man living on his investments who, when the interest on his capital no longer give him enough, begins to make a dent in his savings. Ruin is logically at the end of the procedure.

Planète Vivante 2002, the report of the WWF (World Wide Fund for Nature), is extremely alarmist: the Earth will soon no longer be able to produce enough for the growing needs and productive rhythms of a humanity expanding demographically and technologically. Humanity's 'bio-ecological imprint' (the surface necessary to produce resources and absorb waste products) surpasses the capacities of the planet for a continually growing number of areas. In 2002, already 20 % more than the Earth can give us is being exploited.

Here are some examples. The Earth possesses 11.4 billion productive areas on land and sea, or 1.9 hectares a person. The 'bio-ecological imprint' (productive area under use) for each American is 9.6 hectares, 5 hectares for each European and 1.4 hectares for an inhabitant of the Third World. All these statistics keep on getting worse, however, all the way to the coming breaking point. For example, the bio-ecological imprint of France has grown by 47 % since 1960, while the population has only grown by 27 %. Feryel Gadhoum comments in *Le Figaro Économie* (5 December 2002): 'The ecological imprint of the Hexagon increased in 1999 to 309.9 million hectares while its biological capacity was only 169.5 million hectares. In other words, if everyone lived like the French, we would need more than two planets and if we consumed like the Americans, we would need more than five planets.'

The official objective of Western (and world) civilisation is for all humanity to reach the level of consumption of rich countries, a situation ecologically and physically impossible. The WWF estimates that the situation is only going to get worse. Because of the planet's demographic growth — which will continue until about 2060 — and its technological and economic 'development', the WWF report predicts that 'humanity's bio-ecological imprint is capable of reaching 180 % to 220 % of the Earth's biological capacity by 2050.'

In other words, if demographic and economic development continues at this rhythm, the Earth, emptied of its resources and ecologically ravaged, will no longer be able to supply humanity. The famous 'development' will collapse by itself. To avoid this catastrophe scenario, the experts and sages of the WWF propose three measures: 1) produce more economically and pollute less; 2) stop demographic growth; 3) world governments should agree to preserve the ecosystem and modify from top to bottom the current logic of the world economy that is sending us full speed ahead towards disaster, like a runaway horse or an airplane without a pilot.

***

Dreaming is useless. There will be no international agreement to stop the infernal machine and change the process of economic development. Egoism and pusillanimity will always prevail, as we saw at the Rio and Kyoto summits. The USA does not want to listen to talk about the environment (since they believe in the right to pollute and consume, as well as the infallible logic of the short-term goal) and the Third World is not ready to make sacrifices for the rest of the world.

So let us not delude ourselves. The solution of this unsolvable equation will be catastrophe, that is, the violent 'adjustment variable', which will automatically aim at humanity and not at Nature. Let us use an image. Man is asking too much from nature that cannot be supplied. But nature (the Earth's ecosystem) is much more powerful and enduring than the fragile human species. So it is up to the human species to lower its pretentions or disappear. By overexploiting the Earth's natural resources, humanity is not putting nature at risk, but nature's provisional capacity to nourish humanity. Humanity is putting itself at risk. It is highly unlikely that in 2050 nine billion people can live in a civilisation of economic development and growth as we do today. No massive technological progress can be seen on the horizon that will lower the burden of the energy, farming and fishing levies on the capital of the Earth. The ecosystem in itself is in no way threatened. The Earth still has 4 billion years before it and can regenerate all its forces — without mankind! — thanks to the chemistry of carbon, oxygen and hydrogen. A ravaged ecosystem will regenerate itself very rapidly, that is, in less than 100,000 years.

***

Let us talk again about the famous 'adjustment variable'. The unsolvable equation we discussed earlier can be solved only by two spontaneous and automatic phenomena, which will escape every human will and every constructivist utopia: 1) a drastic reduction of the number of people on Earth; 2) the end of the worldwide techno-consumerist civilisation based on a high degree of bio-energy usage.

The terrestrial ecosystem's inability to meet humanity's demands in the Twenty-first century will end in shortages and so will lead to crises, conflicts, famines, wars, epidemics, etc. The human population could automatically in one or two decades be reduced by 50 % to 75 %. Today's techno-industrial civilisation could collapse and no longer survive and perform except in very limited areas, while most humans would return to a way of life like that of the upper Neolithic Age. This scenario is more plausible than pursuing 'development' and 'progress' *ad infinitum*, the materialist version of the dreams of salvation religions.

The Fraud of the 'New Economy'

Everyone talks about the 'new economy', the economy of multimedia telecommunications and computer services based on the Internet, which is supposed to begin a second Golden Age. This magical concept is the occasion for smug optimists to repeat old progressivist and scientistic illusions. It is, however, a question of a fraud by neo-liberal circles, a scarecrow of more than one modernity in decline, for the 'new economy' could well end in disaster.

In reality, the Internet and the 'new technologies' introduced no 'revolution', but a simple evolution and perhaps an even bigger fragility. The real 'new economy' (based on the globalisation of exchanges, techno-science and instantaneous communications) is more than a century old.

'Online' sales on the Internet are only an improvement of the old mail order catalogues, which were introduced in … 1850; they do not represent a *structural change*. Similarly, the Internet, multimedia cell phones, cable television, smartcards and the general computerisation of society — even genetic engineering — do not represent structural changes. They are all only developments of what already existed. There is nothing in all this to compare with inventions that really turned the world upside down, the real techno-economic metamorphoses introduced between 1860 and 1960 that revolutionised society and the framework of life: internal combustion engines, electricity, the telephone, telegraph, radio (which was more revolutionary than television), trains, cars, airplanes, penicillin, antibiotics, etc. The 'new economy' is behind us! No fundamental innovation has taken place since 1960. Computers only allow us to accomplish differently, faster and more cheaply (but with much great fragility) what was already being done. On the other hand, the automobile, antibiotics, telecommunications and air travel were authentic revolutions that made possible what before had been impossible.

This is one more reason not to succumb to the siren song of this 'new economy' that is supposed to ensure the end of economic crises, while it is in fact well on the way to produce the exact opposite. Let us cite the judgment of the economist Frédérique Leroux, who criticises the 'new economy's' fashionable economic optimism and mirages: 'The dominant thought of market economists lacks breath and inspiration. Under the yoke of the prevailing conformism it has abandoned its iconoclastic dimension. ... Linear projection has thus become the authoritative predictive tool. ... Every moment we are getting closer to the zero degree of economic thought.'

While criticising the fascination of those who imagine that the Internet and start-ups are going to inaugurate a new era without recessions and without business cycles, she notes, 'We are not sure if the expression "new economy" designates new technologies or a new mode of economic functioning (perpetual growth without inflation as opposed to alternating phases of growth and recession). In either case it suits everyone, since it allows them all to speak with expert enthusiasm of what they have, however, renounced understanding.' The 'new economy' is only a phrase that refers to no concrete reality, neo-liberalism's ideological ruse. Leroux writes, the 'new economy' is an expression that serves to allow us to pardon our renunciation of any effort of economic conceptualisation in favour of non-reflection. It is the marketing slogan of those who have opted for complacency out of intellectual frustration, ignorance, conformity, sloth or chance' (*Le Figaro*, 24 July 2000).

Like Francis Fukuyama with his idea of 'The End of History' (after the fall of Communism with the concomitant belief in a planet unified by a universal liberal capitalism finally freed from political conflicts), the apostles of the 'new economy' want to make us believe that we have entered a miraculous period of perpetual growth, without crises and without recession.

Thanks to the Internet, start-ups, computer jobs, globalisation, etc., they imagine that the economy will avoid large-scale crises. These are religious — soteriological — visions of the economy, disguised by pseudo-scientific language. The 'economic cycle', however, always exists, for the root of the economy is human, purely psychological and not 'technological'. Euphoria is always followed by panic and despair.

**

Many factors seem to proclaim that we are experiencing the end of a cycle of illusory growth and are on the edge of an economic catastrophe much worse than the crisis of 1929, because the world economy is more fragile, more globalised, and even more speculative than then. It is the logic of the house of cards or falling dominoes. We are not at all in a 'new era without norms', as the sorcerer's apprentices of transnational neo-liberalism would have us believe. Already in the 1920s, a magnificent period of growth without inflation, it was thought that the new technologies (the automobile, radio, airplane, telephone, electricity, etc.) were going to abolish definitively crises and recessions. We saw what came of that … October 1929 and its aftermath is infamous precisely because that crisis was an important factor in the unleashing of the war. Today we are succumbing to the same *belief in miracles* with computers and the 'new economy'.

The Dangerous Fragility of Globalised Liberal Capitalism

In the United States, we see the bankruptcies of Enron and WorldCom (with their fraudulent exaggeration of profits and assets), then the filings for bankruptcy of United Airlines (America's second-largest airline company), unable to pay back $875 million of debt, and US Airways (America's seventh largest airline). AOL Time Warner, number one worldwide in media and Internet services, is accused of have improperly swollen its income figures by $49 million to reassure the markets. IBM was obliged to fire 15,600 employees in the first half of 2004, or 5 % of its workers. In Europe, the unusual French company

Vivendi Universal, the world's second largest telecommunications company, lost 12.3 billion euros from January to July 2003 and was forced to fire 30 % of its workers while its stocks lost 70 % of their value since December 2000. Crédit Suisse, the second largest Swiss bank, has lost 396 million euros ... The list is long, very long. *The Christian Science Monitor* (3 July 2002) estimates that 25 % of American firms deliberately misrepresent their profits in their annual reports in order to deceive their stockholders.

Ultra-liberal and free market economists explain to us that all this news does not portend a giant crisis of the globalised capitalist economy, but are simply the up and downs of the market; most firms with worldwide economic holdings are in good shape. Really? There are two worrying phenomena: 1) Some very large and successful businesses (British Airways, for instance) could change in a year from profits to colossal losses; 2) Highly localised events (like the 11 September 2001, attacks or a regional war that could break out anywhere tomorrow) are enough to shake the world economy and provoke disasters for ruined investors or fired workers.

This *fragility* of free-market ultra-liberalism — perfectly capable of provoking a worldwide economic collapse — is not a characteristic of the 'market economy' in itself, but of a purely speculative financial system based on short-term gambling on the stock market. The majority of large businesses are not 'enterprises', but in reality *casinos*, run on a day-to-day basis by overpaid administrators, who are media savvy and sit in ejection seats. The present speculative economy is no longer based on the logic of the 'vocation' (a product is made or a service performed), but on the aberrant American logic of the *holding* (participle of the verb 'to hold', to have in one's hands). Groups like Vivendi Universal or Bouygues can unite activities with no necessary connection (for example, the distribution of water, television, multimedia, publishing, public works, etc.) into what amounts to a banking system. It is worth remarking that the most successful firms are those that stick to their *métier*[11] and are the least dependent on the stock exchange: Michelin (tires), L'Oréal (cosmetics), Arianespace (rockets), Teisseire (syrups), etc.

The objective of business is no longer productive industrial activity, but the immediate profit of stockholders, whether small investors or big speculators. In these conditions foresight, wisdom in anticipating the future, management, even in the middle term, are no longer possible. Everything can collapse at the slightest breeze, like a row of dominoes.

***

The world economy should be based on completely different foundations, certainly not on the utopias of the 'anti-globalists' of the Left. The market is a good thing, provided it is accompanied by the following correctives: 1) limitations on anonymous market capitalisation by big business; 2) the development of financing by saving at fixed rates to the detriment of stockholders; 3) the obligation of every business of significant size, including 'private' ones, to submit to government intervention; 4) limitation of the free market (merchandise, workforce, capital) in favour of creating self-centred, semi-autarchic and politically organised continental zones.

These are the principles of a 'third way' economy, which in addition also rejects paralysing business with heavy taxation and socialism. These principles have been defended by the two greatest French economists, François Perroux and Maurice Allais. This is the political economy of entrepreneurial capitalism, which is the complete opposite of the present speculative and globalist liberalism. People's minds are not prepared today for this 'third way'. Only a giant crisis and a collapse of the present system will permit such an evolution.

---

11   French: 'calling', as in a trade.

Some Small but Worrying Signals

The troubling economic predictions of Robert J. Samuelson[12] are little-known in France. This heterodox American economist is launching an important debate in the United States, which has been reported in the British, German, Spanish and Italian press. Not a word of all this, however, has appeared in the French press. French journalists, who understand no foreign languages, are concerned only with French (or Arabic or North African) gossip. Samuelson has developed this theory in an article in *Newsweek*,[13] where he wrote that the economic and political behaviour of the United States could end in a world crisis worse than the depression of the 1930s: 'The global trading system is in trouble — mainly because it became overdependent on big U.S. trade deficits. From 1996 to 2002, the American trade deficit jumped from $191 billion to $485 billion. We Americans are buying vast amounts of foreign-made pots and pans, cars, CD and DVD players, bicycles, clocks, umbrellas, socks and shoes. In 1996, the United States imported $1.31 of goods for every $1 it exported; now, the import figure is approaching $2 (it's $1.79 so far in 2003).' For Samuelson this contradiction, between what claims to be an 'imperial' world superpower (strategically and militarily) and a speculative economy in deficit, can only end in catastrophe.

***

In the *International Herald Tribune*,[14] economist Thomas L. Friedman[15] emphasises the growing economic dependence of the United States on China and Japan: 'As we and our government continue to spend and

12 Robert Jacob Samuelson (b. 1945) has been an economic columnist for *The Washington Post* since 1977.

13 Robert J. Samuelson, 'A Crackup for World Trade?' in *Newsweek* (25 August 2003).

14 Thomas J. Friedman, 'Read My Lips' in *The New York Times* (11 June 2003).

15 Thomas Friedman (b. 1953) has written for *The New York Times* since 1981 and as a columnist since 1995. He is known for his strongly pro-American and

invest more than we save, we will become even more dependent on the outside world to finance the gap.' Friedman explains that foreigners are taking greater control over US businesses and have become the creditor of the state. 'And do you know on whom we'll be most dependent for that? China and Japan. Yes, that China — the one the Bush team says is our biggest geopolitical rival.' Not only do China and Japan finance the private sector, but, a more serious matter, according to financial analyst Robert Hormats, 'Now, with these looming deficits, China and Japan are being asked to finance our government's actual operations.' These facts imply a growing economic dependence on China and Japan and therefore a strategic dependence on China, which, in the next two decades, could become the leading economic power in the world.

***

The worldwide infatuation with the Internet will perhaps turn out to be only a flash in the pan. The idolators of a technology always forget that it is inherently fragile. The Internet is already running up against two major problems: 1) the exponential proliferation of Web sites, which are surpassing the capacities of search engines and is ending by 'drowning' information; 2) the doubtful reliability of this information. But there is a third problem, the proliferation of viruses.

The British daily *Metro* (10 December 2001) published the following analysis under the title, 'Viruses Could Lead to the Death of the Internet': 'One expert in computer security estimates that e-mail and the Internet could disappear if viruses continue to proliferate at the current rate. In 2001 viruses that infect e-mails involved 1 % of postings, as opposed to only 1 in 1,400 in 1999. In 2008 we are on the verge of reaching the figure of 10 %, which will make e-mails inoperative. Alex Shipp, an anti-virus technician from the business MessageLabs,

---

pro-Israeli stances in the Middle East, and for his belief that national governments will eventually have to give up some of their sovereignty as part of globalisation.

told us, "servers are already overloaded and neutralised by viruses that propagate themselves. They can perhaps totally paralyse the Internet.'"

The Spectre of Poverty

The fact is overwhelming. Nothing is stopping the increase of poverty in the world and the gap between rich and poor. Despite the objectives solemnly proclaimed at the Millennium Conference to reduce poverty by half by 2015, UNCTAD (United Nations Conference on Trade and Development), in its annual report for 2003 on less-developed countries (LDCs) predicts that, on the contrary, by 2015, 420 million persons, that is, many more poor people than today, will be living on less than a dollar a day.

The trend is depressing. Poverty has doubled in the course of the past thirty years and today involves 307 million persons. The gap reaches its nadir with Africa, which contains 34 of the 49 poorest countries in the world. The proportion of the African population living below the poverty threshold has passed from 56 % to 65 % in recent years. UN Secretary-General Kofi Annan told the conference, 'The gap between rich and poor countries is growing, despite numerous efforts to help developing countries to have access to new technologies and integrate into the world economy.'

It is useless to indulge in wishful thinking. All efforts will continue to be in vain. The procedure called the 'HIPC initiative',[16] the treatment of the debts of the most indebted poor countries, has been a complete failure, according to Habib Ouane, UNCTAD spokesman. The debt reduction so dear to Jacques Chirac has not worked, since all the current mechanisms of the world economy are vitiated. No one seems to understand that the cause of the current disaster is the absurd

---

16 The Heavily Indebted Poor Countries initiative was begun by the International Monetary Fund in 1996, providing debt relief, low-interest loans from the World Bank, and assisting with the cancellation of debt payments for those countries whose debt is deemed unsustainable. As of 2024, there were 39 designated HIPCs.

idea of a single globalised model of 'development' in the framework
of free trade and a single type of consumer techno-scientific society
extended over the entire planet.

This growing poverty of one part of humanity is only going to
accelerate, because economic disjunctions are going to be joined
by ecological disorders and epidemics in growing intensity. Radical
Islamism (which prospers among poor people) and the pressure of
migration into the North will be only encouraged by the problem of
world poverty.

***

What is the situation of poverty in the world and what causes it? World
poverty has doubled in thirty years! The myth of 'progress' is taking
another punch on the jaw. Despite the solemn commitments of the
United Nations to reduce poverty by half by 2015, the most recent
annual report from UNCTAD on LDCs predicts that, in 2015, 420
million persons will be living on less than a dollar a day. This statistic
is a reality today for 307 million persons. Africa is most affected and
getting poorer every day, including 34 of the 49 most impoverished
countries in the world (despite its enormous natural resources). Since
1990, the proportion of its inhabitants living below the poverty line has
passed from 56 % to 65 %. UN Secretary-General Kofi Annan told the
conference, 'Despite numerous efforts to help developing countries to
have access to new technologies and integrate into the world economy,
the gap between rich and poor countries is growing.' Habib Ouane,
spokesman for UNCTAD, has no solution except this disillusioned
truism: 'We must replace the strategy of debt reduction with a strategy
of economic development.' In other words, rather than helping underdeveloped countries, they must develop themselves. Yes, of course,
provided that they are capable of doing so …

For example, the LDCs cannot process the raw materials they
produce. Mali produces 500,000 tons of cotton a year and processes
only 1 % of it. UNCTAD notes that some thirty countries that have

benefitted from HIPC have seen their debt increase! Obviously, as soon as their debt is cancelled, they contract more debt, *ad infinitum*. According to UNCTAD, 87.5 % of the inhabitants of the 34 LDCs in Africa live on less than 2 dollars a day, as do 68.2 % of the Asian LDCs. What has caused this poverty that has obviously provoked mass immigration into Europe? Ultra-liberalism? Shameless exploitation of the Third World by the global North? Not really. There is a reasonable argument that these peoples can never adapt themselves to the industrial model that was mistakenly imposed on them. Third World poverty is the product of Western globalism and its utopia of extending the norms of its civilisation to peoples that were simply not made for them. In the past, in their rural and pastoral societies, with a small population, they could fend for themselves and live in a prosperity adapted to their way of life determined by natural rhythms. But, following the demographic explosion provoked by Western medicine that suddenly lowered infant mortality, they find themselves in no position to produce enough to feed themselves and enrich their excessive population or fit into the new situation. The example of Africa is emblematic. Despite its enormous natural resources, Africa is ravaged by famines (today from Angola to Mozambique by way of Zimbabwe) that are not caused by 'droughts', as the media keep saying, but by incessant tribal wars of an appalling barbarism. It is the Africans who are primarily responsible. There is not much Africa can do. Despite the still existing colonial infrastructures, despite more than forty years of foreign aid, improved education, technology transfers and investments from countries of the global North, Africa continues to sink, with its only hope being emigration to Europe. Everyone in international institutions knows this, but no one dares to say it. The equation is unsolvable, but it will solve itself. And it is going to hurt.

Cancelling the Debts of Poor Countries Is a Farce

It is time to stop sending foreign aid to the Third World. The latest fad is cancelling the debt of poor countries. Pseudo-humanitarian Third Worldism strikes again. It is a real tearjerker. Monsignor Lustiger[17] proclaimed in *JDD* (23 April 2000): 'The Pope has taken up a command from the *Bible*: he asked for the cancellation of the debts of the poor countries. Economists have raised serious technical objections. Economics is not practiced with good sentiments!' The progressivist Catholic association, Jubilee 2000, after having received, they say, 17 million signatures, thundered, 'Thirteen babies die every minute from the consequences of debt.'

After Algerian President Bouteflika[18] travelled to France, where he played the role of an aggressive beggar, the French government offered to cancel 400 million francs in debt in exchange for investments in Algeria. President Bouteflika was not satisfied, however. He demanded the unilateral cancellation of the entire debt.

French President Jacques Chirac declared in Cairo that it was right to cancel as much as 195 billion francs of debt in addition to the 500 billion francs planned by the 1999 G8 summit at Cologne. After Pope John Paul II, the rock star Bono and the former boxer Mohammed Ali, all of them well known as important economists, picked up the slack of this enthusiasm for charity. Nigeria, for instance, spends, according to the official ideology, five times more to pay interest on its debts than it spends to educate its children. Even without its heavy debts, however, would Nigeria be able to educate its children? The millionaire Bernard Pinaud has launched a publicity campaign: 'For the year 2000, let us cancel the debt!' And everyone joins in this stupid demagogy.

---

17   Jean-Marie Lustiger (1926–2007) was Archbishop of Paris from 1981 until he resigned in 2005.

18   Abdelaziz Bouteflika (1937–2021) served as President of Algeria from 1999 until his resignation in 2019.

In fact, the explanation is simple: It is squaring, or rather the logic of the vicious circle. HIPCs (heavily indebted poor countries) ask for reductions or cancellations of their bilateral debts (loans from state to state, 56 %), multilateral debts (from the IMF or the World Bank, 26 %) or private commercial debts (16 %), so they can apply for new loans and subventions! Later they will demand the 'moral' right not to pay them back.

We are encouraging a large number of Third World countries to live as permanent welfare recipients, just like the immigrant populations in Europe. Are we really helping them? No, we are doing them a disservice. And we are showing contempt for them. When we cancel their debts, we are considering them 'underdeveloped and therefore under-competent.'[19] Basically, cancelling Third World debt is sort of racist. It is treating them as congenital incompetents. How long are taxpayers, workers, entrepreneurs of the northern hemisphere going to put up with financing at a loss (in order to obtain a relative peace) the southern hemisphere, and especially Africa?

Let us tell the truth. The 'poor countries' are poor because they have chosen to be poor and not because they are exploited. These lands have often been blessed with enormous natural resources. Wealth, however, is created by hard work and not by begging. Let the 'poor countries' take the responsibility for their destiny into their own hands. After all, what debts did the IMF or the World Bank cancel that allowed the Dutch, the British or the Germans to become rich countries?

We also need to do away with stupid theories of 'colonial and post-colonial exploitation' of poor states. We have had enough ethno-masochism. We keep hearing that they are 'great civilisations'. Let them prove it! Are they not really history's eternally handicapped people? Enough charitable exaggeration of our faults and a little more responsibility! The peoples of the Third World represent for us a growing economic and ethnic burden. It began with the stupid colonialist

---

19   This phrase was coined in *Europe-Action*, a journal edited by Dominique Venner in the 1960s.

enterprise of the Nineteenth century, which certainly cost us more than we received.

We face another problem, but very few people are thinking seriously about it. Are all these 'poor' countries culturally in any condition to participate in an industrial economy? Probably not. Would it not be a better solution for these countries to return to their ancestral traditional subsistence societies? The great future world crisis that is forming, the convergence of catastrophes, will bring, perhaps with suffering, the true solution in the course of this new century: a two-tier world economy on a planetary scale.

CONCLUSION

A NEW MIDDLE AGES

For the first time in its history mankind is threatened by a convergence of catastrophes.

A series of 'dramatic lines' are approaching one another and converging like a river's tributaries, with perfect accord (between 2010
and 2020) towards a breaking point and a descent into chaos. From
this chaos — which will be extremely painful on the world scale — can
emerge a new order based on a worldview, Archeofuturism, conceived
as *the post-catastrophic age's conception-of-the-world*.[1]

Let us briefly summarise the nature of these lines of catastrophe:

1) The first is the cancerisation of the European social fabric. The
colonising of the Northern hemisphere by the peoples of the South
for purposes of settlement, which is increasingly serious despite
the reassuring commentary of the media, is pregnant with explosive situations, especially those connected with the collapse of
the Christian churches in Europe, which has become a land Islam
plans to conquer; the failure of the multiracial society, which is

---

1   Faye defines conception-of-the-world in *Why We Fight* as: 'The ensemble of values and interpretations of reality — implicitly or explicitly distinct to a specific
human group — whether a people, a civilisation, a family of thought, political
or not, a religion, etc.' From Guillaume Faye, *Why We Fight: Manifesto of the
European Resistance* (London: Arktos, 2011), p. 99.

becoming increasingly multi-racist and neo-tribal; the progressive ethnic and anthropological metamorphosis of Europe, which
is a true historic cataclysm; the return of poverty to Western and
Eastern Europe; the slow but constant growth in criminal activity
and drug use; the continual erosion of family structures; the decline of the educational infrastructure and the quality of academic
programs; jamming the transmission of cultural knowledge and
social disciplines (*barbarisation* and loss of skills); the disappearance of popular culture due to the degradation of the masses, who
have been made passive by *electro-audiovisual media* (Guy Debord
committed suicide because he had seen the future too clearly in
The Society of the Spectacle, published in 1967);[2] the continual decline of the urban and communitarian fabric in favour of sprawl-
ing suburban zones lacking transparency, coherence, legality and
safety; the installation, especially in France, of an endemic situation of urban rioting — a low-key May '68[3] but more dangerous;
the disappearance of all civil authority in the lands of the former
USSR beset by economic decline. All this is taking place at a moment when nation-states see their sovereign authority decline and
have no success in halting poverty, unemployment, crime, illegal
immigration, the rising power of mafias and the corruption of the
political classes; just when our creative and productive elites are
tempted by the great journey to America. An increasingly egotisti-
cal and savage society on the road to primitivism, but paradoxically disguised and offset by naïve and pseudo-humanist talk of the

---

2   English translation: Guy Debord, *The Society of the Spectacle* (New York: Zone
    Books, 1994).

3   In May 1968, a series of strikes by radical left-wing student groups in Paris were
    joined by a strike of the majority of the French work-force, shutting down France
    and nearly bringing down the government of Charles de Gaulle. Although the
    strikes ended in failure and had evaporated by July, they are still seen as the
    decisive moment when traditional French society was forced to give way to the
    more liberal attitude that has come to define France in subsequent years.

'unique morality', becomes clearer year after year until it reaches the breaking point.

2) But these factors of social breakdown in Europe will be aggravated by economic and demographic crises that are only getting worse. By 2010, the number of active workers will be insufficient to finance the retirements of the 'grandpa boom'. Europe will collapse under the weight of old people. Ageing countries will see their economies slowed down and handicapped by financing healthcare and retirement expenses for unproductive citizens. In addition, ageing will dry up technological and economic dynamism. The egalitarian ideology of the (old) modernity has been unable to remedy this situation, because of two dogmas: first the anti-natalism (this *ethnomasochism*) that has censured voluntary attempts to raise the birth rate; then the egalitarian refusal to move from the system of social security paid for out of each year's taxes to a system of capitalisation (pension funds). In short, we have not seen the worst. Unemployment and poverty will only get worse, while a small minority class will prosper because it is connected with world markets and supported by the class of bureaucrats and protected white-collar workers. We have a date with economic catastrophe. Egalitarianism, proving that it is the inverse of *justice* in the Platonic sense, is creating societies of socio-economic oppression by the law of unintended consequences. The social democratic welfare state, founded on the myth of Progress, will collapse just as surely as, but with a much louder crash than the Communist system. *Europe is becoming a Third World society.* We are facing a crisis, or rather the collapse of the socio-economic edifice that is taking the place of civilisation.

America, an immense continent devoted to pioneering migrations and used to a violent culture and a contentious system of ethnic and economic ghettoes, appears to be less vulnerable than Europe. Americans can put up with a breakdown of equilibrium, at least on the level of social stability, but it will not escape an eventual general maelstrom.

3) The chaos of the global South is modernity's third dramatic line of catastrophe. By industrialising against the grain of their traditional cultures, the countries of the global South, in spite of a deceptive and fragile growth, have created in their lands a social chaos that is going to get worse. The recent events in Indonesia are an omen. The Anglo-French businessman, Jimmy Goldsmith,[4] renouncing with perspicacity the way most businessmen think, has analysed it perfectly: emergence of gigantic mushrooming metropolises (Lagos, Mexico City, Rio de Janeiro, Calcutta, Kuala Lumpur ...) that become hellish jungles; coexistence of poverty that is one step from slavery with rich and insolent authoritarian bourgeois minorities supported by 'police armies' intended for internal repression; accelerated destruction of the environment; rise of socio-religious fanaticisms, etc. The countries of the global South are powder kegs. The recent genocides in central Africa, the increase in violent civil conflicts in India, Malaysia, Indonesia, Mexico, etc. (based or not on religious extremism and often stirred up by the United States) are only the foretaste of a dark future. The egalitarian ideology disguises this reality by congratulating itself on the 'progress of democracy' in the countries of the South. The talk is deceptive, since these are only sham democracies. Anyhow, is not 'democracy' of the Hellenic and European type pregnant with tragedies from unintended consequences (Jules Monnerot's[5]

---

4   Sir James Michael 'Jimmy' Goldsmith (1933–1997) was a magazine publisher, financier and politician who represented France in the European Parliament between 1994 until his death. He also founded the Referendum Party in the UK. He published a book, *The Trap* (London: Macmillan, 1994), in which he argued that global free trade, which results in widespread competition over cheap labour in the Third World, is a threat to worldwide social stability.

5   Jules Monnerot (1908–1995) was a French sociologist. He remains largely unknown in the English-speaking world.

heterotelia)⁶ and mental incompatibility, if forced upon the cultures of the South? In short, grafting the Western socio-economic model on the countries of the South has turned out to be explosive.

4) The fourth line of catastrophe, recently explained by Jacques Attali, is the threat of a worldwide financial crisis, which will be much more serious than the crisis of the 1930s and will bring on a general recession. The fall of the East Asian stock markets and currencies, like the recession striking this region, will be its harbinger. This financial crisis will have two causes: a) Too many countries are indebted in relation to the world's banking credit capacities, and not only poor countries. The cost of servicing the debt of European nations is troubling; b) The world's economy increasingly rests on speculation and the logic of the flow of profitable investments (stocks, fiduciary societies, international pension funds, etc.); this dominance of currency speculation over production runs the risk of causing a 'general panic' in the case of the collapse of currency rates in one sector. If international speculators withdraw credit, the world economy would end up 'dehydrated', with investments in free fall, because of the collapse of capital markets where industrial businesses and states borrow. The consequence will be a harsh global recession, a gloomy result for a civilisation that rests entirely on economic employment.

5) The fifth line of catastrophe is the rise of religious fanaticisms, principally but not exclusively Islamic, since Indian polytheists are part of the problem. The rise of radical Islam is the backlash to the excesses of the cosmopolitanism of modernity that wanted to impose on the entire world the model of atheist individualism, the cult of the market, the loss of spiritual values and the dictatorship of the spectacle. Reacting to this aggression, Islam has become

---

6 Faye defines *heterotelia* as '[t]he outcome and consequences of an action whose effects are radically contrary to its intended or proclaimed aim.' From Guillaume Faye, *Why We Fight*, p. 157.

radicalised, at the same time that it again became dominating and conqueror, in conformity to its tradition. More and more people practice it all over the world, just when Christianity is in decline, having lost its commitment to aggressive proselytism — even in South America and Black Africa — after the suicide of the Second Vatican Council,[7] the biggest theological blunder in the history of religions. In spite of the reassuring denials of the Western media, radical Islam is spreading everywhere like wildfire and threatens new countries: Morocco, Tunisia, Egypt, Turkey, Pakistan, Indonesia, and elsewhere. The consequences are the coming civil wars in bi-religious countries, like India, and confrontations in Europe — especially in France and Great Britain — where Islam is likely to become in twenty years the most practiced religion, and the multiplication of international crises involving Islamist states, some of which could possess 'dirty' nuclear weapons. In this regard, I must denounce the asininity of everyone who believes in the possibility of a 'Westernised Islam respectful of republican secularism'. It is impossible because Islam is consubstantially theocratic and repudiates the idea of secularism. Conflict seems inevitable, outside and inside Europe.

6) A confrontation between the global North and South, with ethnic and religious roots, is on the horizon. It is replacing and is much more probable than the risk, for the moment conjured away, of an East-West conflict. No one knows the form it will assume, but it will be serious, because it is founded on collective stakes and sentiments much stronger than the former bellicose polarity between the United States and the USSR, capitalism and Communism, which was artificial in nature. The powerful roots of this threat are, first of all, the tenacious *ressentiment*, inhibited and disguised,

---

7 The Second Vatican Council, or Vatican II, was convened in the 1960s in an effort to bring the doctrines of the Church more in tune with the problems of modern life. Many traditionalist Catholics regard it as a surrendering of the Church to secular pressures.

of the countries of the global South before their old colonisers. The *racialisation of discourse* is impressive. Recently an Asian Prime Minister called the French government 'racist', at the end of an ordinary economic dispute in which an Italian investor was chosen over a business from the Asian country. This racialisation of human relations, the concrete (but *heterotelic*) consequence of modernity's 'antiracist' cosmopolitanism, is obviously found in the West also. The American Black Muslim leader, Louis Farrakhan,[8] like rap groups in the United States and France (NTM, Ministère AMER, Doc'Gyneco, Black Military, etc.) never stops implicit calls for 'revenge against Whites' and civil disobedience. Egalitarian cosmopolitanism has paradoxically created *globalised racism*, which for the moment is under the surface and implicit, but not for long.

Crowded together, touching one another in the 'global village' the Earth has become, peoples are preparing to confront one another. And Europe, the victim of a colonisation aimed at settlement, may well be the principal battlefield. Those who claim that a general race mixing is the future of the world are mistaken: it is the rage only in Europe.

The other continents, principally Asia and Africa, are increasingly forming *impermeable ethnic blocs* that are exporting the surplus of their populations without importing others.

The chief point is that Islam is becoming the emblematic standard of this revolt against the global North, the Freudian revenge against 'Western imperialism'. This key idea is set up in the collective unconsciousness of the people of the South: 'Mosques are being established in Christian lands.' This is the old revenge for the Crusades, the *return of the archaic*, the return of history, like a boomerang. The essence of Islam, like that of medieval Christendom,

---

8   Louis Farrakhan (b. 1933) is the leader of the Nation of Islam, which is the most prominent Black supremacist organisation in the United States.

is *imperial theocratic totalitarianism.* As for those who reassure themselves with learned explanations that the Muslim countries are 'disunited', they should know that they are less disunited among themselves than united against a common foe, especially when emergencies arise.

This colonisation of the North by the South appears as a *soft colonialism*, without legal permission, relying on appeals to pity, asylum and equality. It is the 'fox's strategy' (as opposed to the lion's) noted by Machiavelli.[9] In reality, however, the coloniser, who justifies himself with the 'modern' Western ideology of his victim, whose values he pretends to adopt, does not share those values at all. He is anti-egalitarian, domineering (while claiming to be oppressed and persecuted), aiming at revenge and conquest. This is the clever ruse of a way of thinking that has remained archaic. To counter it, will it not be necessary to *become mentally archaic again* and rid ourselves of the demoralising handicap of 'modern' humanism?

Another foundation of the North-South conflict is a *global political and economic quarrel.* The conflict will be war for markets of scarce resources on the verge of exhaustion (drinking water, fishing resources, etc.), the rejection of anti-pollution quotas by the recently industrialised countries of the South, the needs of these countries to direct their surplus population to the North. In history, it is the simple patterns that stand out. A South that is full of complexes, poor, young, demographically prolific is putting pressure on a North that is unarmed and ageing.

---

9   In Chapter 18 of *The Prince,* Machiavelli writes: 'A prince, therefore, being compelled knowingly to adopt the beast, ought to choose the fox and the lion; because the lion cannot defend himself against snares and the fox cannot defend himself against wolves. Therefore, it is necessary to be a fox to discover the snares and a lion to terrify the wolves.' From the translation by W. K. Marriott (London: Dent, 1911), pp. 137–138.

And let us not forget that the South now possesses nuclear weapons while the pusillanimous North keeps talking about 'disarmament' and 'denuclearisation'.

7) The seventh line of catastrophe is the development of uncontrolled pollution over the planet, which is threatening not so much the Earth (which still has four billion years ahead of her and could start evolution over again from scratch), but the physical survival of humanity. The collapse of the environment is the fruit of the liberal-egalitarian (but once also Soviet) myth of universal industrial development and an energy-intensive economy for everyone. Fidel Castro, for once truly inspired, proclaimed in his speech to the World Health Organization (WHO) at Geneva (14 May 1998): 'The climate is changing, the oceans and the atmosphere are warmer, the air and waters are contaminated, the soils keep eroding, the desserts are expanding, the forests are dying, water is in short supply. Who will save our species? Perhaps the blind and uncontrollable market laws, the neo-liberalization going global, an economy growing by itself and for itself as a cancer devouring man and destroying nature? That cannot be the way, or it will only be for a very short period of history.' It could not be better expressed …

Castro, when he pronounced these prophetic words, must have been thinking of the irresponsible arrogance of the United States that refused to reduce their carbon dioxide emissions (at the summits of Rio and then Tokyo). But was this 'paradoxical Marxist' also thinking of the adhesion of every people to the profit model of a market which thinks entirely in the short term, and which encourages pollution, deforestation, the devastation of the oceans' fish reserves, the pillaging of fossil fuel and agricultural resources with no global planning? Without knowing it, Castro was appealing here, not to a Marxism as destructive as liberalism, but to the ancient *Platonic wisdom of justice.*

8) It is only right to add that the 'backdrop' of these seven converging catastrophic lines is saturated with aggravating factors, accelerators, so to speak. They include, in no particular order, destabilisation of the techno-economic systems by computers (the notorious Y2K bug); nuclear proliferation in the East (China, India, Pakistan, Iraq, Iran, Israel, Korea, Japan, etc.) by countries in intense rivalry with nervous and unpredictable reactions; the growing weakness of states faced with the power of mafias that control and expand the drug trade (both natural drugs and, increasingly, designer drugs), but also rely on new economic sectors that range from weapons to real estate including agribusiness; these international mafias, a recent UN report warns, are better armed than the international authorities that are trying to stop them. Let us not forget the return of old viral and microbial diseases. The myth of immunity from disease is disappearing. AIDS was the first breach. We are threatened, especially because antibiotics are becoming less effective and immigration is increasing, by the return of a worldwide health disorder. Recently, in Madagascar, fourteen cases of pulmonary plague could not be treated.

In short, is there not every reason to think that modernity is going to the wall and the *planetary accident* is irreversible? Maybe not, but then perhaps ... The essence of History, its motor, is it not the fuel of catastrophe? But now, for the first time, catastrophe could become global in a globalised world. Robert Ardrey, a brilliant American ethologist and dramatist, prophesised in 1973: 'The modern world is like a train full of ammunition running in the fog on a moonless night with its lights out.'

These impending catastrophes are the direct fruit of modernity's incorrigible belief in miracles. Let us think of the myth of the high standard of living possible for everyone on a global scale, and the generalisation of economies with a high energy consumption. The dominant paradigm of materialist egalitarianism — a society of 'democratic' consumption for ten billion people in the Twenty-first century *without* a generalised devastation of the environment — is a primitive utopia. This hallucination runs headlong into *physical impossibilities.* So the society that it has produced cannot last a long time. *The paradox of egalitarian materialism is that it is idealist and materially unrealisable* for reasons that are social (it deforms societies) and especially ecological. The Earth cannot physically support the general development of an economy with high energy use that is accessible to all humans. The 'progress of science' cannot meet the demands. It is not necessary to reject techno-science, but we do have to refocus it in a non-egalitarian perspective. We shall see this later ...

The problem, therefore, is not knowing *if* the planetary civilisation erected by egalitarian modernity is going to collapse, but *when.* We are therefore in a *state of emergency* (the *Ernstfall*[10] Carl Schmitt spoke of when he explained that liberal egalitarianism had never understood or made sense of this important notion, since it thinks of the world in a providential and miraculous manner, dominated by the rising line of progress and development). Modernity and egalitarianism have never envisaged their end, never recognised their mistakes and never understood that civilisations are mortal. For the first time there is a certainty. A global order of civilisation is threatened with collapse because it is founded on a paradoxical and bastard *idealist materialism.* We need a new worldview for the post-catastrophe civilisation.

---

10 *Ernstfall,* one of Schmitt's key concepts, is often translated as 'state of exception' or 'emergency case'. Schmitt's use of this concept is complex, but in brief, Schmitt regarded the rule of law in any society as always being a temporary state of affairs and that modern, liberal concepts of law in particular are insufficient when confronted with a situation that falls outside the routine situations which they were designed to regulate. As such, it is the responsibility of the leaders of a society to determine when the law must be suspended in order to deal with an exceptional situation. Schmitt regarded the National Socialists' abrogation of the Weimar constitution as being a legitimate use of the *Ernstfall.* Schmitt discusses this idea at length in his book *Political Theology.*

Chaos and Post-Chaos

You need to get used to the idea that the relatively comfortable individualist consumer society, in which you are still living, will probably not last for a very long time. Your middle class way of life is experiencing perhaps its last days. Your (even today only relative) 'peace and quiet' will soon be only a distant memory. In a not so distant future the second half of the Twentieth century will be called a Golden Age. We are far from the End of History. The present young generations are going to experience the Return of History, that is, the return of tempests.

I know that my predictions and ideas are looked upon with horror by Parisian intellectuals, the same people who did not foresee the fall of Communism, who believe that the peaceful 'assimilation' of immigrants is possible, who expatiate all page long on abstruse questions, who drone out truisms on 'democracy' and pious asininities on the 'republic'. I am not backing down, however: war is coming and announcing itself with unheard-of violence: war in the streets, civil war, widespread terrorist war, a generalised conflict with Islam and, very probably, nuclear conflicts. This will probably be the face of the first half of the Twenty-first century.

And we have never been less prepared: invaded, devirilised, physically and morally disarmed, the prey of a culture of meaninglessness and masochistic culpability. Europeans have never in their history been as weak as at this very moment when the Great Threat appears on the horizon.

***

Chaos is the state of disorganisation and anarchy of a whole, whatever it may be, after its decomposition in a 'catastrophe'. Post-Chaos is the phase of reconstruction of a new order, according to the logic of metamorphosis.

It is the eternal cycle of life, death and rebirth expressed by Nietzsche in his theory of the *eternal return* of the same,[11] but also by mathematician René Thom in his *catastrophe theory*. The society we know cannot be patched together again, the system cannot be saved by repair. This is the illusion of conservatives of every stripe. The solution, health, can come only from a situation of chaos — civil war, giant economic crisis, and so on — which will turn our ways of thinking upside down and make acceptable and indispensable what was not envisaged before. This is what will change all the givens and, alone, will permit the construction of another order, the post-chaos order. Solutions are only found in crisis. In order to build a new home, we need to knock down the old one. Recognising this fact is not being a pessimist, but a realist.

Humanity, the 'Adjustment Variable'

You do not have to believe that I am predicting the 'end of mankind' in this book. In fact, I am neither an optimist nor a pessimist. I am just describing what I see. A 'catastrophe' is neither good nor bad. It is the brutal change of the state of a system. All civilisations are mortal, Paul Valéry[12] said, thinking of *local* civilisations. Well then, why should the *global*, planetary, worldwide civilisation that we know not also be mortal?

Unlike the Romans, but like the Incas or the Aztecs, our civilisation shall collapse very violently, in twenty or even ten years. Of course, it

---

11   'What if some day or night a demon were to steal into your loneliest loneliness and say to you: "This life as you now live it and have lived it you will have to live once again and innumerable times again; and there will be nothing new in it, but every pain and every joy and every thought and sigh and everything unspeakably small or great in your life must return to you, all in the same succession and sequence..."' From Friedrich Nietzsche, *The Gay Science* (Cambridge: Cambridge University Press, 2001), p. 194. This is one of Nietzsche's central ideas.

12   Paul Valéry (1871–1945) was a prominent French poet and essayist.

will be a cataclysm unlike any humanity has ever known. But life on Earth has seen so many others. The human species will begin again, on new foundations.

***

Simply, it is necessary to note this point, which will drive to despair or scandalise the incorrigible humanists. This catastrophe — in my opinion unavoidable, that is, it cannot be halted by the illusory attempts of a few people at the present hour to reorganise or improve the world — will wreak enormous demographic havoc. Humanity will lose many people. We shall perhaps return to the population of the Eighteenth century (a likely hypothesis, in my opinion) and the level of technology will collapse.

It is a question of a constant feature in the history of civilisations: Since humans are not capable of solving their own problems, *nature* and the logic of things take charge in their place. One way to solve an unsolvable problem is the disappearance of the person who posed it.

The historians of the future, living in the new Middle Ages, will say that it was impossible in the Twenty-first century to make almost ten billion people live together peacefully on this little planet with an ever-increasing energy consumption. The idea was the product of hallucinatory ideologies. So the solution will be found by the logic of the living: *humanity will be the adjustment variant.*

In fact, epidemics, wars, ecological and climate disasters, a collapsing standard of living and healthcare will inevitably provoke a worldwide demographic collapse as the end of this civilisation, and this spontaneous *adjustment* will solve the problem. The Earth (Gaïa) is not 'threatened' by mankind, who is her guest. The Earth possesses several billion years ahead of her and can create other species on the path of phylogenetic evolution. And, after all, the Earth has known ecological disasters so much worse ...

Mankind is threatening itself with his behaviour. Natural law finds the solution close at hand. Gaïa will not rid herself of mankind (again), but is going to inflict on him a severe punishment, in the course of this dramatic Twenty-first century.

***

The unheard-of paradox of our present worldwide civilisation is precisely that it has the appearance of a civilisation without being one. It is a question of a *system*, a machine within which different civilisations cohabit, crowded against one another, all constantly dependent on one another. This kind of historical configuration has never been seen before in history.

Two contradictory movements have come into existence in the course of the Twentieth century: a movement of *homogenisation* of humanity around a Western, techno-economic model; and a movement of *heterogenisation* on the ethno-cultural level, of which the rise of Islam is a good example. This mixture of two opposed principles is explosive.

***

No one can predict what the future will be like, but one can at least predict what it will not be like. Starting from these results, it is possible to construct hypotheses.

In 2050, the future will not be a worldwide civilisation two or three times as 'developed' as ours today. The dreams of the 1960s are not really relevant. We are going to live through — and I mean see clearly in our lifetime — the collapse of the world that we know today with an extremely violent fall in our standard of living and our relative security. What we are beginning to experience today is nothing in comparison with what awaits us. We have seen nothing yet. We are living in the 'final beautiful days', the Indian summer of a civilisation.

The catastrophic events that are going to occur will be much more significant than the ones that precipitated the end of the Roman Empire, because they will involve the entire world and they will be much more rapid. I am willing to bet that the year 2050 will resemble the year 500 much more than anything we believe we have been promised. We are at the end of a pluri-millennial cycle, which began with the Neolithic Age.

The Drunken Boat

Our leaders see nothing and understand nothing. Their degrees and education have not prepared them to comprehend either the present or the future, because everything has encouraged them to prefer *administration* to *foresight*. Their careerism also blinds them. They believe that they are still in a stable world, although it has never been less stable. They are also paralysed by the humanist and optimist ideology, like the Americans, but without American pragmatism.

There has never been so much talk of 'forecasting', never such practicing of 'rationality'. There are lectures on 'sustainable development' and there even ministries with that name. There are countless international institutions that multiply seminars, colloquia and conferences. The realisation that humanity has entered a very bad patch, like a boat whose navigator is drunk and disabled, is not lacking and the most authoritative voices express it. It is obviously difficult to say, as I am doing: *it is too late*. We are not going to escape crashing into the reefs because we are too close.

It is necessary to present an optimistic façade and encourage people to believe that the situation can be miraculously restored with 'good will', 'cooperation', and 'rationality'. In reality, however, this now globalised planet, where a global civilisation reigns for the first time, has been and is incapable of governing itself, even in the middle term. Everything is based on the short term, especially in an economy which rests only on the imperatives of 'growth', 'development', and, naturally, on the maximisation of profits, that is, on a generalised *myopia*.

Who is going to persuade the Chinese that it is *ecologically impossible and suicidal*, when we take into account the terrestrial ecosystem, that their 1.3 billion inhabitants reach a standard of living equivalent to that of the West in the 1960s, which is, however, their official objective, and India's as well? Who has been able to persuade the Americans to ratify the Kyoto Protocol on limiting greenhouse gas emissions? Nobody. Their own immediate interests — industrial, financial and political — are too strong. Forests are chopped down, marine and fishing reserves are pillaged, petroleum (the key of the world economy) is pumped as if the reserves were inexhaustible, fresh water is wasted ... The list is a long one. Even Parisian environmentalists who deplore the overconsumption of energy cannot do without their 4 X 4, daily shower and electric household appliances.

No one takes global catastrophe seriously, because, just like the Sunday driver who thinks, 'Accidents happen to other people', this worldwide civilisation has too much confidence in itself. It believes that it is immortal. It is still permeated by Western myths of progress (which by definition will never come to an end). These myths are very active in Third World countries as they were in Nineteenth-century Europe. Confidence in the omnipotence of techno-science, which will solve all problems, never leaves us and blinds us. We are victims of a linear and ascending vision of history, while the law of life is *cyclical*, with a phase of ascent, then of maturity and finally of decline, at first slow and then violent. The present world civilisation is in the same state as an old man, who believes he is in good health, but who feels all the same disturbing signs and alarming aches and pains, but who refuses to draw the natural conclusions from them; or of a tree that appears strong, but which is eaten away from within and suddenly falls.

***

It is impossible to stop the headlong race of contemporary planetary civilisation to the abyss, because there exists no power with the decisive will to do so. How to change the direction of six billion people? The world state is only a mischievous myth. Humanity is, in fact, globalised, without having learned how to govern itself, since enormous masses cannot be governed, only a limited number of people. International institutions are completely powerless to stop the linked sequence of the lines of catastrophe.

There is no reason to be surprised, since it is not in man's nature to *anticipate*. This instinctive tendency was accentuated by the exaggerated individualism of contemporary civilisation. 'Wisdom' is not a characteristic of human beings, except, in the best situation, for self-conscious elites who, in any event, do not practice it. The name of *Homo sapiens sapiens* applied to our species is inappropriate. Mankind is handicapped by its *hybris*, its aggressive lack of moderation, and one can even ask whether our species is not an evolutionary dead end.

***

We must not ignore the phenomenon of premonitions. For forty years in literature, comic books, movies, and so forth, some authors have foreseen an end of our civilisation and an enormous regression. Let us be careful never to despise the intuition of poets.

It is quite certain that it is not possible to predict in detail *how* the planetary system of the present world civilisation is going to collapse, nor the precise date of the catastrophe — which in any event will take place over several years. We can be sure, however, that the event will take place and will strike us dumb. All of a sudden everything will stop and the magic will end. The TVs will stop working. The cell phones will not respond. The police will not be there to stop the pillaging. The whole fragile system of our civilisation will fall down like a row of dominoes — and perhaps from one end of the Earth to the other.

Quite unlike the scenarios of the 1960s and 1970s, which were based on the Cold War and the spectre of a nuclear confrontation between East and West, it is not at all generalised nuclear war that is to be feared and that will overthrow our civilisation, but a piling up of crises that are already at work today. Global nuclear conflict will not take place (for example, between China and the USA). A limited nuclear conflict between two middling powers (for example, India and Pakistan) is not very likely and, if it did take place, it would not be enough by itself to bring chaos over the entire Earth. On the contrary, it is very probable that we shall see nuclear attacks against big cities, which will entail tens of thousands of deaths and which will contribute to the general destabilisation.

Catastrophe Scenarios

Here is what I foresee. These prognostications could turn out to be correct, at least approximately so. Let us suggest three scenarios, a first 'soft' one, a second 'hard', and a third 'very hard'. Let us start with the probable assumption that the great crisis that issues from the convergence of the lines of catastrophe will take place between 2010 and 2020. These dates seem near, but we are currently experiencing a considerable acceleration of historical events and modifications.

1. The 'Soft' Scenario

In two or three years the European economy collapses and enters a se-vere recession. It is undermined by the following factors: colossal state debt (the 'Argentina' situation); the considerable burden of retirements and welfare payments for unemployment and sickness that prevents investment; the flight of young, educated people out of the continent; unsupportable tax burdens; the lower quality of the workforce; ac-celerating deindustrialisation and outsourcing. France is the country most affected by these trends. Real unemployment reaches 20 % and the general standard of living sinks in two years by 30 %. The crisis in Europe surpasses in extent that of 1929.

To this situation is added the pressure of increasingly high immi-gration, which the European Union is incapable of halting; a crime wave that can no longer be controlled; and the explosion of ghettoes and refugee zones for the well-off classes. The overwhelmed forces of order face a 'low-key civil war'. Islamist attacks become common, but no 'giga-terrorism' takes place. Everywhere Muslim voters start vot-ing for their own 'ethnic' lists that elect an increasingly large number of representatives with growing communitarian demands. Islam has become the most practiced religion. Faced with this, native nationalist parties and parties of the 'extreme Right' grow inexorably.

The entry of new members — including Turkey — into the European Union has made it unworkable and unmanageable, and the EU is on the edge of splitting apart. Although the situation is dramatic, it never reaches the *breaking point*, however. The system lasts and adapts to the new situation.

In a word, the European Union has simply become a Third World country, in which hopes for a moderate life slowly begin to vanish, where the shrinking of the GDP and the standard of living become larger year after year; where the political crisis is permanent and insecurity is worse than today. Catastrophe, or collapse of the situation into chaos, has not (yet) taken place.

***

This weakening of Europe and its economy obviously has a very negative impact on the rest of the world economy, which, however, does not enter into recession, but continues to grow.

The situation of the planet is not good, however, since other crises get worse and their effects reverberate, each affecting the others:

1) Climate catastrophes accelerate dramatically starting from 2010, affecting especially the countries of the South to which are added recurrent famines and the progression of epidemics, especially AIDS, which continues to ravage the Third World.

2) Islamic fundamentalism is established in a growing number of countries. The Middle East is on fire and enters into a state of total war, poisoning all international relations. Murderous attacks (like what happened at Madrid)[13] occur several times a year, striking

---

13 On 11 March 2004, a series of simultaneous commuter train bombings in Madrid killed 191 people and injured thousands, three days before the national election. The attack was blamed on Islamist terrorists.

the USA, Europe and certain Muslim countries that are in a state of civil war.

3) Black Africa sinks into anarchy, wars and economic recessions while the UN is increasingly powerless.

**

On the world level and in France and Europe, however, the rope does not break. The situation, although very serious, remains *under control*. A situation of generalised continuing crisis is established. The present civilisation maintains itself painfully, but it resists. Collapse is feared, but put off to the Greek calends[14]. The Twenty-first century follows its happy trail. The demographic growth of the planetary population slows down noticeably, however, because of the generalised rise in mortality rates.

The fragility of this immense banking system is not so great that it can cause its fall. In 2020 the worst is avoided, for the moment ... No serious measure is taken, however; no lesson is learned. Destiny grants the tragedy one more act ...

2. The 'Hard' Scenario

The same elements and the same causes as those evoked in the previous scenario are at work, but they happen more suddenly and their linking and concomitance have much more severe consequences.

Here are some examples: the European economic recession is much more severe than before; the standard of living falls in a few years by half. The threshold attained by ethnic civil war in several countries is no longer low-key, but frank and open. All over the world, conflicts involving Islam reach a dramatic intensity. Shortages of petroleum and the exhaustion of agricultural and food reserves begin to be seriously felt. All the parameters remain the same as in the previous

---

14 A Latin expression, meaning a time that will never come.

scenario, but they are getting worse. The conflagration in the Middle East takes on dramatic proportions. Localised nuclear wars break out. Giga-terrorist attacks have nuclear episodes. Epidemics, famines and climate episodes are linked to one another.

We witness a *psychological destabilisation* of humanity, which has devastating effects, all the way to the collective unconsciousness. Mankind, in a state of torpor, gives up. No voluntary change takes place and a sort of 'low-key chaos' is established, but controlled chaos.

***

The global system of world civilisation is holding up, but a radical *metamorphosis* happens, without a real *fractal break*. After a few years the following situation occurs:

The European Union disappears, pure and simple, because it has become completely unmanageable. Europe is organised as a sort of neo-medieval kaleidoscope, extremely fluid, although in theory the juridical existence of nation-states still subsists. Some Islamic areas become autonomous republics and there are hyper-protected areas reserved for rich Europeans. Conflicts are incessant, but never go beyond a tolerable threshold. The standard of living of inhabitants of Europe continues to sink slowly, but a small wealthy class maintains itself.

The global system manages to survive. The stock market is still functioning. The law of adaptation is in play. People live in the ruins or semi-ruins of the old world, but after all they are still living. The techno-scientific level regresses, although not in a drastic manner. There is, however, no more talk of technological 'progress'.

Poverty on the planetary scale reaches astronomical levels, especially in the Third World. The human population regresses rather rapidly, as do polluting emissions (but it is too late), because of massive economic regression. On the international scale, local wars, macro-attacks, incessant encounters with Islam follow one another without respite. The movement to democratisation of the world is halted.

3. The 'Very Hard' Scenario

This is the scenario that, in my opinion, is the most likely and perhaps the most desirable.

The fractal break happens, the rope breaks. The edifice of world civilisation can no longer resist. The factors discussed in the previous two scenarios undergo a still more heightened intensity, especially in the area of climate where a cataclysmic break intervenes around 2015. Everything collapses like a row of dominoes. The collapse happens between 2010 and 2015, but the shipwreck takes ten year to finish. In 2030 the state of the planet has nothing in common with what the 'experts' and today's authorised savants had foreseen.

1) The world's population shrinks drastically. It shrinks from more than six billion to a billion and continues to decline very rapidly. The causes are simple: the collapse of the supply systems of food and drinking water, as well as the end of access to medicine due to the end of pharmaceutical industries and medical structures. At the middle of the Twenty-first century, the human species stabilises at a little less than 300 million inhabitants. Everything happens as if humanity had served as an adjustable variant to pass from one non-viable system to a viable one. Africa is the continent most affected by depopulation. The level of population in Africa recovers at a pre-colonisation level.

Humanity (by the law of cycles) finds itself propelled into the 'equilibrium situation' that it knew countless centuries ago.

2) The survivors flee towns and metropolises *en masse*. Urban buildings, invaded by vegetation, begin to degrade. Only gangs survive in the deserted cities, from which they make raids into the country. In the country, where the remnants of the population have taken refuge, people live on subsistence farming and arts and crafts.

3) In effect, all industry is finished. A fantastic and violent technological regression begins, that only gets worse since the transmission of knowledge is no longer possible.

Three types of 'levels of civilisation' are noticed: first of all, some areas (essentially in the present Third World) where life has returned to the Neolithic Age, with a primitive agricultural economy; second, other areas — for example, in Europe and the old developed countries — where life returns to the situation of the early Middle Ages (from the Sixth to the Tenth century); finally *subsistence islands* (it is not possible to predict their location decades before the catastrophe) that preserve behind barricades part of the technology acquired from the old civilisation. The islands are founded in part on the recycled materials of gigantic cast-offs left by the old culture. Since these machines need petroleum, however, it is not unthinkable that they are established near current extraction points.

These subsistence islands maintain a highly variable technological level, which only rarely (and not in all matters) surpasses the level of the beginning of the Twentieth century. It is possible, however, that, using the most recent technologies of the Twentieth century, in use just before the collapse, a super-technological 'micro-civilisation' will subsist somewhere in the world. These separate areas resemble 'city-states' and will probably be run by military dictatorships.

4) On the political level, all nation-states have collapsed as well as international institutions. Humanity knows — or rediscovers — a situation at once medieval and tribal.

The imperatives of subsistence, protection and hunting are the general law, and therefore war. These incessant struggles no longer put the Earth in peril. The weapons of mass destruction — nuclear, biological, and chemical — no longer exist. In zone A (Neolithic), there is the kingdom of tribes and the return to what mankind has known for millennia. In zones B and C (see above) the situation is more complicated. Feudal societies are formed and new political relationships are established, rather similar to what was seen at the beginning of the Middle Ages. In some sense, it is a repetition of the past, but according to a different modality, since history is an 'approximate' eternal return.

5) In the religious and spiritual domain, we witness a true explosion. Writing remains. The great religions of the old civilisation continue to be handed down, but they are modified and return to their sources. The collapse, over the entire Earth, of the individualist society of consumption marks the end of materialism and the development of spiritualism. New cults and syncretisms are born, including resurgences of ancient pagan cults. To the collapse of the material domain of the old world corresponds the development of the spiritual domain of the new world, not contrived (as in our days), since it corresponds to extremely difficult conditions of life, especially because of the severe climate conditions.

***

A new humanity is in the process of being born everywhere, founded on radically new bases. Slowly the law of life is re-established. The Earth breathes. Pollution has ceased — the Kyoto Protocol is respected, painfully, at the price of a gigantic human hecatomb[15]. It is the victory of Gaïa, the Earth. Of course, the effects of the terrible pollution of the Nineteenth and Twentieth centuries, and the beginning of the Twenty-first century, continue to be felt. But the Earth absorbs it and becomes healthy once again. A new cycle begins. Are the people who

---

15 A hecatomb is a large-scale sacrifice. In Classical Greece, it meant the sacrifice of 100 cattle to the gods.

have survived less happy or happier than their parents and ancestors? Probably more.

The End of Contemporary Humanity, Predicted by Tradition

The convergence of catastrophes and the violent end of the present civilisation can be deduced from the observation of different phenomena, as we have just done. It would be dishonest, however, not to mention that several traditions, from the Druids to the Tibetans, and including India, seem to have predicted a similar collapse that will affect all humanity and which has already been seen in the past without being mentioned in official history. In all the ancient traditions, the idea returns that mankind knows successive ages, punctuated by catastrophes, but the one we are about to experience will be the greatest.

The scholar of Indian traditions Alain Daniélou[16] in *Le destin du monde d'après la tradition shivaïte*,[17] writes: 'According to the Shaivite Tradition, since the world has been habitable, several human species have already existed. Each had its period of glory, technological development, knowledge, then decline, and found its end in a cataclysm. We belong to the seventh species. The Earth has already known six successive human species that have disappeared, leaving to the following one some traces of their knowledge and sometimes the memory of their glory. After the end of the present species, on seven more occasions the Earth will know the human species, or species like humans, before becoming uninhabitable. All living species develop like entities, like individuals. They have their own gestation, infancy, adolescence, maturity and decline.'

---

16   Alain Daniélou (1907–1994) was a French author who spent 20 years living in India, taking up the practice of Shaivite Hinduism while there. He wrote many books based on his experiences. Several of his books have been translated.

17   Alain Daniélou, *Le destin du monde d'après la tradition shivaïte* (The Destiny of the World According to the Shaivite Tradition) (Paris: Albin Michael, 1992).

Daniélou distinguishes clearly between the *human species* that follow one another and the successive *civilisations* that each knows in its heart. He believes that, in the sacred narratives of the Puranas,[18] he has deciphered the description of the end of a human race that preceded ours, that of the Assours, 60,000 years ago, which bears an astonishing resemblance to what the Shaivite tradition calls the *Kali Yuga*, that is, the Dark Age in which we have now entered and which will end in the final phase of the present human race. We shall not escape the law of cycles. The linear and ascending vision of human history that modernity possesses, inherited from Christianity, has no reason to exist.

Daniélou writes: 'The history of the Assours is at one and the same time a tale of the past and a prediction of the future. There is an obvious parallelism between the events, religious conceptions, ideologies and social and moral theories that provoked the destruction of the Assours and those that, since the beginning of the *Kali Yuga*, characterise current humanity and, it seems, must end in the "provoked catastrophe" that eventually awaits us.' Daniélou believes that there are minorities today who can reject the anti-values that are destroying the current humanity and prepare the rebirth of new vital values: 'which could allow some to traverse the cataclysm and participate in the Golden Age of the future humanity.'

***

Daniélou, by transcribing faithfully the sacred texts of the *Shiva*, *Vishnu*, and *Linga Purana* gives a narrative of the end of the Assours that bears a strange resemblance to what could be our end, especially in what concerns the moral causes of the decline.

---

18 The Puranas are a series of ancient Indian texts that are important to the Hindu, Buddhist and Jain traditions alike. They relate the history of the cosmos. In Hinduism they are regarded as second in importance only to the Vedas themselves.

A false god (Aryat, or 'destroyer of pious people') begins by 'condemning the castes and the duties of the different ages of life'. Egalitarianism and non-violence is imposed everywhere. Non-violence is interpreted to mean forbidding opposition to invaders. The decline of this powerful human race began in this way, according to this text, which is also a prediction of what will happen again: 'The number of princes and farmers gradually declines. The working classes want to assume royal power and share the knowledge, the feasts and the beds of the old princes. Most of the new leaders are of working class origin. They hound the priests and the possessors of knowledge.' So everywhere the economic and mercantile function is substituted for the spiritual function.

The sacred text, cited by Daniélou, continues: 'The foetus is killed in the mother's womb and heroes are murdered. The *Shudra*[19] can behave like *Brahmans*[20] and priests like workers. Thieves will become kings and kings will be thieves. Leaders confiscate property and put it to evil use. They stop protecting the people. Food already cooked will be put on sale. ... Gangs of bandits are organised in the towns and countryside. There will be many people with no home, wandering from one country to another. Merchants will make dishonest deals. They will be surrounded by pretentious false philosophers [those who try to mask the decline with reassuring lies]. Everyone will use harsh and vulgar words and no one can be trusted. The people of the *Kali Yuga* will claim to ignore race differences and the sacred character of marriage, the relation of teacher and pupil and the importance of the rites. Farmers desert their work of sowing and harvesting to become unspecialised workers and assume the mores of those outside the castes. [Is this an allusion to the agro-alimentary business that replaces farming?] There will be a lack of water and fruits will not abound.

---

19 In the Hindu caste system, the *Shudras* are at the lowest level, consisting of servants and labourers.

20 In the Hindu caste system, the *Brahmans* are at the highest level and constitute the priesthood.

Many will be clothed in rags and tatters, without work, sleeping on the ground, living like the destitute. People will believe in illusory theories. False gods will be worshipped in false ashrams, where fasts, pilgrimages, penitential acts, gifts of property and austerities will be decreed in the name of the false religions.'

The sacred text then relates that, when he learns of this horrible decadence of the human race of the Assours, the god Shiva used a 'weapon of fire' that destroyed all life. Survivors, according to the myth, fled into the 'Mahar world', that is, the extraterrestrial world. Later, they returned to Earth, after having preserved certain elements of the wisdom of the Assours in secret, before transmitting them to a new human race ... ours. Today, we are reliving exactly the same end of the cycle. All this happened 60,000 years ago ...

***

Of course, we are keeping our distance from this Hindu sacred text, which can give rise to wild prophecies. It is, however, neither scientific nor honest to despise the texts of the ancient traditions and to declare in peremptory fashion, that 'the Assours never existed', for every myth, as Mircea Eliade[21] has shown, rests on a memory, a partial truth, even if transfigured.

Pierre-Émile Blairon, a disciple of Daniélou and Eliade, and the editor of a very serious traditionalist journal, *Roquefavour*, has doubts about the truth of the official history and the archaeology behind it: 'Alain Daniélou takes seriously the hypothesis of all the honest experts in ancient civilisations, that is, that it is not very likely, since mankind has inhabited our planet, that we have to accept the linear thesis of a unique human race, whose origins archaeologists, anthropologists and ethnologists never stop pushing back in time, without drawing

---

21 Mircea Eliade (1907–1986) was a Romanian scholar of comparative religions. In 1956 he moved to the United States, where he remained as a Professor at the University of Chicago. He became one of the most prominent scholars of comparative religion of the Twentieth century.

the consequences. Namely, that the official theses, in their frenzied dogmatism, refuse to admit even the idea that dozens, perhaps hundreds of civilisations, spiritually and technologically as developed as ours, could have appeared and disappeared without leaving a trace, or else, since these traces exist, to refuse to take them into account' (*Roquefavour*, February 2003).

Blairon believes that 'the similarity of the two declines, that of the Assours and our own, is flabbergasting. So could we attribute some credit to the predictions of the Sanskrit texts that discuss the present human race?' Analysing chapter 40 of the *Linga Purana*, Blairon thinks that this current human race will perish, rather soon, in the course of a monstrous generalised war that will only be the climax of the convergence of all the catastrophes now existing, its final *leitmotiv*. This final catastrophe will be at the same time a purification and the tentative beginning of a regeneration, according to the law of cycles.

Here, in fact, is what is written in this famous chapter: 'In the twilight period that ends the *Kali Yuga*, the righter of wrongs will come and slay the evil ones. He will be born from the dynasty of the Moon. His name is War (Samiti). He will wander over the face of the whole Earth with a vast army. He will destroy the Mleccha (Western barbarians) by the thousands. He will destroy those of the lower castes who have seized royal power and will exterminate the false philosophers, the criminals and those of mixed blood.'

These sacred Hindu texts obviously appear shocking to our minds as Westerners. It is not intellectually honest, however, to pass by them in silence.

***

Now here is what Daniélou writes in the book from which we have quoted. Commentary would be superfluous: 'According to the theory of cycles that regulate the evolution of the world, we are today approaching the end of the *Kali Yuga*, the age of conflicts, wars, genocides, embezzlements, aberrant philosophical systems, the baneful development of knowledge that falls into irresponsible hands. There is mixture of races and castes. Everything tends to seek the lowest level and levelling in every area is the prelude to death. At the end of the *Kali Yuga* this process accelerates. The phenomenon of acceleration is one of the signs of approaching catastrophe.'

Out of Chaos into the Light

This 'convergence of catastrophes' should not drive us to pessimism. On the contrary, it should, perhaps, prepare us for what Daniélou in the article we cited calls 'the Golden Age of a future humanity', even if we stand a good chance of witnessing for the first time in our history the global collapse of a worldwide civilisation, with all the suffering and crimes that this supposes. How can we not rejoice, however, at the end of a world that is detestable on the ethical level and eroded by its own contempt for life?

Every civilisation is a *cycle*, which contains three parts: a slow rise, a brief apogee and a sudden fall. Up to the present, this model has been applied to civilisations that are geographically separate — Egyptians, Romans, Amerindians, and so on. Today, for the first time, it concerns the whole of humanity. At least, 'for the first time' in the known historical period, for, as we have just seen, Tradition[22] states that this cataclysmic catastrophe of humanity will not be the first one.

In other words, we are perhaps arriving at the end of a general cycle of human history, a history that was led astray into a dead-end, one that we are living through today. We may very well be at the end of an Iron Age, on the imminent eve of chaos. But from this chaos will arise a new period of humanity, one perhaps spiritually superior, no longer held down by materialist and individualist burdens. This new humanity will correspond to the emergence of a 'new race' (in the

---

22 Faye is here using Tradition in the same sense as René Guénon and the traditionalists, which refers to the timeless and unchanging esoteric core which lies at the heart of all genuine spiritual paths rather than to a specific tradition.

metaphysical sense, not the biological one), thanks to which civilisation will take off again, will be reborn on foundations that are much more stable and ethically higher. Will the lessons of the great cataclysm of the Twenty-first century have been understood? In *Patterns in Comparative Religion*,[23] Mircea Eliade wrote: 'Men disappear periodically in a deluge or flood because of their "sins"… They never perish utterly, but reappear in a new form, return to the same destined path, and await the repetition of the same catastrophe which will again dissolve them in water.'[24]

In *The Myth of the Eternal Return*,[25] Eliade notes, '[D]eluge or flood puts an end to an exhausted and sinful humanity…[but] even the disappearance of an entire humanity (deluge, flood, submersion of a continent, and so on) is never total, for a new humanity is born from a pair of survivors.'[26]

***

---

23   Mircea Eliade, *Patterns in Comparative Religion* (New York: Sheed & Ward, 1958).

24   'The Waters and Water Symbolism', in *Patterns in Comparative Religion*, p. 211.

25   Mircea Eliade, *The Myth of the Eternal Return: Cosmos and History* (Princeton: Princeton University Press, 2005).

26   Mircea Eliade, *The Myth of the Eternal Return: Cosmos and History*, p. 87.

To paraphrase the visionary poet Hölderlin,[27] we are entering the night, the 'world's midnight'.[28] We are at twilight. But after the ordeal of the night, what will follow can only be the morning, since the Sun is always reborn. *Sol Invictus*.[29] The term 'catastrophe' should not be perceived in the sense of 'apocalypse', but of 'transformation' and 'metamorphosis'. We are not yet in the times of Death. The sun is not ready to go out. Simply, humanity is arriving at a crucial point of its millennia-long history and must wait for the plunge into the abyss, but at the same time for a rebirth and regeneration, which will be based on a *new type* of human.

What I have tried to express in this book in a scientific and rational manner is this objective *acceleration* of the symptoms of the end of a cycle, which has also been observed by poets and people of faith for several centuries. Although I am not very well versed in esotericism and my approach has always been rational and observational, I believe that it is not right to underestimate or neglect intuitive perceptions, those that come from an irrational method, which is rooted in another dimension.

In all the great 'religions', whether it is a question of Islam, Christianity, Buddhism, Celtic cults, and so on., this idea, this vague intuition that mankind is heading toward a *global collapse*, from which a new cycle for the entire race will be reborn, has always been present and prophesied. This time, this moment, which has been foretold for so long, perhaps we have finally reached it in the Twenty-first century. A general decadence, a tragedy, those that appear today on the horizon

---

27 Friedrich Hölderlin (1770–1843) is considered one of the greatest German poets of the Romantic era.

28 Faye is most likely referring to Hölderlin's poem 'Bread and Wine'. The night is used to symbolically represent our age, when the ancient gods of Greece and Christ have left the world and it is only the poets who attempt to keep their memory alive until their return. Many translations exist. Martin Heidegger discusses this poem at length in his famous essay 'Why Poets?', translated in *Off the Beaten Path* (Cambridge: Cambridge University Press, 2002).

29 Sol Invictus, or 'invincible sun', was the Sun god of the ancient Romans.

and have been proclaimed for a long time by what can be called the voices of 'Tradition' will be replaced by *something else*, which it is still impossible to describe. Predicting the new civilisation is risky and uncertain. What is certain, however, is that today's civilisation is on the verge of death and its death will take the form, before the middle of the Twenty-first century, of an appalling cataclysm. My diagnosis is ruthless. But every death is followed by a birth, a reincarnation.

***

Despair is not appropriate. The end of the world is good news, even if it will occur soon with distress and suffering. After the coming shadows will come the light. Human history is far from reaching its end. Preparing for catastrophe and rebirth means transforming oneself *from the inside*. The tragedy on the horizon is perhaps the will of what is called God or fate. We are ruled by forces which we do not understand and which play dice with us. A new world is about to be born. Man is despairing, but despair is inhuman. The future is thrilling because it is catastrophic. We are dice in God's hands. Who is God?

OTHER BOOKS PUBLISHED BY ARKTOS

	A Handbook for Right-Wing Youth
	Metaphysics of Power
	Metaphysics of War
	The Myth of the Blood
	Notes on the Third Reich
	Pagan Imperialism
	Recognitions
	A Traditionalist Confronts Fascism
GUILLAUME FAYE	*Archeofuturism*
	Archeofuturism 2.0
	The Colonisation of Europe
	Ethnic Apocalypse
	A Global Coup
	Prelude to War
	Sex and Deviance
	Understanding Islam
	Why We Fight
DANIEL S. FORREST	*Suprahumanism*
ANDREW FRASER	*Dissident Dispatches*
	Reinventing Aristocracy in the Age of Woke Capital
	The WASP Question
GÉNÉRATION IDENTITAIRE	*We are Generation Identity*
PETER GOODCHILD	*The Taxi Driver from Baghdad*
	The Western Path
PAUL GOTTFRIED	*War and Democracy*
PETR HAMPL	*Breached Enclosure*
PORUS HOMI HAVEWALA	*The Saga of the Aryan Race*
CONSTANTIN VON HOFFMEISTER	*Esoteric Trumpism*
	MULTIPOLARITY!
RICHARD HOUCK	*Liberalism Unmasked*
A. J. ILLINGWORTH	*Political Justice*
INSTITUT ILIADE	*For a European Awakening*
	Guardians of Heritage
ALEXANDER JACOB	*De Naturae Natura*
JASON REZA JORJANI	*Artemis Unveiled*
	Closer Encounters
	Erosophia
	Faustian Futurist
	Iranian Leviathan
	Lovers of Sophia
	Metapolemos
	Novel Folklore
	Philosophy of the Future
	Prometheism
	Promethean Pirate
	Prometheus and Atlas
	Psychotron
	Uber Man
	World State of Emergency

OTHER BOOKS PUBLISHED BY ARKTOS

OTHER BOOKS PUBLISHED BY ARKTOS